STUDIES IN FRENCH LITERATURE

XXIII

ÉLÉGIE

The Fortunes of a Classical Genre in Sixteenth-Century France

by

JOHN E. CLARK

1975

MOUTON

THE HAGUE · PARIS

LIBRARY OF CONGRESS CATALOG CARD NUMBER: 74-79851

Printed in The Netherlands by Mouton & Co., The Hague

PREFACE

There are a number of ways of justifying our undertaking a study of the sixteenth-century French elegy. Perhaps most obvious is the fact that the sixteenth century thought of poetry in terms of genre. If the *arts de seconde rhétorique* of the waning middle ages contented themselves with an outline of verse forms, beginning with Télin in 1534,[1] all the *arts poétiques* attempt to see a happy unity of form and substance. It is rather strange, therefore, that scholarship during the last century has not delved more vigorously into a study of the genres which interested French renaissance poets. Some monumental works have been produced but much remains to be done.

It is also strange that the elegy should be one of the genres still lacking a full-length appraisal. One would have thought that the classical ring to the word 'elegy' would have made it of keen interest to students of classicism in the renaissance and to students of the problems of inspiration and imitation. Surely a study of the elegy is bound to shed important (if necessarily only partial) light on the enormous problem of the relationship between the sixteenth-century poet and his sources and his ideals. Since the elegy did not exist in French before 1500, one expects it to be the birth of something new in French letters. One can only wonder about the success of the enterprise and about its actual nature.

Another obvious point of interest is to see the vicissitudes of a genre as it undergoes the rather quickly changing styles in taste. How does the elegy, for instance, react or become defined as it goes its course from the still medieval styles of 1500 to the often baroque

[1] See J. E. Clark, "An Early Sixteenth-Century Art Poétique, by Guillaume Télin", *Bibliothèque d'humanisme et renaissance*, XXXI (1969), 129-137.

character of the poetry of 1600? Awareness of those changes in literary fashion can be revealed in more than one way, of course, but mirrored in a single genre they are not without a certain drama.

Altogether, these aspects of the elegy and of sixteenth-century poetry are not easily clarified by the study of single authors. Thus, while material exists concerning major poets like Marot[2] and Ronsard,[3] the study of the whole century still seemed to be desirable. A recent monograph by Christine M. Scollen indicates by its title, *The Birth of the Elegy in France, 1500-1550*,[4] that the broad perspective can only be gained by going well beyond 1550, while the situation of the elegy at the end of the century reveals our reasons for not continuing further.

In dealing with our chosen period, we have been guided by a major principle which must be emphasized. It seemed essential to our purpose that we consider those poems only which were called *élégie* in the sixteenth century. This has not always been the case in either modern editions or studies. In his excellent work on Pernette du Guillet, V.-L. Saulnier calls five of her poems 'elegy' although only one of them has a sixteenth-century source for that title;[5] Abel Lefranc gives the same title to a whole group of poems by Marguerite de Navarre despite the fact that the manuscript on which his edition is based does not once mention the word;[6] Dora Frey in her study of Ronsard's elegies finally leaves aside the poems so named by Ronsard to study other poems which fit *her* definition of the genre;[7] Warner Forrest Patterson, after studying thoroughly the

---

[2] V.-L. Saulnier, *Les Elégies de Clément Marot*, nouvelle édition augmentée (Paris: SEDES, 1968).

[3] D. E. Frey, *Le genre élégiaque dans l'œuvre de Ronsard* (Liège: Thone, 1939); R. E. Hallowell, *Ronsard and the Conventional Roman Elegy* (Urbana: Illinois U. P., 1954).

[4] Genève: Droz, 1967. Necessarily our study will overlap to some extent with Mrs. Scollen's work, but we have made every attempt to limit our discussion of poets about whom she has written. Certain differences in viewpoint, however, have necessitated the reconsideration of certain writers.

[5] V.-L. Saulnier, "Etude sur Pernette du Guillet", *Bibliothèque d'humanisme et renaissance*, IV (1944), 1-119. See pp. 19-20.

[6] Marguerite de Navarre, *Dernières Poésies*, edited by Abel Lefranc (Paris: Collin, 1896).

[7] Frey, *Le genre élégiaque dans l'œuvre de Ronsard*.

arts poétiques of the sixteenth century, finally chooses as his first example of the elegy a poem by Bonaventure des Périers which was not called elegy by the poet and which is not typical of the French elegies of the period.[8] Now that, at the end of our work, we have seen the sort of poem entitled elegy at every period of the century, we would feel fairly confident at choosing or rejecting untitled poems as elegies, but this book did not seem the appropriate place for editing of this sort.

Another main principle in our general approach has been to ignore the tracking down of sources for every line and image in a poem. Indeed, such an approach would still tell us little about the elegy as a genre. What we have been concerned with is a study of form and theme, manner of expression and sources which have influenced the composition of the poem as a whole and not simply a few lines of it. In this way, it should be possible to discuss the elegy in terms of genre and also to determine whether or not foreign elegies had any important influence on the French poems. A fairly recent study of the influence of the Roman elegy on Ronsard concludes that Ronsard was very much influenced by his readings of the Augustan elegists.[9] The precise borrowings of Ronsard from their writings are found, however, just as much among the poems which he did not call elegy as among his elegies, and the writer is not able to show that Ronsard's elegies as a whole are similar to the Latin elegies which Ronsard knew so well. Results of this sort are inevitable if one is concerned simply with the passing idea or the particular image.

Concerning the format of this study, the only unusual feature is the use made of Catalogues, one of sixteenth-century elegies excluding Ronsard and one of Ronsard's elegies with all the pertinent data concerning publication and title-changes. The Ronsard Catalogue was required because of the complexity of studying his elegies, and it existed in the original form of this book. The general Catalogue is a new feature and was chosen as a way of shortening considerably a seven-hundred page thesis and of making the history of the elegy a more pleasant reading experience. Our chapter notes, however, al-

---

[8] Warner Forrest Patterson, *Three Centuries of French Poetic Theory*, 2 vols. (Ann Arbor: University of Michigan Press, 1935) II, 398.

[9] Hallowell, *Ronsard and the Conventional Roman Elegy*.

ways refer to the Catalogue instead of giving bibliographical information, thus inviting the reader to an immediate acquaintance with many of the 'hard facts'. The Catalogue also includes many poets who are not discussed in the main text: for various reasons their elegies no longer seemed to merit special discussion.

In writing and preparing a work of this kind, many people inevitably contribute various types of help and encouragement. May I acknowledge here particular gratitude to: the late I. Macdonald (Queen's College Oxford), D. B. Wilson (University of Durham), V. E. Graham (University of Toronto) and A. L. Gordon (University of Manitoba). My thanks must go as well to the Canada Council for its generous support.

CONTENTS

INTRODUCTION

As a context for a study of the French elegy in the sixteenth century, there are two essential preliminary areas which should be considered. There were no poems in French called elegy before 1500, but it was a genre which had already come into being elsewhere and which continued to appear in languages other than French during the sixteenth century. A knowledge of these elegies is as obviously interesting to our subject as is the study of the French arts of poetry which give advice to poets on the proper manner of composing elegies.

1. THE FOREIGN ELEGY

A French poet could potentially be familiar with four sources for his own elegies: Italian, neo-Latin, Greek and classical Latin poetry. Of these four sources only one will be of special interest, and as our study will prove, even this one source is in some ways more useful in defining the French elegy by contrast rather than by similarity.

The Italian elegy certainly could not have much impact on a Renaissance Frenchman since the title elegy was very rarely used in Italian poetry. Care must be exercised in this area because many of the 'elegies' of Italian poets are the result of modern editorial liberty. Certainly, sixteenth-century editions of the strambottists, of the popular anthologies and of much read poets like Bembo, Ariosto, and Sannazaro provide us with no elegies. Correction: *one* anthology, by Dionigi Atangi, includes two elegies (so named only in the index) dealing with religious themes and imitating the classical elegiac distich, a hexameter followed by a pentameter.[1]

This last point is strange because the few other examples of the Italian elegy that we have found have been consistent in their use of one form, the *terza rima capitolo*, and this preference is given critical approval by Lodovico Dolce in his discussion of the problems of adapting classical forms in the vulgar tongue:

Percioche possiamo dire, che in uece dell'Hessametro et Pentametro, con che essi formauano le loro Elegie; noi habbiamo quella sorte di uersi detta Terzetti, perche per lo piu di tre uersi lo Scrittore ua chiuedendo la sua sentenza. Onde in questa età alcuni discriuendo in si fatti Terzetti le loro amorose passioni, quelli Elegie nominarono.[2]

Dolce has mentioned as well the subject that he expects to find in the elegy, love, and, indeed, love is the theme most frequently treated by Luigi Alamanni,[3] the Italian poet most interested in the elegy, and by Bernardo Tasso in four of his five elegies.[4] In his preface, Alamanni defends his choice of subject and refers specifically to Tibullus and Propertius as his masters.[5] As well as love, however, he writes a few mythological poems,[6] and the whole of the fourth book is devoted to religious poems, not personal poems, but poems dealing with the Annunciation, Nativity, Crucifixion and Resurrection. The impression nevertheless remains that the elegy was principally a love-poem, presumably inspired directly from the classics although certainly more chaste in expression.[7] Stylistically,

---

[1] *De Le Rime Di Diversi Nobili Poeti Toscani, Raccolte de M. Dionigi Atangi, Libro Primo* (Venetia: Lodouico Auanzo, 1565), in-8.

[2] *I Quattro Libri Delle Osservationi Di M. Lodovico Dolce, Di Nuouo Da Lui Medesimo ricorrette, & ampliate, & con le postille* (Vinegia: Gabriel Giolito de' Ferrari, 1562), in-8, 194. *Terza rima* was, however, very widely used for a great number of different themes and in poems often bearing different titles, and so it has been rash for modern critics to call untitled *terza rima* poems elegies.

[3] *Opere Toscane*, first published in Lyons by Gryphius in 1532-33. We have used the edition published in Rome by Caetani, 1806 (2 vols.).

[4] *Libro primo de gli Amori di Bernardo Tasso — Hinni et ode di Bernardo Tasso* (Vinegia: Joan. Ant. da Sabio, 1534), in-8.

[5] Alamanni, *Opere Toscane*, I, xvi.

[6] Alamanni, *Libro Terzo*, III "Dello Specchio di Flora" and VI "Natale di Flora".

[7] For a discussion of Alamanni's debt to the classics, see H. Hauvette, *Un Exilé*

he imitates one of the principal characteristics of the classical elegy,
the frequent use of mythological adornment:

> O biondo Apollo, e pur fra noi talora
> Già venisti anco tu caldo nel foco,
> Che ben su s'a ragion quaggiù s'adora.
> Ah bella Dafne e cruda, a poco a poco
> Distruggi quel, che'l mondo alluma e'l cielo,
> E per te vita cangi, e forma, e loco.
> Questo è 'l caro Signor, cui Delfi e Delo
> Vivon suggetti, e frondi e fior produce,
> L'aria addolcisce, e doma i venti, e'l gelo. (II,i,ll. 43-51)

Alamanni is a potentially important source for French poets since
he enjoyed a position of favour at the courts of François Ier and of
Henri II. Curiously, however, no important influence has ever been
traced of Alamanni on French poets,[8] and, in any case, his example
merely provided a less sensual version of the classical elegy with a
particularly Italian prosodic form.

The case of the neo-Latin elegy is quite different: instead of one
or two poets being involved, virtually all writers in Latin wrote
elegies, and, instead of one type having special importance, the neo-
Latin elegy is bewildering in its refusal to show any marked preference. There is, obviously, the common form of the classical elegiac
distich, but there is no feeling of genre in the choice of themes or
even tone. As Van Tieghem puts it:

L'élégie se prête à tous les sujets, adopte tous les tons; long récit, épanche-
ment amical, espoir, plainte ou regret; c'est la forme par excellence de la
poésie personnelle.[9]

The neo-Latin elegy is thus a prosodic form and, because of its
somewhat personal nature, a rather familiar and (for the period)
humble utterance.[10]

---

florentin à la cour de France au XVIe siècle: Luigi Alamanni (Paris: Hachette,
1903), 202-7.

[8] Hauvette; see the concluding chapter.

[9] Paul van Tieghem, *La Littérature latine de la renaissance* (Paris: Droz, 1944),
86.

[10] As well as Van Tieghem, see D. Mururasu, *La Poésie néo-latine et la Renaissance des lettres antiques en France 1500-1549* (Paris: Gamber, 1928), and Christine M. Scollen, *The Birth of the Elegy in France 1500-1550* (Genève: Droz,
1967), 153-6.

Among its various uses, the subject of love, most closely associated with the Roman elegy, is certainly to be found, although to a much lesser extent in France than in Italy. Especially in the early years of the sixteenth century, Frenchmen writing in Latin were inclined to shun love as a suitable subject for their verse, and we find many elegies dealing rather with religious subjects. Guillaume du Bellay, for instance, writes a poem on the birth of the Virgin Mary: "De beatissimae virginis mariae natiuitate elegiœ".[11] Of a moral rather than a religious nature is Robert Gaguin's poem on the seven ages of man.[12] Near the beginning of the century, however, some love elegies are to be found even in France. The first writer of them is Remacle d'Ardenne, who published his *amores* in 1513.[13] The subjects of his love-elegies are themes common to all love-poems,[14] and even in this collection there are a number of poems dealing with subjects other than love.[15]

Perhaps a consideration of Joachim du Bellay's Latin verse will best illustrate the tendencies of neo-Latin elegies. First of all, the *Poemata*[16] are divided into four sections: *Elegiae, Epigrammata, Amores* and *Tumuli*. The elegiac distich is not, however, reserved to the first section: forty-eight of the sixty-four epigrams are in elegiacs,

---

[11] *Guillemi Du Bellay, Peregrinatio Humana. Item de beatissimæ virginis mariæ natiuitate elegia De dominica annunciatione Sapphicum Carmen De sancto betrando Sapphicum Carmen De cappessenda virtute Sapphicum Carmen De venere & auaricia Asclepiadæum Carmen Ad sanctam genouesam Ode dicolos distrophos. Venale inuenitur opusculum apud Egidium Gourmontium Erigione collegij cameracensis* (Parisiis, 1509), in-4, folio h. iv recto.

[12] *De variis vite humane incommodis Roberti gaguini elegia* (Parisiis: apud D. Gerlier, nd.) in-4.

[13] *Remacli Arduenne florenatis amorum libri, Venundantur in ædibus Ionnis parui: & Iodici Badii Ascensii* (Parisiis, 1513), in-4.

[14] *Ibid.*, "Amoris impatienta morti proximus extrema quæ pati mallet", folio a vi recto; "Incertitudine amoris circumuentus sola spe sustinetur: quid tamen speret non habet", folio c vii recto.

[15] *Ibid.*, "De obitu serenissimi Philippi Regis Hispaniem cum orbis totius mœrore extincti", folio b iv verso; "Carmen nuptiale mistum ex epheborum & puellarum contentione", folio b vi recto; "Tumulus Balbanus Lucensis salutem", folio g ii recto.

[16] *Ioachimi Belaii Andini poematum libri quatuor quibus continentum elegiæ, varia epigr., amores, tumuli* (Parisiis: apud F. Morellum, 1558), in-4. The Latin works of Du Bellay are also found in *Poésies Françaises et Latines de Joachim du Bellay*, edited by E. Courbet, 2 vols. (Paris: Garnier, 1918), I, 419-535.

twenty-five of the thirty-three poems in the *Amores* are elegies, as
are forty-five of the fifty-seven death-poems. The elegiac distich is,
therefore, the major metrical form used, and, as the sections indicate,
it is used for a variety of subjects. What is perhaps most curious
about the use of the elegy by Du Bellay is the fact that the section of
verse called *Elegiae* contains poems which we might least expect to
be called elegies. Rather than with love and death, Du Bellay's book
of elegies deals with his stay in Rome, his reactions to this city
(elegies I and II) and his homesickness for France (elegies III-V).
These elegies are not a constant complaint, however: although the
city illustrates Du Bellay's "déchéances et ses propres misères",[17]
there is as well a feeling of enthusiasm for the past glory of the city
and for its colourful and varied present.

More interesting to consider are the *Amores* of Du Bellay since
the poet also composed three French elegies dealing with love. The
Latin poems form a story of the writer's love for a single woman,
Faustina, who is unobtainable at first because of her marriage to an
ugly old man. The poet spends the night at her door but does not
gain access; he is later separated from her when she is sent to a
convent by her husband. The theme of absence is, thus, the essential
one, and it is a common theme in all love-poetry. As we shall see,
however, the themes of the door, which separates the lovers, and the
old, suspicious husband are common classical elegiac themes, and,
according to Sutherland, the convent is a transposition of the temple
of Vesta.[18] Even more important than the themes, however, is the
tone. Typical of most neo-Latin love-poetry, and unlike most of the
poetry in the vulgar languages of the period, Du Bellay's love-elegies
have a "caractère terrestre et fougueux":[19] in general, writers allowed themselves greater licence in Latin than they dared in their native
tongue.[20] Certainly the case of Du Bellay is an interesting example
of the elegy's taking on a distinct character according to the language

[17] George M. Sutherland, "Étude littéraire comparée de la poésie latine et
française de J. du Bellay", Thèse de doctorat d'univerité, Paris, 1952 (unpublished), 48.
[18] Sutherland, 84.
[19] Sutherland, 47.
[20] See Van Tieghem, 59-85.

in which it is written. However autobiographical his *Amores* might be, many of the themes and the erotic nature of the verse are classical; as we shall see later, his three French elegies belong to an entirely different tradition.

What is true of Du Bellay, the gulf between his Latin works and his French works, appears to be generally true during the sixteenth century. That is not to say, of course, that there was no imitation of any sort of neo-Latin poems in French. In some cases, a new type of poem is created from the Latin (for example, the *baiser* poems); a glance through the sources of Ronsard and Du Bellay shows an interesting list of fifteenth- and sixteenth-century Latin poets. Most of the sources reveal, however, imitation of a very limited sort, and the vigorous neo-Latin literature does not appear to have greatly influenced developments in the vulgar literature. In the case of the elegy, the neo-Latin example was far too varied to suggest any idea of genre, and, when dealing with love, its expression was too sensual and erotic for the prevailing habits in French.

The case of the Greek elegy is different again. It is like the neo-Latin elegy in that it deals with a variety of subjects, but except for a very few writers, the reader of the Renaissance, like the modern reader, could know only a limited number of short fragments of most of the Greek elegists. Again it is not likely that the poet would have a clear idea of the Greek elegy as a genre; the fragments would be more suggestive of the epigram.

In the earliest Greek elegies we find military themes (Archilochus and Tyrtaeus), convivial poems (Callinus), many sepulchral elegiacs devoid of lament, a touch of hedonism (Mimnermus) and, perhaps most noteworthy, a tendency to treat very serious themes of a moral and social nature. Tyrtaeus outlines qualities desirable in the good citizen, but it is especially Solon and Xenophanes who are important for this use of the elegy. With them the elegy becomes an instrument of society and politics and takes on a didactic nature.

There is very little to do with love and lamentation, therefore, in the early Greek elegy, and, although the Alexandrian poets are reputedly the creators of the erotic elegy, one can hardly find the evidence for this fame today. Indeed, after reviewing the dossier, A. A. Day decides that it is inadmissable to credit the Alexandrians as the originators of the subjective love-elegy.[21] What we find in their use of the elegiac distich is the collecting of stories from mythology and legend to embroider a basic theme which is, admittedly, frequently connected with love. The embroidery is the *raison d'être* of the poem, however. In the *Lyde* of Antimachus the lament over the death of the beloved is quickly smothered by the flood of illustrious examples of similar grief, and the style of Antimachus will be eagerly followed. Even Callimachus appears to have an undeserved reputation in the history of the love-elegy:[22] more serious than Antimachus, Philetas, Phanocles and their like, Callimachus is the creator of the aetiological elegy, verse that not only collects and preserves old legends but studies them in some depth for an understanding of the poet's own world.

If not proper 'elegies', the Alexandrians did compose many erotic (and other) epigrams in elegiacs, epigrams which use a rather limited number of themes. These epigrams will form the most important single source for the elegies of the Augustans[23] for whom such themes as the brevity of night, the ravages of love, the suspicion of magic, will become every bit as commonplace.

The Greek use of the elegiac distich is thus extremely varied and is mainly preserved for us even today in short fragments. A poet like Solon who remains for us in comparatively long fragments will be of interest to poets of the sixteenth century and will be translated a number of times; many of the others will be available in compilations but they will not be widely copied or referred to.[24]

The Roman elegy is different again and is the source of most interest to us. Tibullus, Propertius, and Ovid each produced a sizable body of complete, not fragmentary, poems, and all three poets were much published in France and Italy throughout the Renaissance.[25]

[21] Archibald A. Day, *The Origin of Latin Love-Elegy* (Oxford: Basil Blackwell, 1938), 1-36.
[22] Day, 26-36.
[23] Day, 105.
[24] Most unexpected, for instance, is a reference to Mimnermus and a quotation from him in Pierre Le Loyer's *Erotopegnie, ou Passetemps d'amour – Ensemble une Comédie du Muet insensé* (Paris: A. L'Angelier, 1575), in-8, folio iii verso – iiii recto.
[25] For a list of editions, see Robert E. Hallowell, *Ronsard and The Conventional Roman Elegy* (Urbana: University of Illinois Press, 1954), 7-11.

As with the Greeks, the Latins did not have a word which meant
elegy in the sense of a generic form-theme unity: *elegus* means one
distich of hexameter and pentameter lines. Twice Ovid creates a
personification, *Elegeia*, which is intended as a representation of a
genre, but the personification has a different meaning each time.[26]
However, although there is a certain variety of theme to be found in
the Latin use of elegiac distichs, the *Amores* of Ovid and the elegies
of Propertius and Tibullus suggest overwhelmingly a love-poem of
rather clear characteristics.

First of all, the elegy is a pseudo-personal poem[27] with a common
fund of theme.[28] All three poets make a clear distinction between
their preoccupation with elegiacs and the loftier hexameter, appropriate for epic themes of war. Propertius proclaims his muse to be
neither Calliope nor Apollo but his lady (II, i, 3-4) and this because
his talents are not suited to grander themes (III, ix, 1-4). The love-
war dichotomy is clear, therefore, and contrasts sharply with a certain epic presence still evident in the Greek elegy. As well, it
broadens out considerably from a theme of poetic gift and preference to a special view of life. The elegist is a certain type of man,
not particularly in tune with his age. As Müller puts it,

Paupertas, inertia, infamia und Todesgedanke charakterisieren die Le-
bensform der Elegiker. Diese passive Haltung steht im schärfsten Gegen-
satz zum Geist der Zeit, dem unermüdlichen Streben nach Ruhm, Ehre
und Reichtum, das oft zu Habgier und Krieg führt. Auf literarischer
Eben steht der Elegiker im schärfster Opposition zum Epiker.[29]

Müller allows that each of the elegists has his own manner of dealing
with this motive, but what is here of most importance is the elegist's
opposing himself to his milieu and using the elegy as his means of
expression. Sometimes the poet defends himself (Ovid I, xv, 1-2);

[26] See Ovid, *Amores* III, i and III, ix. The text consulted is *Heroides and Amores*,
edited and translated by Grant Showerman (London: Heinemann, 1947).
[27] Perhaps sometimes sincere: see Georg Luck, *The Latin Love Elegy* (London:
Methuen, 1959), chapters 4, 7, & 9. According to Richard Müller, *Motivkatalog
der Römischen Elegien* (Zürich: Juris-Verl., 1952), 26-7, the poems are completely
literary.
[28] These commonplaces have been thoroughly discussed by both Müller and
Hallowell, and so we shall simply review the most frequent ones here.
[29] Müller, *Motivkatalog*, 47.

sometimes he boldly speaks his mind in sharp criticism of his contemporaries (Tibullus I, x).

Love is the centre of life for the elegists, whose muse is Venus,
Cupid or Elegia, or else the mistress. The women celebrated in these
poems put their suitors through remarkably similar tortures. So
similar are the three groups of elegies that Hallowell has been able to
describe in a business-like fashion the typical love-affair, which begins with the poet's avowal of love and runs through many difficulties and a few precious moments of security and joy.

The main concern of the poet is, of course, to win and then to
maintain the love of his chosen mistress. Some of the troubles are
directly concerned with the woman, as, for example, her haughtiness
and pride (Ovid II, xvii, 5-10) or her greed. Tibullus is particularly
bitter about the lady's venality. In II, iv, he tells the Muses that he
wants their aid only in gaining opportunities for him to see his
mistress. But the Muses cannot help, and so he is forced to steal
even from temples in order to satisfy his mistress's desire for presents.
This greed is only encouraged by the woman's *lena*, a sort of bawd
who seems to control the young courtisan. It is on the advice of this
much cursed hag that the mistress deserts the poets for some young
warrior recently returned from a distant campaign with much wealth
or, as in Propertius II, xvi, for a praetor of a distant province. The
appearance of a rival, of course, means two things: the door is
closed to the poet, and he is overcome with jealousy. The door-
theme is found in Greek epigram and in Catullus (LXVII, in elegiacs)
and continues to find a place in Augustan elegy. As in Catullus, it
takes the form of a direct address to the door or, as in Ovid *Amores*
I, vi, to the door-keeper. The theme of jealousy is interesting because
it is not always on the side of the poet only. The mistress is sufficiently in love with the poet that she too feels jealous if he seems to
be going astray. Propertius I, iii, records the angry words of Cynthia when he arrived at her room in the early morning.

The reasons for dissatisfaction are often more exterior. From
time to time the beloved decides to go on a voyage. In I, viii,
Propertius tries to dissuade Cynthia from going to Illyria, and, in I,
xi, he is apparently writing to her since she appears to be already at
Baiae. Illness is another reason for the poet's anguish, although dur-

ing the lady's indisposition the poet is able to demonstrate his fidelity (Propertius II, ix, 25-8), which he boasts of retaining always despite the tortures to which he is put. At other times, however, the poet proclaims his liberty and praises the joys of free love. Ovid gives a list, in *Amores* II, iv, of the types of women who please him, the obvious conclusion being that he is susceptible to *all* feminine charms, even the most opposite. But the exasperation of the poet does not always lead to his seeking comfort elsewhere. It happens occasionally that he strikes his mistress (Ovid I, vii, 1-6), and when he does decide to renounce his beloved, it is often with tears rather than gaiety at the thought of his new freedom (Propertius III, xxv, 3-4, 7-8).

It is interesting to remember that the elegy was sometimes an expression of joyful success, when the mistress complied with the wishes of the poet (Propertius I, viiia, 27-30). The poet also considered himself to be an authority on the art of love and on the curing of it, and so we have from time to time didactic elegies: the two long poems by Ovid in elegiacs, *Ars amatoria* and *Remedia amoris*, do not form any real exception to Augustan conventions of subject-matter in the elegy.

The same is true of another of Ovid's long works in elegiacs, the *Fasti*, which recalls the Alexandrian type of poem most clearly represented by the *Aetia* of Callimachus. This tradition of aetiological verse written in distichs not only is found in Ovid's *Fasti*, but also makes its appearance in the shorter poems, expecially Book IV of Propertius. In IV, i, Propertius declares his intention to write a series of poems celebrating the history and institutions of Rome. Elegies IV, ix, and x, outline the history of the *Ara Maxima* and the Jupiter *Feretrius* cult; others (like IV, ii, concerning the god Vertumnus) have less to do with Rome specifically.

As well as celebrating cities and tracing the history of temples and cults, the poet sometimes sang the praises of a contemporary. The Emperor Augustus was, of course, a favourite choice (Propertius IV, vi) or the patron (Maecenus in Propertius III, ii). In addition, various holidays and festivals were celebrated. The birthday of the poet's mistress or patron was certainly not forgotten: Tibullus in I, vii, pays fine tribute on Messalla's birthday, and in III, x, Propertius honours Cynthia. General days of festivity are also considered fit subject for description (Tibullus II, i; Propertius II, xxxi).

So far, nothing has been said about the death-elegy in the work of the Augustans because it is scarcely more in evidence here than it had been in the earlier history of the elegy. There are a few examples, however. Propertius is the only one to lose his mistress (IV, vii); two other death-poems from his fourth book show rather different moods and techniques. The fifth elegy is a very unsympathetic curse on the tomb of a *lena*; and xi is inspired by the death of a Roman noblewoman, the words being put in her mouth as in Greek epitaphs. As well as his celebrated elegy on the death of Tibullus (III, ix), Ovid gives us a 'parrot poem' (II, vi) intended to rival the Catullus lament on the death of Lesbia's sparrow.

The Propertius elegy on the death of Paetus (III, vii) is interesting because it shows the way in which the elegy sometimes broadened into a poem of moral comment. Paetus is dead, and his death is unfortunate, but the cause of his death was greed:

> Ergo sollicitæ tu cause, pecunia, vitæ!
>   per te immaturum mortis adimus iter;
> tu vitiis hominum crudelia pabula præbes;
>   semina curarum de capite orta tuo.
> tu Pætum ad Pharios tendentem lintea portus
>   obruis insano terque quaterque mari. (1-6)

As we have said above, the Augustan elegy was also the expression of an attitude towards life, and, as it happened, an attitude rather different from the one generally accepted by the poet's contemporaries. Money, power, and fame were the preoccupations of the day, and at least the first two of these were scorned by the poet. Death at sea, the end of so many merchants searching for riches, was a thought haunting the poet's mind, leading him to fear all voyages. What difficulties came to disturb the course of his love because his mistress wanted more wealth than the poet could give! Tibullus sees this as a special feature of his time and puts in the mouth of Priapas (I, iv, 57-60) a curse on the one who started the buying of love. Another favourite complaint concerns the use of cosmetics (Propertius I, ii and II, xviiib). Thus, despite the poet's seeming obsession with his own love-affair, his poem often took on a broader significance.

As has been stated, fame was one of the main pursuits of the Augustan age, and this is one concern which the poets did not deny. They set themselves apart rather in their conception of what would give them fame. Great exploits, they thought, were not necessary; their verse would suffice. Thus we find the very common theme that it is by the poet's art that both the beloved and the lover will retain youth, beauty and, above all, remembrance in the world (Tibullus I, iv, 63-6).

A final point that must be mentioned in connection with the classical elegy, Greek as well as Latin, is a formal matter: from the beginning of its history the elegy has had the character of an address. In the case of the Greek elegy, it is its relationship with epic poetry which explains the use of address. As Jebb comments:

The elegiac measure, derived from the epic, suggests that the poet, like the old minstrel, is addressing a circle of listeners. Even when he speaks ostensibly to one person only, as Theognis to Cyrnis, the tone is still frankly social; the things said are such as might be said in a gathering of friends.[30]

This characteristic of address distinguishes the Greek elegiac from iambic verse and from the hexameter when used for inscriptions and epitaphs.

The Augustan elegy almost always has an address as well, but, in keeping with the Latin elegy as a personal love-poem, the address is not general, not to a gathering, but is directed to a single person. There are exceptions: a number of the later Propertius elegies and some of Tibullus do not contain an address, but it is still frequent enough to be considered a characteristic of the elegy as a whole. An interesting variation on the address is the epistolary form common in Ovid and sometimes found in his predecessors.[31] Ovid might well have been influenced in this by his own *Heroides*, which he was composing in part at the same time as the *Amores*. It will be remembered, too, that his last works in elegiacs, the *Tristia* and *Epistolae ex Ponto*, are also letters.

The Latin elegy is, then, in its general lines, a personal poem

[30] R. C. Jebb, *The Growth and Influence of Classical Greek Poetry* (London: Macmillan, 1893), 120.
[31] See, for example, Propertius, IV, iii.

addressed to the poet's mistress or to a friend.[32] The subject usually treated is love; only a few poems have other subjects, and it will be recalled particularly how few poems are death deplorations. An essential point in connection with the theme of love is that the love depicted is not romantic so much as erotic, and this characteristic was recognized in the sixteenth century.[33] The erotic nature of the elegy is perfectly in keeping with classical literature as a whole, but it is an important difference with regard to post-classical Western literature. When the classical elegist refers to his lady as his "domina" and to himself as her slave,[34] the meaning is quite different from that embodied in the same terms in Petrarchan love-poetry, nourished by the idealism of courtly love. Finally, the classical elegy has, above all, the unity of a single and distinctive metrical form: to the classical writer, the use of the elegiac distich was the first essential for a poem which he might have thought of as belonging to a distinct genre but for which he never found a word.

2. FRENCH THEORISTS OF THE ELEGY[35]

When Frenchmen of the sixteenth century refer to the art of the elegy, its history and its recipes, the only sources clearly avowed and recommended for study are the classical Latin poets and occasionally a French poet: Sebillet suggests the study of Marot, Laudun d'Aigaliers suggests Ronsard, and Vauquelin de La Fresnaye refers vaguely to contemporary poets who have written elegies. Otherwise the poets that we have emphasized in the preceding pages are precisely the ones whose names come up so frequently. Sebillet recom-

---

[32] See especially the first book of elegies by Propertius.

[33] In his *Apologie pour Hérodote*, Henri Estienne says: "Car entre les payens quelles gens sçaurions-nous trouver plus lascifs...que les poëtes et principalement les latins elegiacques?" (quoted in A. Delboulle, *Matériaux pour servir à l'histoire du français* [Paris: Champion, 1880], 110).

[34] See Luck, *The Latin Love Elegy*, 122.

[35] The principal theorists are: Thomas Sebillet, Claude de Boissière, Joachim du Bellay, Barthélemy Aneau, Jacques Peletier du Mans, Pierre de Ronsard, Pierre de Laudun d'Aigaliers, Jean Vauquelin de La Fresnaye. See the Bibliography for the editions used and to which our page references apply.

mends Ovid;[36] Vauquelin prefers the brevity of Propertius; Peletier
(as well as noting Ronsard) thinks of Tibullus and Propertius as
appropriate models; and Du Bellay mentions all three Latin elegists
as worthy of the attention of the apprentice elegist. The Greek,[37]
Italian and neo-Latin poets never appear in discussions of the elegy.

Although the Latin poets are cited as models, only one theorist
recommends the most essential distinguishing characteristic of the
Latin elegy, the elegiac distich. Like a certain number of French
poets, Jacques Peletier du Mans sees in a couplet consisting of an
alexandrine and a decasyllabic line a satisfactory approximation of
the classical, quantitative hexameter-pentameter couplet.[38] To this
he adds the further observation that the sense of the verse is usually
made to fit the couplet form:

En l'Elegie, les clauses sont communement finies an chaques deus vers:
e quasi james le verbe ne se và chercher au troesième.[39]

His further advice on using *rime croisée*, however, is entirely
original and was not to have any obvious influence on poets.

Peletier remarked that he had seen an elegy by Ronsard (his
second) which alternated the alexandrine with a decasyllabic line,
but Ronsard as poet and theorist was to prefer a different and much
more common solution to the problems of naturalizing the classical
distich. Like Peletier, he says that the sense should be complete in
two lines and not run on into the third.[40] Otherwise the couplet
structure is differently emphasized: instead of line length it is the
simple *rime plate* which is to suggest the nature of the distich. Further
emphasis is attained by Ronsard's idea that there should be regular
alternation of masculine and feminine rhymes,[41] and the secondary

---

[36] I do not understand Scollen *The Birth of the Elegy*, 14, where she quotes
Sebillet ("Or si tu requiers exemples d'Elegies, propose toy pour formulaire
celles d'Ovide escrittes en sés trois livres d'Amours...") but concludes that
Sebillet was talking about the *Heroides*. Sebillet could not be clearer in referring
to the *Amores*.

[37] Callimachus and Philetas are occasionally referred to but the source is
probably Propertius III, i. 1-2. There are other references to these Alexandrians
in Propertius and also in Ovid.

[38] Pp. 181-5.

[39] P. 183.

[40] XVIII (1), 246.

[41] XIV, 9. Ronsard is concerned about the problem of setting the elegy to
music and thus reveals in his *Abbrégé* his view that the elegy is a lyric form.

importance of the line length is proved by his allowing either decasyllabic or alexandrine couplets.[42]

In one way or another, Ronsard's attitude is the one we find in the other theorists. Sebillet[43] and Boissière[44] opt for the decasyllabic couplet and point out that the couplet-*épître* is much freer in choosing the length of its lines. After Ronsard, Laudun d'Aigaliers will prefer decasyllabic couplets to alexandrines[45] but, like Vauquelin de La Fresnaye, he will admit the use of both. Rather eccentrically, Vauquelin also says that *stances* and verses "ioints autrement" are admissible.[46] In practice, however, they will be rare.

The form of the elegy normally recommended is thus the rather commonplace couplet. When it comes to the question of appropriate subject-matter the theorists usually try to define the elegy according to classical theory and practices. Peletier du Mans, Ronsard, and Vauquelin de La Fresnaye all recount how the elegy was originally a death-lament before becoming involved with "choses joyeuses, c'èt assauoer aus propos d'Amour"[47] – or, in fact, with "toute chose".[48] It is love, however, which is recognized as the important subject, and thus the elegy becomes a poem whose purpose is to "conter sa passion".[49]

Love is the dominating theme according to the other theorists as well – implicitly in Du Bellay, since he lists Ovid, Tibullus, and Propertius as models for the "pitoyable" elegy;[50] with condemnation in Aneau;[51] and with some insistence in Sebillet: the elegy, he says, "traitte singuliérement lés passions amoureuses, lésquéles tu n'as guéres veues ni oyës vuides de pleurs et de tristesse".[52] In

[42] XIV, 26.
[43] See pp. 155-6. Curiously, in another chapter (Livre I, Chapitre V), Sebillet has a quite different idea about the French equivalent of the "vers Elégiaque": here, the decasyllabic line is the same as the hexameter and the octosyllabic takes the place of the humbler elegiac meter.
[44] Folio 13 verso.
[45] P. 103.
[46] ll. 519-522.
[47] Peletier, 182.
[48] Ronsard, XVIII, 244.
[49] Ronsard, XVIII, 246.
[50] Pp. 207-8.
[51] Folio 102 recto.
[52] P. 155.

another chapter, however, Sebillet shows a less exclusive view: since the elegy simply means complaint, he says, it is thus a generic term for all "complaintes et déplorations"[53] – and he is thinking not only of love but also of death. Boissière naturally follows suit, but it is interesting to note that death is never particularly emphasized as the appropriate 'modern' theme of the elegy. It is a possibility but not at all a characteristic subject. Laudun d'Aigaliers first sees the elegy as simply an *épître* which stresses love;[54] in a later chapter he allows the elegy, as well as the sonnet, the madrigal, the ode, the quatrain and the *huitain*, as a form which can be used for deploration.[55]

Further suggestions from the theorists, concerning such matters as the appropriate tone and style in the elegy, are much influenced by the curious fact that the elegy is normally defined in terms of some other genre. Most frequently it is with the *épître* that the elegy is said to have a close connection. Sebillet treats both of them in the same chapter and warns the reader from the beginning that "la différence en est tout petite, qu'il t'y faut aviser de bien près pour la discerner".[56] After looking closely, he concludes that the *épître* is a generic term which includes the elegy, a specific type of letter: "Pren donc l'*élégie* pour epistre Amoureuse".[57] Or, as he allows in another chapter, the elegy may deal with death. In both cases the nature of the poem is sad ("triste et flébile"[58]), and thus the tone, he concludes, will be less popular than in the *épître*; and because it is so personal in its expression of emotion it will be simpler than the *épître*: the "superscriptions et soubzscriptions" disappear, and the theme is dealt with "simplement et nuément".[59]

Boissière follows Sebillet in viewing the elegy as a limited *épître*;

---

[53] P. 178.
[54] P. 103. His remarks are inspired by the example of Ronsard.
[55] P. 107.
[56] P. 153.
[57] P. 155.
[58] As Gaiffe, Sebillet's editor, points out (154), this description is probably a reminiscence of Ovid. Cf. *Heroides* XV, 1.7 ("Flendus amor meus est, elegia flebile carmen") and *Amores* III, ix, 1.3 ("Flebilis indignos, / Eligeia, solve capillos").
[59] P. 155.

Peletier tries to make a difference between the two genres by recommending a formal difference as well as the usual observation that the subject-matter of the elegy tends to be limited. The good work of these writers in building up distinctions is nicely trampled underfoot at the end of the century by Laudun d'Aigaliers:

> Il y en a qui font difference entre epistre et elegie, à la vérité, si l'epistre est en prose, et l'elegie en vers, il y a difference; mais si toutes deux sont en vers, il n'y en a point, et ce ne sont que deux noms à une mesme chose.[60]

Because of the habits of the Prince of Poets, Laudun is little impressed by the usual idea that love is the predominant theme in elegies.

Not all the theorists view the elegy as an *épître*, however. Du Bellay in fact makes a sharp distinction between the two genres, condemning the *épître* and recommending "un style coulant et non scabreux"[61] for the French imitation of the Latin elegists and the enrichment of the style with mythology. Interestingly, at the end of his life Ronsard will also recommend that the poet decorate the expression of his feeling by "quelque fiction rare".[62] It is strange, however, that he should also come to view the elegy as a brief poem rather in the style of an epigram:

> Sois toujours simple & un, que ta fin pregnante
> Tire sur l'Epigramme un peu douce & poignante.[63]

Vauquelin also prefers brevity and points to Propertius as the best model of it. He confuses the picture of the elegy considerably, however, by claiming the medieval *lai* to be the foreshadowing in French of the classical type of elegy and by saying that long elegies are the same as *discours*.[64]

For reasons that we have shown, sixteenth-century French poets were bound to find the classical Latin elegy the most instructive for acquiring an idea of the genre. When theory about the elegy is written in Renaissance France, the drift of thought is guided by

[60] Pp. 102-3.
[61] P. 207.
[62] XVIII, 246.
[63] *Ibid.*
[64] ll. 531-4.

knowledge of these same classical writers, but with further observations coming from an awareness of what French poets had themselves done in the elegy. What they had done proved in many ways to be different from the habits of Ovid, Tibullus, and Propertius.

I

THE BEGINNINGS: 1505-1544

Et Marot vint. Such is the general attitude concerning the birth of the elegy in France. In a restricted sense, it is probably true that the elegy owes its real life to the example of Marot, but it is not absolutely true that Marot was the first French poet to use the title elegy. Before Marot, the idea to do so came to at least two poets belonging to the much accursed group called the *rhétoriqueurs*.

1. ELEGIES BEFORE MAROT

It is well known that the word *élégie* came into the French language in 1500 thanks to the prolific pen of poet-historiographer Jean d'Auton.[1] He was also the first to give us an elegy, or rather one should say a poem to which the word elegy is attached, because the poem in question scarcely distinguishes itself from the general run of *rhétoriqueur déplorations*, and the real title of the poem is not, in fact, *élégie*, but the more conventional *complainte*: "La complaincte de Gennes sur la Mort de Dame Thomassine Espinolle, Genevoise, Dame Intendyo du Roy, Avecques l'Epitaphe et le Regret".[2] In the prose immediately following the poem, however, d'Auton refers to his poem as an "elegye", and its main section (which follows a highly allegorical introduction and precedes the epitaph and "Regret") is called "Complaincte elegiacque". This

---

[1] For a history of the word, see V. L. Saulnier, *Les Elégies de Clément Marot*, nouvelle edition augmentée (Paris: SEDES, 1968), 161 *sqq.*
[2] See Catalogue 1.

seems sufficient justification for its being placed here at the beginning of our study.

This study begins, then, in 1505 with the death of the beautiful – and married – Italian lady Tommasina Spinola, who loved the French king not at all wisely and much too well since she departed from this world at the rumour of his death.[3] It is an extraordinary story and extraordinary people are involved, and so the poem's account of the gods of the zodiac preparing to receive and to deify Tommasina hardly seems out of place. Personified Genoa is not consoled by all this godly activity, and thus her lament and her call to others to lament form the basis of the second and principal section of the poem. Grief and praise are the two themes here, and their elaboration in 180 lines proves something about the poet's ability to lengthen his material, an acceptable, even admired, quality in poetry of the sixteenth century.[4] Genoa's tongue finally tires, however, and she allows the defunct to speak her own epitaph, which ends by an address to the king. The king in turn, in a *ballade* and a *rondeau*, affirms his respect and sorrow, and thus ends the poetic tribute to Dame Thomassine.

The poem is not highly original. Although it lacks the dream setting so common in the lengthy *rhétoriqueur déploration*, it manages to include almost all the other characteristics of such poems – elaborate allegory, personification and prosopopoeia, mixture of the pagan and Christian, moralizing in abundance, variety of stanza forms and fixed-forms in the different parts of the whole, the usual stylistic traits of the *rhétoriqueurs*. What is new is simply the attaching of the word elegy to the poem, and probably this is done as casually as he refers to the final *rondeau* as an epigram ("Cy finira

---

[3] For the details concerning this story, see d'Auton's *Chroniques* (Maulde La Clavière's edition), III, 76-85 and IV, 9 *sqq*. See also H. Kühnholtz, *Des Spinola de Gênes, et de la Complainte...* (Paris: Delion, 1853) and the edition of d'Auton by Paul L. Jacob, 4 vols. (Paris, 1834), I, iv.

[4] See Pierre Fabri, *Le Grand et vrai art de pleine rhétorique*, ed. A. Héron, 3 vols. (Rouen: Cagniard, 1889-1890), I, 69-73. Fabri lists nine acceptable ways of lengthening one's material, supposedly to avoid obscurity, but obscurity appears to be almost necessarily linked with brevity. Fabri's techniques are well known to poets of the sixteenth-century – "interpretation", circumlocution, comparison, apostrophe, prosopopœia, example, "demonstration", "reduplication" (the same thing expressed in two different ways), digression.

ma piteuse epigrame"). A certain love of new words (and words with a classical resonance) is what we find in d'Auton. That he singled out this particular poem as an elegy is perhaps not because it dealt with death but because there was a highly romantic tale behind the event so lamented. In our first example, then, we have a certain ambiguity: its most obvious theme is a death complaint, but its interest is in the story of the dead lady. Not unfittingly, perhaps our poem unites the two major themes associated with the elegy in world literature.

They are not the only themes to be found in the earliest French elegies, however. D'Auton himself attaches the word *élégiaque* to a poem[5] which is entirely different from his death lament but which resembles the second of three elegies by that shadowy figure Guillaume Michel de Tours.[6] The d'Auton poem is called "Epistre elegiaque par leglise millitante transmise au roy trescrestien loys douziesme"; Michel more elaborately calls his prosopopoeia of the church "Les elegies thre(n)es et lamentations de Leglise contre les gens ecclesiasticques dissoluz et aultres".[7] Although separated by a maximum of only six years, the poems speak of two different French kings and two different popes. In d'Auton the hero is very much Louis XII and the villain Julius II. If the church is to survive the threat of the Turks and the inner division and corruption of the church, it will be through the continued and increased services of the French king. Michel is concerned by the same two problems, but in his elegy he emphasizes the decadence of the clergy. These themes are expressed with a daring of metaphor and allegory which is equalled only by twentieth-century literature. Michel begins often enough with a conventional idea, but once he adopts a metaphor he does not easily let it go, and it is in his development of a commonplace that the classical ideal of decorum is transgressed. The idea of a marriage between God and Holy Church is not shocking, but the elaboration of this metaphor becomes singular as Michel refers to

[5] The poem is to be found in a manuscript in the Leningrad library. See Catalogue 2.
[6] See the recent article by Elizabeth Armstrong, "Notes on the works of Guillaume Michel, dit de Tours", *Bibliothèque d'humanisme et renaissance*, XXXI (1969), 257-281. This article supersedes all previous material on Michel.
[7] See Catalogue 4.

the church's "serviteurs" as the fruit of this union and to point out that fecundity is not the problem but simply parental authority. The church is, of course, the female partner in the union, and the idea of the lady in distress is treated in a way that resembles a thriller of the silent movies: through grief the lady's hair changes from gold to brown (symbol of the clergy's fall from saintliness through greed); she is pictured holding a baby in her arms and facing the hazards, on one side, of "bestes qui sapprochent / Pour me Rauir" (ll. 95-6) and, on the other side, of a great fire (the Turks and inner corruption threatening the church and the Tiers Etat). The husband of Eglise is transformed later in the poem into Pope Leo, and in this passage Michel indulges in the medieval and renaissance delight in name-magic. As pastor, the pope is given a Virgilian shepherd's name, Meliboeus; Leo is made to refer to the lion of the tribe of Judah (Revelation V, 5), a symbol of Jesus suggesting royal power and strength; and Medici, the pope's family name, obviously allows a development of the idea that the pope heals the "playes et maladies" (l. 167) of his charges.

These two elegies, then, do not deal with the themes usually associated with the genre. Like d'Auton, Michel does devote an elegy to death, a lament on the death of Claude de France belatedly published in 1526,[8] but this is his third elegy, and the first one that he wrote is, like the second, on an unexpected theme. The poem in question appeared in 1516 in a book which is Michel's first original published work.[9] The main part of this book is a very long allegory of the moral life of nobles in terms of a hunt, but preceding the allegory we find a more prosaic statement of the poet's theme, and this is called "Elegie sus le propos de peche et vanite". It is a perfect 'kill-joy' of a poem: addressing young nobles, Michel develops the point that they risk perdition through pride in their youth and social position and through their pursuit of the delights of Venus. The remedy is to see all earthly existence as vanity and to be constantly prepared for death. Grim lesson indeed, but the vision of

[8] See Catalogue 5.
[9] See Catalogue 3. There is a second edition of this work (1520) which gives "Eglise" rather than "Elegie" as the title of our poem. This is not a variant, however, but an obvious error.

Heaven given to tempt the young to virtue is anything but ascetic. The author in his naive way has perhaps hit on the sophisticated principle of deferred pleasure. His Heaven is strangely sensuous in nature –

Lieu plain de liqueur de laic table
Pluente miel dodeur et basme (ll. 263-4)

– and, in this context, the replacement of Venus by the Virgin strikes the modern reader versed in the lore of the subconscious as perhaps a little suspect.

To conclude about the elegy before the appearance of Marot's examples, one must first emphasize the lack of pattern in the two poems by d'Auton and the three by Michel. All the poems resemble various already established forms – the *déploration*, the *épître* (*artificielle*), the rhymed sermon; the style shows no effort at renewal or change. The function of the word *élégie*, then, seems to be to suggest simply a tone of complaint and not a genre. Let us remember that d'Auton prefers the adjective *élégiaque* to his own noun *élégie* – *complainte élégiaque, épître élégiaque* – and that Michel twice links the word *élégie* with words like *threnes, complaintes* and *lamentations*.

If the word *élégie* simply suggests a tone rather than a subject and/or a prosodic form, it is not surprising for instance that d'Auton's two poems are not only different in theme but different in form as well (stanzas in the first, couplets in the second). In the case of Michel, however, there is more uniformity in his choice of form: all three of his poems are in couplets, octosyllabic in the first case and decasyllabic in the other two examples. Especially in *La Forest de Conscience* it is noteworthy that the elegy is almost alone in eschewing the use of stanzas. One can come to no categorical conclusion about Michel's conception of the elegy, but the formal similarity is suggestive of some preference. Perhaps one could hazard that for him it was a complaint on any subject in couplets.

2. MAROT

When Marot does finally enter the picture as a writer of elegies, he does so dramatically: his first offering lavishes twenty-one examples on the world of French letters, and a mere four years later he adds a further half-dozen to their number (see Catalogue 6 and 13). If Marot is not the first writer of elegies in France, his poems are certainly the most important of the early examples – by their number, by their quality, and by the prestige of the author himself. Nevertheless we shall have occasion to question the degree of influence these poems actually had upon contemporary poets.

What can be said about the elegies of Marot? Perhaps not a great deal that is new: the elegies are not generally much read but they have been quite often studied and commented upon.[10] These studies are often in disagreement with one another, however, and so it does not seem impertinent to review a few particularly important matters concerning the nature of this part of Marot's poetry.

Basic indeed to our understanding of these poems is determining whether they distinguish themselves from the poetry of their time in any way other than by their title, and the first thing we notice is a number of precise associations between the twenty-seven elegies and other French genres: the three death-elegies are intimately connected with the poet's epitaphs, and most of the love-elegies are only too clearly associated with the *épître*.

The association between the death-elegy and the epitaph is, of course, to be found in editions which precede 1538 and in manuscripts. It is true that XXIII appears in the Montmorency manuscript[11] under the title "Elegie de Jehan Chauvin, ménestrier, qui fut noyé en Seine", but it appears in a group of epitaphs. It is to be remarked that this is the only Marot elegy to be so called when found in a printed book or manuscript before its appearance in either the 1534 or the 1538 editions. The other two death-poems, XXI and XXII, are both to be found in the section of epitaphs called *Cimetière* (*Suite*, 1534), and XXII appears in three manuscripts as an

---

[10] Among recent publications notice must be made particularly of V.-L. Saulnier, *Les Élégies de Clément Marot*; Christine M. Scollen, *The Birth of the Elegy in France 1500-1550* (Genève: Droz, 1967); Clément Marot, *Œuvres Lyriques*, édition critique par C. A. Mayer (London: Athlone Press, 1964). These works also list the important earlier studies on Marot's elegies.

[11] See Saulnier, 12. This manuscript (Musée Condé, Chantilly) was a gift from Marot to Anne de Montmorency.

epitaph: in B. N. fds, fr. 17526, 17527 and 24020 (in this last manuscript the poem is entitled "Le grand trésorier de France seigneur de Semblançay" but is found in a series of epitaphs). One wonders why these particular three epitaphs should upset in 1538 the exclusiveness of the Marot elegy as a love-poem. The answer seems to be that their original title did not suit them particularly well: removing them from the rest of the epitaphs helped the unity of that area of Marot's writing even though it somewhat confused the single-mindedness of the book of elegies.

Of these three deplorative elegies, two are identical in conception. In XXI and XXIII an imaginative and supernatural reason is given for the death of the person in question. Anne L'Hulier (XXI)[12] had the misfortune to be burned to death in her bed, but it was no simple accident. Because Anne refused to serve Venus, the latter angrily sought the aid of Vulcan, who set the bed on fire. The nature of the event provides the opportunity to make use of the Petrarchan image of putting out fire with tears:

> Mais qui de son Mary
> Eust alors les larmes qu'espandues
> Il a depuis, pas ne fussent perdues,
> Comme elles sont, car de ses yeulx sortir
> En feit assez pour ce feu amortir. (ll. 34-38)

The elegy on the death of the unidentified minstrel Jehan Chauvin (XXIII) follows a similar pattern. From the facts that the dead person was a musician and that he drowned, Marot creates the myth of Chauvin's being carried into the waters by the aquatic gods to prevent his charming the Naiades from their proper domain. The adoring sprites are most upset and see to it that their charmer is taken back to land for a proper burial.

The elegy on the death of Jacques de Beaune (XXII) is of a different nature since it is much closer to medieval traditions. The dead person speaks of his glory before Fortune turned against him (ll. 1-8). In his "blanche uieillesse" he finds himself on a scaffold, a

---

[12] See Saulnier, 23-7 for biographical and historical details concerning these three elegies. All quotations of Marot will be taken from the edition by Georges Guiffrey and Jean Plattard, 5 vols. (Paris: Jean Schemit, 1876-1931). The elegies are found in vol. V. IX bis is the ballade "Amour me voyant sans tristesse".

sight so pitiable that even his enemies weep. The description of the venerable old man hanging at Mountfaulcon is the most moving part of the poem:

> Là où le uent, quand est fort et nuysible,
> Mon corps agite, et quand il est paisible,
> Barbe, et cheveulx tous blancs me faict branler
> Ne plus ne moins que feuilles d'arbre en l'air.
> Mes yeulx, iadis uigilans de nature,
> Des uieulx corbeaux sont deuenuz pasture:
> Mon col, qui eut l'accol de Cheualier,
> Est accollé de trop mortel collier:
> Mon corps, iadis bien logé, bien uestu,
> Est à present de la Gresle batu,
> Laué de Pluye, et du Soleil seché,
> Au plus uil lieu qui peult estre cherché. (ll. 39-50)

The poem continues to contrast Semblançay's prosperous existence with his horrible death. The moral is obvious: wealth, which gives pleasure, gives even greater pain.

When one looks at the three sections of Marot's death-poems, one readily sees how inappropriate the elegies would be among them. The *Epitaphes* (*Adolescence*, 1532) are all facetious, even cruelly comical in tone. The *Cimetière* (*Suite*, 1534) originally contained two of the elegies, but apart from these elegies all the *Cimetière* epitaphs but one[13] stress their generic nature by the use of inscriptional formulae ("Cy gist...", "Passant..."). The three elegies do not, therefore, fit in with the general conception of the *Cimetière* poems. Nor would they be in appropriate surroundings with the five *complaintes*.[14] Although these poems seem radically different from one another, they all follow the general precepts for deplorative poetry, which is theoretically a structure normally of five parts: "Praise, demonstration of loss, lamentation, consolation, exhorta-

---

[13] "De Jean L'Huillier, Conseiller" (Guiffrey, IV, 366). This epitaph is not, however, like the three elegies. It is a curious poem of eighteen lines in which the poet recounts the wish of L'Huillier's wife to die; the wish is granted a year after her husband's death, and so Death was not able to undo what Love had wanted to unite.

[14] It was Constantin who first gathered these poems together into a single section: *Les Œuures de Clement Marot, de Cahors, Vallet de Chambre du Roy* (Lyon: à l'enseigne du Rocher, 1544), in-8 (B. N. Rés. 1484-1485). The *complaintes* begin on p. 437.

tion".[15] A certain leeway is permitted, of course, and one notices that Marot goes from strict adherence to all the parts in the Louise de Savoie lament to perhaps excessive abbreviation in the complaint of the niece. The elegies, however, are quite different in structure and conception – they are odd pieces that seemed, finally, to require a new title.

The love-elegies present an entirely different situation. These twenty-four poems form an impressively homogeneous group. Let it be mentioned immediately that in the 1534 and 1538 editions we have the elegy in ballade-form; in all sixteenth-century editions we have the presence of an elegy in sextains (XVIII). Apart from these two poems, however, the remaining twenty-two elegies are composed in decasyllabic couplets (like the three death-elegies). As well as a unity in prosody, the love-elegies are virtually all clearly associated with the well-established genre of the *épître*. Three of the titles in the 1534 edition state this connection explicitly: "La premiere Elegie en forme d'Epistre", "La troisieme Elegie en forme d'Epistre", and "La IIIe Elegie en Epistre". As well, the section following the elegies in 1534 is headed "Les Epistres differentes". Even more interesting, however, is to see how the poems themselves adopt certain expressions as a result of their epistolary character. In fact, there are only four of the love-poems (not counting the *ballade*, of course) which make no reference to the act of writing (VIII, X, XI, XVII). Even in these cases, the rhetorical character of the address would seem to presume the *épître* form, or, at least, a written complaint which may be thought of as a letter. It is not surprising, then, that all but one of the manuscript copies of the love-elegies use the word *épître* in the title.[16] We can now readily understand that Sebillet was to

---

[15] Scaliger, quoted in O. B. Hardison, Jr., *The Enduring Monument, A Study of the Idea of Praise in Renaissance Literary Theory and Practice* (Chapel Hill: U. of North Carolina Press, 1962), 113. Hardison gives an excellent discussion of all the conventions of deplorative poetry.

[16] For a discussion of the manuscripts, see C.-A. Mayer, *Bibliographie des Œuvres de Clément Marot*, 2 vols. (Genève: Droz, 1954), I, and Saulnier, 147-149. The exception is XVII, which is called a "Complaincte" in B. N. n. a. 477. The value of these manuscript titles remains in their general indication of what the poems appeared to be to contemporaries of Marot. While it is possible that these anonymous manuscripts are based on authentic earlier versions of the elegies, there is no proof of this.

find himself in an embarassing position when he came to define *épître* and elegy. He was perhaps more observant of the real nature of the bulk of Marot's elegies than many critics have been when he stated that Marot (or the printer) had simply set aside as elegies the *épîtres amoureuses*. He says, then, "Pren donc l'élégie pour epistre Amoureuse et la fay de vers de dix syllabes toujours..."[17] In the works of Marot, this definition has few exceptions indeed.

Let us just stress two further points about the elegy of Marot as *épître amoureuse*. First of all, the sections devoted to *épîtres* and elegies are surprisingly tidy: there is no real overlapping. Among the *épîtres* there is no poem which deals with love in the pseudo-personal way of the elegies. The "Epistre de Maguelonne à son amy Pierre de Prouence, elle estant en son hospital"[18] and the "Epistre des Iartieres blanches" are the only *épîtres* which deal with love at all, and they have nothing to do with the style and approach of the elegies.[19] Therefore, Marot, or his printer, has given generic significance to the book of elegies by the very homogeneity of the poems: in form and theme the elegies make up a logical group and are to be distinguished from the rest of Marot's poetry.

---

[17] Thomas Sebillet, *Art poétique françoys*, edited by Félix Gaiffe (Paris: Cornély, 1910), 155; see also 153.

[18] Obviously I differ from Scollen with regard to the influence of the *Heroides* on Marot. I see its influence certainly in the case of the Maguelonne *épître* but not in the elegies, which are far more likely to be distantly inspired by the *Amores*. I find it interesting to note that even in textual similarities the *Amores* are more in evidence in the elegies than the *Heroides* (Scollen, *The Birth of the Elegy*, 45-47). And surely the difference between the *Amores* and the *Heroides* is clear. Although Mayer in his edition of the *Œuvres lyriques* is encouraged to include the Maguelonne letter in this volume because of the *Heroides* influence, I note that he does not feel inclined to place it with the elegies. He does, however, feel justified in giving the *épître* "Bien doy louer la divine puyssance" as "Elégie XXIV". The difference between this poem and the Maguelonne *épître* is clear and it is the same sort of difference that exists between the *Amores* and the *Heroides*. One also remembers at this point that it is specifically to the *Amores* that Sebillet refers: "Or si tu requiers exemples d'Elegies, propose toy pour formulaire celles d'Ovide escrittes en ses trois livres d'Amours: ou mieus ly lés élégies de Marot: desquéles la bonne part représente tant vivement l'image d'Ovide, qu'il ne s'en faut que la parole du naturel" (155). Why does Scollen, when commenting on this passage, insist on referring to the *Heroides* (14)?

[19] The "Epître à une Dame" ("Bien doy louer la divine puissance") is an exception but it is posthumous (1841). It is indeed similar to the elegies but there is no sixteenth-century source for that title.

The second point to be stressed is that the elegy as an *épître* is likely to be governed by certain important conventions. Sebillet again is to be attended to carefully when he states that "en un mot, l'Epistre Françoise n'est autre chose qu'une lettre missive mise en vers..."[20] Since the middle-ages there was a whole art to letter-writing, which found painstaking expression in Fabri's monumental and popular rhetoric.[21] It is eminently useful to recall some of Fabri's lore, all the more so perhaps since, among the types of *épître*, he refers to "...les aultres d'amour comme les epistres de Ouide, Properse...":[22] in Fabri's mind, obviously, the same laws applied to prose and verse.

Fabri is generous in precepts and examples, but basic to the whole discussion of letter-writing is the following:

Toute epistre est partie en trois, comme vng argument qui est de maieur, mineur et de conclusion, que les orateurs disent la cause, l'intention et la consequence.

La cause est ce qui nous meult ou contraint a escripre a aultruy, en luy voulant signifier nostre volunté. L'intention, c'est de luy signifier par lettre nostre volunté; la consequence, c'est quant est premise nostre intention et declaree, nous faisons conclusion en bien ou mal, ou proffit ou dommaige, etc...[23]

A proper letter, whether it be about love or any other subject, is a sort of syllogism: rhetoric propounded a five-part structure for the deploration but a tidy three-part argument as a basis of the letter. As in the deploration, not all parts have to be explicit, and the argument need not be so tidy that the three steps follow necessarily in their syllogistic order. Poetic – and even prosaic – licence is permitted. Another particularly fundamental point Fabri makes about letters is that they contain – always, he says – a request, and since this is the case one must (a) show the request to be "juste", (b) show that the person addressed is capable of satisfying the request, and (c) indicate the "remuneration" which will follow the granting of the request (I, 203). Since letter-writing is begging, one

[20] Sebillet, 154.
[21] Fabri, *Le Grand et vrai art* ..., I, 194-293.
[22] Fabri, I, 197.
[23] Fabri, I, 199.

should "user d'humble langage", advises Fabri (I, 214). Make every effort to gain "beniuolence" as well, an essential characteristic of almost all letters. It is this characteristic which Fabri stresses for the letter "d'amour vitieuse", as he so charmingly calls it. Specifically for the *épître amoureuse*, he recommends the following three-part structure:

En la premiere, l'en acquiert beniuolence a celuy ou celle a qui l'en rescript, en le louant de trois choses: premierement, de vertu moralle ou de science, etc., se il en y a; secondement, de noblesse, se elle est noble; de richesse ou fortune, se elle est riche; tiercement, de beaulté corporelle, etc. Et, se en la personne ne sont les choses dessusdictes, l'en dira: "Combien que tu ne soys pas noble ne de grans parens, si es tu en meurs, en courage plus noble que les aultres, ou semblable, etc."

En la seconde partie, nous acquerons a nous beniuolence, en demonstrant sans arrogance notre ieunesse, noblesse, richesse, etc., pour inciter a nous aymer; en après, le plus honnestement que l'en pourra, nous dirons l'amour de quoy nous l'aymons.

En la tierce partie, nous luy prierons qu'il luy plaise nous accorder nostre requeste, en nous aymant ainsy que nous l'aymons, disant que l'amour est plus diuin que humain, en admenant quelque exemple de celles a qui bien est venu par bien aymer. Et puis fault declarer quelque crainte de dommage la ou elle pourrait venir, se elle ne veult aymer, en confermant de exemples d'aulcunes qui non voullant aymer sont mortes miserablement, en luy suadant non choir en tel inconuenient, luy promectant honnestement et secretement la garder et luy faire tout seruice et playsir.[24]

With these few indications it will be sufficiently clear that Marot's elegies are not really free poems at all but follow a rather precise set of precepts. The themes of praise (of the lady and of oneself for fidelity and service), the constant begging, the humble pose – these points are immediately clear. More interesting is the basic structural solidity which Fabri prescribes for the *épître*. It would be tedious to go through the elegies of Marot one by one to prove the presence of this tripartite argumentation, but let us just point out how clear this structuring is, for example, in X:

1. I must correct my previous statement (IX bis): you are the most beautiful in the world.

[24] Fabri, I, 229.

2. my heart is free of all treachery etc.
3. therefore, receive my love and love me in return.

These are the three parts of Fabri's *lettre d'amour vitieuse*, and Marot uses his own poetic whim simply by stating the request of the third part after each of the other parts: thus we have a sort of 'logical' refrain, as distinct from a verbal-prosodic refrain. In IX the argument is really the same:

1. your beauty is so great it inspires love (ll. 23-38)
2. I am faithful in my love (ll. 11-22)
3. therefore I ask to be treated as you would be treated in love (and she is unhappy because of another)

The ordering is more imaginative, however (and let us recall Fabri's allowing any order in the parts): Marot's pattern is 3-2-1-3. One further example: in V Marot recalls to the lady that she has made a promise (therefore his request is a just one), that it is in her power to satisfy his request (see especially ll. 12-14) and that she will receive a proper reward:

> Le tien office est de me faire grace:
> Le mien sera d'aduiser que ie face
> Tes bons plaisirs, & sur tout regarder
> Le droict chemin pour ton honneur garder. (ll. 27-30)

Thus Marot gives us in the logical order the three parts of a letter of request as Fabri recommends.

The elegies, then, are very precisely *épîtres*. Before it is decided that their classical-sounding title is pure whim, one should consider whether or not Marot renewed an old form by means of stylistic or thematic novelty. It appears that this is a delicate subject to approach. Among the early scholars of these poems we find diametrically opposed points of view: for Henry Guy,[25] Marot's elegies stem directly from earlier French poetry; for Alfred Roedel,[26] the influence of the classical elegy is essential. In more recent years the same opposition is still to be found: Mayer ranks the elegies among the most medieval of Marot's poems[27] and Saulnier tends to

---

[25] Henricus Guy, *De fontibus Clementis Maroti poetae* (Fuxi: Gadrat, 1898).
[26] Alfred Roedel, *Studien zu den Elegien Clément Marots* (Meiningen: Keyssner'schen, 1898).
[27] See his edition of the *Œuvres lyriques*, 19.

nuance intelligently the extreme position of Roedel.[28] Let us briefly review the evidence.

First of all, there are several close similarities between Marot's elegies and the style of the *rhétoriqueurs*. It is well known that Clément began his poetic career under the tutelage of his father.[29] That he was never completely to give up the poetics taught him in his youth need not surprise since he always spoke of his predecessors with reverence.[30] As far as the elegies are concerned, their comparatively early writing (the bulk of them between about 1525-1534)[31] made the signs of *seconde rhétorique* inevitable. Three of these characteristics are obvious in the first elegy, and they are not restricted to it by any means. First of all we have the allegorical figures, the argument of *Doubte* and *Ferme amour*, which provides the lengthy introduction to the poem; we have the moral developments so dear to the *rhétoriqueurs*, as in lines 127-144 which deal with war and fortune; and we have touches of *rhétoriqueur* versifying:

> Comme Mallars, Merles, Mauluiz, Mesanges,
> Pinsons, Piuers, Passes et Passerons. (ll. 122-123)

In a different vein are the many passages in the elegies which delight in a peculiar physical dissection: the eye or the heart is taken away from the living organism as a whole and given independent existence. In the third elegy, the heart is seen as the centre of the love-experience. This is not, of course, unusual in love-poetry of any period, but here it is the development which creates a rather special effect. The poet bids his lady to accept his heart and to treat it well if it be loyal and to reject it if unfaithful:

> Vous y uerriez uostre face au uif paincte,
> Vous y uerriez ma loyaulté empraincte,

---

[28] Saulnier, 105: "... (Marot) a remis en forme l'épître amoureuse latine, la naturalisant française. Suivant moins le texte que l'esprit général de la tradition latine et néo-latine, il n'avait pas à trahir la tradition française: et ses élégies ne sentent jamais l'exercice d'école, la production transplantée."

[29] See most recently F. Joukovsky-Micha, "Clément et Jean Marot", *Bibliothèque d'humanisme et renaissance*, XXIX (1967), 557-565.

[30] See Epigramme CLXXV ("Des poëtes francoys, à Salel"); Elégie XVI (ll. 7-14); "Complaincte du Général Preudhomme" (ll. 35 *sqq.*).

[31] See P. Villey, *Rabelais et Marot* (Paris: Champion, 1923), 341-384, and Saulnier, 136-137.

Vous y uerriez uostre nom engraué,
Auec le deuil qui me tient aggraué
Pour ce depart....   (ll. 17-21)

Also in the third elegy, we have a dialogue between the poet and
his eye, which complains of not having "ceste claire lumiere" to
look upon. This tendency to suggest feeling in concrete terms is
found as well in briefer details of expression. Love and indifference
become fire and ice (II, ll. 15-16); the fire which rages in his heart
will be sufficient to burn the letters which his lady wants to be destroyed (XVI, ll. 59-64). The proper analysis of such passages has
caused some difference of opinion. One is first naturally tempted to
see such imagery as Italian in origin, and certain Italian influences
have been determined.[32] Recent research also suggests that in general one must date earlier the presence of Petrarch's influence in
France.[33] The problem is, of course, that Petrarch was himself in-
debted to medieval French poetry, and so for a critic like Guy the
elegies of Marot show virtually nothing but a kinship to the French
medieval chanson.[34] Guy tends to exaggerate. No doubt Saulnier's
elegant conclusion to the debate is the most accurate assessment of
the situation:

Au fond, l'érotique des Elégies est très caractéristique de ce qu'on
aurait le droit d'appeler le pré-pétrarquisme français, dans le sillage
courtois. On connaît déjà Pétrarque: on ne pétrarquise pas encore.[35]

If Marot's poems seem somewhat more exaggerated than the
medieval French style, it is probably simply the result of the long-
life and over-use of the imagery.

---

[32] Saulnier, 97 ft. 1: Saulnier refers to a study, by Diana Magrini, which indicated two Tebaldeo influences in the sixteenth elegy.
[33] See the two articles by C.-A. Mayer and D. Bentley-Cranch: "Le premier
pétrarquiste français, Jean Marot", *Bibliothèque d'humanisme et renaissance*,
XXVII (1965), 183-185 and "Clément Marot, poète pétrarquiste", same place,
XXVIII (1966), 32-51.
[34] Guy, *De fontibus Clementis Maroti pœtæ*, 26: "Præterea, sæpius fit ut quod-
dam Maroti poema, quod, inter elegias admissum, ad antiquam ingenium
referri posse credas, medii ævi litteris penitus imbuatur, et, versa vice, Græcorum
Latinorumve imitationem in versibus recognoscas, qui dispositione rerum
priscis "generibus" gallicis minime sunt dissimiles."
[35] Saulnier, 98.

A few borrowings from Italian poetry do not result in 'Italianate' poetry. One must draw the same conclusion about classical influences. Roedel has been the most assiduous of the critics in pointing out the influence of the Latin elegists, [36]and if later scholars have thrown doubt on the probability of some of these comparisons, certain reminiscences seem secure. Saulnier and Scollen discuss them in detail and come to the same conclusion as Villey:[37] the total number is very small and their effect on the elegies hardly noticeable. If the thirteenth elegy is really inspired by Propertius III, xxi, no reader has the impression when reading Marot's poem that the lines were dictated by anything but the sensibility and feeling of a man living in early sixteenth-century France.

If the few Italian and classical influences do not result in poems clearly modelled on these sources, in our opinion the *rhétoriqueur* and *courtois* elements likewise do not succeed in making Marot's elegies resemble closely medieval poetry. The *épître amoureuse* was certainly known to Marot's predecessors, but a reader would never confuse one of Marot's elegies with an *épître* of Bouchet, for example. The "Epistre de Maguelonne", the "Epistre du Despourueu", even the "Petite epistre au Roy" are medieval enough, but the elegies, written after 1525, are clearly different: they are, with minor lapses, 'marotique'. Marotique means, of course, that they are composed in the new style which develops about a decade after François Ier's accession to the throne and which is perhaps not so much the work of a professional poet like Marot as that of the king and his courtiers. As part of the Italianate evolution of court-life in France after 1515, it became steadily more common for the courtier to compose his own verses instead of employing the services of a professional poet. A reflection of this is to be found in Bourbon:

> Nemo hodie uersus temere non scribit, et audet
>   Tractare illota Musica sacra manu.
> Tam multos passim effutire poëmata cruda,
>   Et uideas fœtus præcipitare rudeis.

---

[36] Roedel, *Studien zu den Elegien Clément Marots*, 52-60.
[37] Saulnier, 92-94; Scollen, 39 *sqq.*; Villey, *Rabelais et Marot*, 52.

Talia Phœbeas lauros tetigisse nefas est
  Ingenia, ad stiuam quæ magis apta forent.[38]

The obvious result of this was that the extraordinary difficulties
of *rhétoriqueur* writing had to be forgotten. As Jourda puts it:

...les allégories héritées du Moyen Age et les difficultées de la métrique
ne conviennent plus: princes et jolies femmes échangent des poésies qui
ne brillent pas par la recherche de la forme, mais disent – au prix même
de gaucheries – des sentiments naturels.[39]

The elegies of Marot are a reflection of this style, a modification
of what preceded it in French letters.

Not all poets writing in this new, simplified style felt compelled
like Marot, to adopt a new title: during the 1520's and 1530's we
find many *épîtres amoureuses* which are identical to the elegies of
Marot in general conception and style. Saulnier points out some
examples: "Epistres" of Roger de Collerye[40] and of François Ier.[41]
The poems in question are difficult to date, but at least some by
François are before 1525 or were written in 1525. We agree with
Saulnier that

...Marot n'a pas imité François Ier, mais François Ier n'a pas imité
Marot. Dans la tradition de l'épître amoureuse française, déjà précise,
ils ont travaillé chacun pour sa part. Et Marot a fait davantage.[42]

But one wonders why he goes on to say (especially in the light of
his discussion of classical influences and of French traditions) that
Marot restored the Latin love-elegy. We prefer to say that Marot's
elegies are 'still' *épîtres* rather than that certain *épîtres amoureuses*
are 'already' elegies. The problem is not accounting for the poems
but rather the title.

There is no way of solving this problem; one can only suggest two

---

[38] Nicolas Bourbon, *Les Bagatelles, présentées et traduites par V.-L. Saulnier*
(Paris: Jacques Haumont, 1945), 68 (VIII, 16). Saulnier offers the following
translation: "Tout le monde aujourd'hui écrit des vers au petit bonheur, et ose
toucher de ses mains sales les objets du culte des Muses. Tu peux, un peu
partout, voir une foule de gens débiter des poèmes mal cuits, accoucher des
enfants avant terme. Sacrilège! Ces têtes-là ont touché aux lauriers d'Apollon,
mieux faites pour conduire un manche de charrue" (69).

[39] Pierre Jourda, *Marot, L'Homme et l'œuvre* (Paris: Boivin, 1950), 54.

[40] Saulnier, 103, ft. 3.

[41] Saulnier, 104-105.

[42] Saulnier, 105.

possible reasons for Marot's classical-sounding title. First of all, by the 1530's there seems to be a certain glamour surrounding antiquity: already the *rhétoriqueurs* (and not just Lemaire de Belges) show a classical interest in their creation of new vocabulary (one recalls the delightful "odes et palinodes" of Michel de Tours) and in their ever-increasing number of classical allusions; Télin's short *art poétique* concerns itself exclusively with classical genres and expresses the theory of poetry as divine; the eglogue gets underway in France through François Ier's admiration of Vida. The word *élégie* itself took on a certain value simply as a word: twice in the early 1530's books (by Bouchet and by Marot) are published promising elegies on their title-page and providing no poem so named.[43] There seems to be, by 1534, a certain cultural atmosphere which may alone account for the elegies of the *Suite de l'Adolescence Clémentine*.

There might also have been the influence of Alamanni's *Opere Toscane*, which appeared in print in 1532-33. Saulnier is inclined to reject the influence of the Italian poet,[44] but it is because he is convinced that Marot had "son idée du genre". Since we do not entirely agree with this, and since we do not intend to suggest that Alamanni's poems were a direct source, it seems quite legitimate to advance that Alamanni influenced Marot, or his printers, in a different way: in the arrangement of his *poems* according to genre (unknown to works in French before the *Adolescence* and the *Suite*) and in devoting one of the sections to elegies. It must not be forgotten how important Alamanni was at the court of François Ier,[45] and it must not be forgotten either how French poets, Marot included, tried to keep up with the king's tastes. We need only recall what the creation of Marot's eglogue on the death of Louise de Savoie owes to François's admiration of Italian pastoral poetry. It does not, therefore, appear improbable that the physical aspects of Alamanni's publica-

---

[43] *Les Opuscules et petitz Traictez de Clément Marot de Quahors...Contenens Chantz royaulx Ballades Rondeaulx Epistres Elegies auec le Temple de Cupido ...nouvellement Imprimees a Lyon par Oliver Arnoullet* (1530 et 1531); *Epistres, Elegies, Epigrames et Epitaphes* (Poitiers: Marnef, 1535).

[44] Saulnier, 102.

[45] See H. Hauvette, *Un exilé florentin à la cour de France au XVIe siècle: Luigi Alamanni* (Paris: Hachette, 1903).

tion had something to do with the arrangement and the use of title in Marot's poems, which nevertheless remained recognizably French in their forms and style.[46]

The Marot elegy, then, is almost always an *épître amoureuse* which expresses a common fund of themes of the period (to be found in the same poet's *rondeaux*) and in the simpler style which develops after 1525. Unlike his predecessors and a good many of his successors Marot nevertheless gives generic unity to his elegies by their insistence on a particular form and theme.[47] Because of the clarity of pattern in these twenty-seven poems by Marot, signs of his influence should be easy to detect.

3. MAROT'S CONTEMPORARIES

Let us state clearly from the outset that it is virtually impossible to see any influence of Marot on the fairly numerous poets who used the title elegy during the period between the publication of the *Suite de l'Adolescence Clémentine* and his death. Just as it is impossible to imagine that d'Auton, Michel de Tours, and Marot were not completely independent in their elegizing, it would require suspect finesse to see in the poets of the 1530's and the first half of the 1540's anything but remarkable independence in the use of the title elegy.

[46] The ordering of the *Opere Toscane* (Lyon: Gryphius, 1532-1533, in-8) is almost strictly by genre (*Elegie, Egloghe, Sonetti, Satire*, etc.) with a few long mythological tales interspersed. It is interesting to compare the *Adolescence* and the *Suite* of Marot. While there is a certain amount of ordering according to genre in the former, the latter is much more carefully arranged. As in the *Opere Toscane*, the *Elegies de l'autheur* come first and are followd by: *Les Epistres differentes, Les Chantz diuers, Le Cymetiere, Et le Menu* (corresponding to Alamanni's *Salmi* and *Selve*?)

[47] Elsewhere, however, Marot does not show any very consistent understanding of the word *élégie*. In "Le Dieu Gard à la Court" (1537), the poet refers to his poem as an *élégie* six lines before the end. But, although he refers to Ovid's exile, which resulted in the *Tristes* and the *Epistolae ex Ponto*, his own situation in the poem is exactly the opposite since it was written on the occasion of his being forgiven by the king. The Montmorency ms. is also curious. Prepared just before the Dolet edition of 1538, the manuscript gives us two of the new elegies of 1538, but it is a poem on death which is called elegy in the manuscript, and *épître* is given to the poem dealing with love. Since in 1534 all the elegies were love-poems, this is a difficult choice of title to understand.

We do not mean to suggest, of course, that all the poems during
the decade under discussion are original in important ways. Gilles
Corrozet in 1536 gives us a very typical *rhérotiqueur* deploration:[48]
it reminds us of d'Auton and of Michel de Tours but also of any
number of other *rhétoriqueur* death-laments. It is an enormous poem,
over six hundred lines in length, but the poet has sought to make
this monument to the dead dauphin as interesting as possible
through the then-popular means of allegory and prosodic variety.
The allegory assures a certain dramatic framework and a pictorial
element which reminds us constantly of the spare and 'essential'
woodcuts of the period; the variety of rhyme-schemes and line-
lengths provides variety in the music – "Et pource que Rhetorique
et Musique sont une mesme chose..."[49] What Corrozet, typically,
does not give us is density of language: the 'poetry' is contained in
the allegory and the music. The rest is a sort of oratorical ritual.
Lautheur, *Pays de France*, and the three ladies of France, *Foy*,
Loyaulté, and *Noblesse*, take us nicely through the hallowed five-
part structure of the deploration with all the attendant commonplaces. Signs of originality are rare, but one notes that the allegorical
figures do not appear to the author in a dream. Indeed, they keep
him awake when he tries to sleep! In the plea to all members of
society to lament France's great loss, we have the usual apostrophe
to writers and artists. What a curious list Corrozet gives us, however. In literature he is conservative almost in the extreme, since
many of his poets had been dead far longer than the dauphin
(Gréban, Molinet, "George" [Chastellain], Crétin, Nesson, Meschinot, La Marche, Bouchet, Gringoire, Taperie [Tasserie?], Marot);
but the painters and sculptors are just as surprisingly modern
(Michelangelo, Raphael, Perugino, Michaut[?], Paganino [Guido
Mazzoni]).

[48] *Triste Elegie ou deploration*, on the death of the dauphin. See Catalogue
7. Although we have accepted the attribution of this poem to Corrozet, it must
be pointed out that his *Deploration sur le trespas de tresnoble Princesse madame
Magdaleine de France Royne Descoce* of 1537 (?) is written in a very different
manner and is much closer to Corrozet's normal style *(Blasons domestiques, Le
Compte du rossignol)*.
[49] Jean Lemaire de Belges, *Œuvres*, ed. J. Stecher, 3 vols. (Louvain: Lefever,
1882-85), III, 197. This is a commonplace among the *rhétoriqueurs* and like most
commonplaces should be taken seriously.

Except for a few interesting details, however, the poem is un-
noteworthy. Its content is standard; its form – and forms – are
familiar. Even its title – *Elegie ou Déploration* – reminds us of Michel
or d'Auton: elegy seems not a generic word so much as a synonym
for unhappiness. It hardly appears that Corrozet had to know
d'Auton or Michel to arrive at his title, however, and certainly Marot does not seem involved here in any way.

Another manifestation of the longevity of *la grande rhétorique* is
Bouchet's *Angoysses et remedes damours* of 1537.[50] Since Bouchet
gives us four elegies here dealing with love, one expects perhaps a
trace of Marot's influence, but the poems themselves resemble
Marot's in no way at all, except of course in their general theme of
love. Bouchet is very medieval indeed. His elegies form a sort of *cas
d'amours*; the approach is either thoroughly moralizing or, as in the
last case, the influence of Ovid's *Heroides* is felt. The poems have
virtually nothing to do with Marot's familiar *épître amoureuse* type
of poem.

Bouchet's elegies are sections of what he terms the *angoisses* of
love. Unlike Corrozet who includes the whole apparatus of his
poem as constituting his elegy, Bouchet, who creates an equally
impressive structure of allegory, intends only the lovers' complaints
to be understood as the elegies. Thus, before the first elegy we have
a description of the young love-sick poet who sets off one morning
down an unfamiliar road and happens upon a grove where he is
able to eavesdrop on our first elegy, the plaint of a young lover
"transy sans espoir". The elegy is not an *épître*, then, but a 'private'
effusion of the sufferer's feelings and thoughts. In the present case,
it is virtually an attack on the experience of love in general. The
trouble with love is that it seems to lead to carnal desire. Therefore,

[50] See Catalogue 11. Prior to 1537 Bouchet published a small work called
Epistres, Elegies, Epigrames et Epitaphes (Poitiers: Marnef, 1535), in-4, B. N.
Rés. Ln 27. 2708 but no poem called elegy appears in it. Scollen, 57-61, decides
to interpret as an elegy the poem called "Deploration de virginité religion et
cloustre..."; we prefer the plural word *élégies* in the title of the collection to be
just another example of the vague use of the word during the 1530's: the allitera-
tion of the title is no doubt the only *raison d'être* for its inclusion there. Bouchet
also claims to have written both eglogues and elegies before 1530, but no trace
can be found of either genre before that date (see A. Hulubei, *L'Eglogue en
France au XVIe siècle* [Paris: Droz, 1938], 247-8 ft. 6).

the lady's exemplary conduct is not the problem but rather the man's lust, for which he does not feel responsible. It is all the fault of "folle amour", of that "faux Dieu damours". This is an appropriate moment to measure the distance which separates the *rhétoriqueur's* attitude from that of the classical elegists! The poor young man continues to lament and to wish for death, but when he finishes the poet has the chance to hear all the circumstantial details of the unhappy love-affair because a knight comes along and the lover is only too happy to relate in the most elaborate allegorical terms the whole story, which ends with the success of *Refuz* over *Bon Espoir*. The elegy, however, is distinct from this allegorical narration and is instead an emotional and pseudo-personal expression of a moral attitude towards love.

The poet is soon distracted by an unhappy voice coming from another part of the grove. As in the preceding case, allegory is very important to the expression here (one remembers that these two poems were conceived at least as early as 1502), but the problem is different: after having argued that love is evil by its very nature, Bouchet presents us here with the social aspect. The lover in this second lament is estranged from his lady because of the envy of others. We are here very much involved with the sublunary, and so Fortune gets the standard drubbing (including a "Couplet [of twelve lines!] dont tous les motz se commencent par f / fors la derniere ligne", stanza 9). The allegory relating the precise events so evilly concocted by Fortune is not without entertaining aspects: we too quickly assume that allegory of this period is necessarily a bore. *Dame Envie*, with the help of *Discorde* and *Accident*, volunteers to help Fortune separate the lovers. Let us quote a small part of the ensuing events:

Tantost apres Enuie sans effroy
Bancquetz feit faire/ & non a son deffroy/
Ou me trouuay/ si feit la dame chere.
Mais Accident remply de male foy/
y feit venir vn quidam empres moy/
Lequel tenoit la dame soubz banniere.
Et sur le poinct quon faisoit bonne chere/
Discorde y vint/ qui pour mectre renchere
Gecta du fruict a chascun en droict soy.

Prendre en voulu par ioyeuse maniere/
Mais le quidam me voulut mectre arriere
Dont il aduint vn merueilleux derroy. (stanza 15)

The beloved lady never does see the innocence of her suitor in this fray, and he is banished. Thus, a second long attack on Fortune and Envy.

The third elegy is a little more special although it seems to start off in a way reminiscent of the first: love awakens desires which are shameful – and unlikely of satisfaction. What makes love so particularly guilty here is that the lamenting lover is an elderly and learned man. He already knows all about the substance of the first elegy, but he is now learning that knowledge ("Rien ne me sert destre clerc/ & scauant", 1. 127) and experience do not save from the assaults of *folle amour*:

Helas/ dont vient la violente oppresse
De folle amour/ qui massault & me presse/
Lors que ie veulx pudicque me tenir.
Veu que passe iay ma sotte ieunesse/
Et que ie suis es faulxbourgs de viellesse/
Tout rechigne/ dont peult cecy venir?
Chaste veulx estre/ & mon corps contenir/
La chair ne veult a mon vouloir se unir/
Mais nuict & iour tellement me tourmente/
Quen moy ie sens guerre tresuehemente. (ll. 1-10)

The description of his weakness, his broken resolutions, his relapses after a feeling of new strength are not lacking in a certain pathos.

Ie desire estre a toute heure / pres delle/
Non pour auoir compaignie charnelle/
Mais seulement baiser/ & deuiser/ (ll. 141-143)

But his kisses are soon "d'ardent desir" (l. 145), and his conversation soon turns to one purpose. The war within him is close to causing his complete collapse.

In the first stanza of the fourth elegy, Bouchet refers to six of the famous pairs of lovers treated by Ovid in his *Heroides*, a hint that this last elegy is not quite like the other three. First of all, the subject is basically different: this time we are not concerned with the betrayal of the god of love but with the betrayal of the perfidious lover.

The situation as a whole is seen in erotic rather than idealistic and chivalrous terms, and it is the precise situation which receives the greatest attention: instead of allegories of the evil forces surrounding true lovers or of apostrophes to Fate and curses on it, all the minute details of the poor lady's predicament are given. These elements correspond to Ovid's manner of dealing with the sad fate of his goddesses and heroines. Bouchet tells his story in strictly sixteenth-century terms, however, and it would not appear that there is any influence of the *Heroides* beyond the general orientation.[51]

The story of the fourth elegy is banal enough – but not in the early French elegy. The lady finally gives in to the carnal desires of her suitor, who then rejects her. Our lamenting lady is pregnant, which encourages the cad to marry someone else. The poem ends with much cursing: the lady curses her love, his desires, her weakness – and she curses *folle amour*, which leads *all* mankind astray:

> Saiges/ & folz/ pauures/ & indigens/
> Princes/ & roys/ monarches/ & regens/
> Preux cheualliers/ & gens plus droictz que sierges/
> Moynes cloistriers/ & docteurs refulgens/
> Theologiens en vertuz emergens/
> Femmes dhonneur/ mariees & vierges/ (ll. 151-156)

In one of his *Épîtres familières* Bouchet was to reminisce as follows:

> ...ne scay chose immonde
> Auoir escript, fors en lan mil cinq cens
> Que folle amour auoit surprins mon sens
> Qui contraignit ma folle main escrire,
> L'aymant transy, voulant amour descrire,
> Dont (non a tort) me repentis soubdain
> Par vng liuret faisant d'amour desdain
> Depuis me suis pour au mal satisfaire
> A mes regards et loups rauissans faire,
> Ou ie conquis le nom de trauerseur.[52]

Obviously, with an attitude like that towards all expression of love

---

[51] We see no justification for a firmer statement of influence and cannot see any influence of Ovid on the third elegy, as does Scollen, 70.
[52] Quoted in Auguste Hamon, *Un grand rhétoriqueur poitevin: Jean Bouchet, 1476-1557* (Paris: Oudin, 1901), 399, ft. 1.

in poetry, one can hardly hope for the subject to be treated in a manner far removed from a sermon. And that is what the *Angoysses et remedes* are, in fact. The elegies are the *exempla* of the *Angoysses*, which were intended to make the reader ardently desire the methods of Reason for controlling that most undesirable experience, love. Especially when seen in the context of the book as a whole, it is obvious that Bouchet was adding still another moral tract to the already enormous stock produced during the fifteenth and early sixteenth centuries. His particular tract happens to voice the usual themes of late medieval love-poetry.

His verse is also in the style of the *rhétoriqueurs*. As he informs us himself in the 1537 preface, his masters in the art of writing are all of the old school: Chastellain, Clopinal, Castel, Lemaire, Octavien de Saint-Gelais, and Meschinot. He uses a variety of stanza forms (no two elegies use the same forms), none of which are new to French poetry. Especially in the first two elegies he expresses himself most willingly in allegorical terms; he does not resist the most trivial, stylistic tricks, such as the stanza in the first elegy in which all the words begin by the letter 'f'.

There is, however, one point worth underlining. His elegies are 'personal' complaints. That is, they are the woeful expressions of an individual who is more intent on expressing his grief and analysing his state (especially the third elegy) than in exposing the facts. This one detail unites him with the post-Marot love-elegy. The fact that the love-complaint eschews the epistolary framework, however, is to remain unusual.

But then, almost everything is unusual about the elegy during these years preceding Marot's death. The two poets we have just discussed at least seem to be unsurprising in talking of death and of love. But Corrozet did not have in 1536 Marot's example and Bouchet differs from Marot more than he resembles him. Among all our other poets of these years we find no proper example of a deplorative elegy[53] and only Marot's enemy Jean Le Blond will speak again of love.

[53] There is an unpublished "Epistre elegiaque sur la mort de feu monseigneur le daulphin..." by Victor Brodeau (B. N. fds. fr. 1700, folio 72 recto): since it is unpublished and uses only the adjective *élégiaque* we are not including the poem

Le Blond is hesitant in his use of the word elegy: the exact titles of the two poems which concern us are "Epistre elegiacque de lhumble esperant a sa dame en Rythme alexandrine" and "Epistre delegie", and in the table of contents both *élégie* and *élégiaque* disappear.[54] However, our expectations are momentarily high concerning a Marot influence since love and the *épître* are united in Le Blond's bashful essay. The theme of separation is also vital in both poems, and we recall that Marot's first four elegies deal in some way with separation. In Le Blond's "Epistre elegiaque", the lady's grief over her suitor's impending departure causes him to inform her that he has changed his plans. In the "Epistre delegie" the lady has had to leave, and the poet grieves at having missed seeing her at an appointed spot as she set out on her trip. The poem is replete with apostrophes to Fortune and a wish-fulfilment dream in which he enjoys the great beauty of his lady, receives a kiss, and is assured of her love.

We must conclude, however, that the general nature of these two poems does not appear to be Marot-inspired. Le Blond constantly embroiders his matter, and it is precisely this over-elaboration of the subject which distinguishes the two poems from Marot's elegies, for, if the latter did not refrain from allegories and apostrophes, his poems are nevertheless generally direct and simple. Indeed, Le Blond's constant apostrophizing points out another difference: with Marot the reader never loses the feeling of the poem's being a (pseudo-) personal address, an intimate letter, whereas with Le Blond, the lady's presence in the situation loses all importance. The literary pretence of personal communication is made so vague that we forget the importance of the word "épître" in both titles.

In addition, if Marot were a real influence on Le Blond, one would

---

in our catalogue of elegies; d'Auton merited inclusion because of the date. Brodeau's poem is not without interest, however, and it is a pity that his works are almost all still unpublished. Another example of a death elegy at this time is Robinet de Luc, "Elegie faicte par ledict Robinet sur l'accouchement de sa femme à angerville du temps de la maladie de Monseigneur Le Daulphin, envoyee a ung sien beau-frere", Catalogue 9. This poem is an *épître* and is much more a narration of a whole series of events culminating in the death of the child than a deploration on its death.

[54] See Catalogue 8. The poems are found on folios Diii verso and Diiii verso.

not expect his shyness over using the word elegy. As well as the
vagueness in the case of the two poems under discussion, one notes
that there are a number of *épîtres amoureuses* in *Le Printemps* which
could easily have been called elegies after the example of Marot and
which retain nevertheless the older title *épître*: "Epistre ou vng
amant faict plaincte que plus voyt sa dame" (folio Dviii recto),
"Epistre dung amant habandone de sa dame" (folio Dviii verso),
"Epistre ou vng amant promet a sa dame de garder tousiours loyal-
le" (folio Ei verso). Le Blond could easily have formed a section of
elegies like Marot. On the other hand, our seigneur de Branville uses
the word *élégie* in two death-poems. In the "Plaincte sur le trespas
de maistre benoist de la ñoe docteur en theologie penitentier Deu-
reux" (folio Ev recto) and in the "Plaincte sur le trespas de maistre
Pierre de Buysson" (folio Eviii verso), he calls upon various per-
sonages of the antique world to make their elegies heard. It will be
recalled that in 1536 Marot had not yet published his three death-
elegies.

It is not easy to see, then, that Le Blond's use of the word elegy
had much to do with Marot's *Suite de l'Adolescence Clémentine*. It
is not difficult, on the other hand, to believe that Le Blond used the
word as a result of his own humanistic culture. After the *Virelays
nuptiaux* of 1537, he was to devote himself entirely to translation,[55]
in which he shows a considerable concern for elegance of style; in
the second edition of *Le Livre de police humaine*,[56] he gives at the
beginning of the second book a defence of the French language quite
similar in its over-all message to Du Bellay's *Deffense et Illustration*.
And Charlier is not justified in suggesting that Le Blond would not
have been concerned with a renewing of French poetry by classical
and Italian imitation, [57]for as early as the *Printemps* of 1536, the
signs of his own contact with foreign influences are obvious.

[55] Except for his last work, a history of Normandy, which remains unpublished.
See Gustave Charlier, "Jean Le Blond et son apologie de la langue française
(1546)", an extract from the *Revue de l'instruction publique en Belgique*, 1912?,
335-6.
[56] Paris: Ch. L'Angelier, 1546, in-8. For a full discussion of this defence of the
French language, see Charlier.
[57] Charlier, "Jean Le Blond ...".

Le Printemps is indeed a peculiar mixture. Just as the poet does not see any inconsistency in placing the indelicate account of his troubles with venereal disease after a monstrous *rhétoriqueur* allegory on chastity,[58] the old and the new in poetry are placed side by side with equal status. The genres represented are almost exclusively familiar French forms: *rondeaux*, *ballades*, *chants royaux*, *dizains*, *septains* and so on. But besides our *épîtres-élégies*, and the mention of the word *élégie* in other poems, we find a curious "Description dune feuillee" (folio Dvi verso) in which the poet tries to paint an idyllic, Horatian scene. In a beautiful natural setting, described with much recourse to mythology, the poet evokes learned conversations among companions under the trees. To fit in with his pagan setting, he refers to the "odes" and "hymnes" (l. 26) which will be composed and enjoyed in these surroundings. Le Blond, had, then, an awareness of the classical world, and, while he did not renounce French styles, he did make an attempt to introduce something new. On a more concrete level we have proof in his use of alexandrines in the first elegy and of terza rima in the "Epistre dung amant ala louenge de sa dame de vers tiercez en la facon italienne" (folio Eii recto). It might be added that the dream in the second elegy is also "en la facon italienne" rather than *rhétoriqueur*: the love-dream replete with sensual details is typical of the strambottists and not of French poets of this period.[59]

Like Marot, Le Blond modifies the *rhétoriqueur* style; unlike Marot, he does not do it in the direction of simplicity (except technically) or of direct, personal statement. If Le Blond resembles Marot occasionally in such poems as the "Epistre à vng drapier" (folio Cvi verso), his style can more often be distinguished from his rival's and from the *rhétoriqueurs'* by his development of mythological ornamentation. Whereas the *rhétoriqueurs* simply referred to classical gods and heroes, Le Blond delights in developing the myths to the point that the main subject almost becomes a pretext. Because of this, his elegies offer an early example of the rich and learned

[58] "Temple de Diane", folio Avi verso and "L'espistre du poure fouldroye enuoyee au dieu damours", folio Biv verso.
[59] See Al. Cioranescu, *L'Arioste en France*, 2 vols. (Paris: Éditions des Presses Modernes, 1939), I, 234, for sources before Ariosto.

style which develops throughout the 1540's and finds its greatest expression in the early years of the 1550's.

Apart from Bouchet and Le Blond, love and death do not receive any further treatment in the elegies before 1545 – except for the curious *Elégie nuptiale* of 1537, no doubt written by Pierre Saliat.[60] Long and colourful, the poem was composed as a souvenir of Madeleine's wedding to James V of Scotland, a wedding which was thought to unite two people very much in love. Thus, without using precise sources, Saliat nevertheless imitates the sensuality of the classical elegy although his themes (the bride's departure from her family, the bearing of children) are more precisely typical of the classical epithalamium.

The poem scarcely merits inclusion, therefore, with the love-elegy – indeed, its theme is unique in the sixteenth-century elegy. All the other elegies of this period treat a considerable variety of subjects, sometimes as unexpected as Saliat's. François Sagon uses the title elegy once, in a petulant defence of himself and criticism of Marot and his friends.[61] But the poem is not an *épître*, as most of the poems in the famous quarrel tend to be: instead Sagon pretends here simply to be giving personal vent to his feelings in a 314-line *complainte* (a word he uses frequently in the poem) which includes a whole barrage of apostrophes along the way (to his Muse, his *esprit*, *coeur*, *conscience*, to all Christians and to his enemies – but not to Marot who remains in the third person). A short poem by Claude Colet[62] is equally untouched by Marot: it is a strophic justification of war as God's punishment and at the same time a prayer to God for deliverance from war. The obscure *Elegie delectable* by Guillaume Deheris[63] clearly points to the fact that a common-denominator in the elegies of this period is not even necessarily an element of complaint or sadness.

One is astounded, then, by the utter lack of Marot's influence on

---

[60] See Catalogue 10. We have an article in preparation on this poem.
[61] See Catalogue 12. Scollen, 71-76, gives a description of the contents of the poem.
[62] See Catalogue 15.
[63] See Catalogue 16. This poem offers another example of allegory which is lively and entertaining.

poets up to the time of his death. No more dramatic example of the independence of these poets can be given than that of Charles de Sainte-Marthe, for Sainte-Marthe was a great admirer of Marot. As well, he and Marot are the only poets of these years to gather a number of elegies together as a significant part of their works: in the case of Sainte-Marthe, the third section of his *Poesie Francoise* of 1540[64] is called "Epistres et Elegies". The reason for Sainte-Marthe's putting the *épîtres* and the *élégies* in the same section will soon become apparent, but he nevertheless went out of his way to distinguish the latter poems. On page 197 we find the title "Les Élégies" in large print, and this is followed by a short preface which informs us that the following six poems are merely a selection of the poet's elegies, which he will someday publish separately, "...tant pour la diuersité, que pour la gratuité des matieres lesquelles y sont comprises". Already the six elegies that he gives us well illustrate what he means by the diversity and gravity of matter. Not one deals with the plaints of a lover; not one is even so frivolous as to mourn the death of an individual. The subjects are either moral or theological, except in the case of the first poem, where the poet allows himself to write a piece of fulsome praise to the dedicatee of the whole collection, the duchesse d'Etampes. Since Scollen has given a lengthy account of these six poems we need only recall briefly here their salient features.[65]

The first elegy, the longest of the set, begins with an idyllic description of the ancient valley of Tempe (ll. 1-36), a description which is made as lush as possible in order to contrast all the more dramatically with the new and even more extraordinary Tempe, the duchy of Etampes, given to Anne de Pisseleu in 1536. The poem is thus based on a pun already exploited by Marot in his epigram "De La Duché D'Estampes". Lines 37-52 make the transition from the old to the new Tempe, and lines 53 to 166 present various comparisons between the two, the superiority of the duchess's domain being clear each time: the modern Tempe is bigger than its predecessor, its charms and attributes are immortal, since they are not based simply on material beauty, and the present duchess has a far better

[64] See Catalogue 14.
[65] Scollen, 77-96.

chorus of poets to praise her domain than the valley in Thessaly had. At line 167 we return to the theme of the spiritual virtues of Etampes and of the duchess herself. The poem ends with a plea that poets who had praised the ancient Tempe reconsider their choice.

The title of the second elegy indicates its complete contrast with the preceding poem: "Elegie en forme d'Epistre, a Monsieur le Cheualier de Monthozier, Que a qui Iesus ayde, rien ne peut nuyre". If its opening and close are sufficiently flattering to suggest the tone of the elegy to the duchess, the main preoccupation of the poem is soon clear and puts it in an altogether different category. The elegy is an answer to a letter which the duc de Montaussier wrote to Sainte-Marthe to congratulate him on his change of fortune.[66] The poet never makes explicit the precise events, but we can presume with fair certainty that what inspired the duke to write was Sainte-Marthe's election to a chair at the collège de la Trinité at Lyons (1540) after years of imprisonment and flight. In Sainte-Marthe's final victory over his adversaries, the duke sees the will of God. Sainte-Marthe agrees:

> Il est bien uray, que si croyons, Fortune
> Nous dominer, dirois que par rancune,
> (Voire à grand tort) à souffrir suis soubmis
> Tant affligé, sans mal auoir commis.
> Mais ie cognoys, que Fortune, ou les Astres,
> (Ce que nous font a croire ces follastres,
> Et ignorants Astrologues, menteurs)
> Ne sont en rien sur moy dominateurs.
> ....
> Ie croy plus tost, estre le puissant uueil
> De celuy la, qui sur nous seul domine,
> Et qui les maulx augmente, ou bien termine,
> Ainsi qu'il ueult, a iceulx mesmement,
> Qui sont Esleux, des leur commencement. (ll. 31-46).

This is the theme of the poem, the clear expression of Sainte-Marthe's convictions, which are seen here to be not simply Reformist but, more exactly, Calvinist.

[66] The letter is no doubt the one reproduced in Ruutz-Rees, *Charles de Sainte-Marthe* (Paris: Champion, 1914), 343. For information about the duke, see Ph. -Aug. Becker, *Aus Frankreichs Frührenaissance* (München: Max Kellerer, 1927), 131, ft. 1.

Sainte-Marthe writes of similarly serious affairs in the third elegy: "Du vray bien, et nourriture de l'Ame". The poem addresses mankind in general, the assumption being that all mankind badly needs the exhortations given: like the second elegy we have here some indication of Sainte-Marthe's jaundiced view of the world. As the title suggests the poem deals with two principal matters: lines 1-84 deal with the definition of "le vray bien" ,and the remainder, lines 85-104, with the soul's nourishment. Sainte-Marthe first emphasizes that whatever is considered good should be permanent (ll. 1-12).In general, however, men choose as their goal the acquisition of material riches, and this is because men do not properly reflect on the destiny of the body. Reflection on death, in fact, constitutes the fundamental principle of gaining a proper perspective in this world. Since only our soul is immortal, the only good is that which profits it (ll. 57-68). The proper nourishment of the soul is clear: "C'est l'esprit sainct, c'est la sacrée Bible" (l. 86). The body rebels, but the soul must bind itself to "son cher Espoux", Christ, and be liberated of the body's dominion. Faith is the key to salvation, as the last lines of the poem make clear:

> Or lisons donc l'Escripture tant belle,
> Or recepuons ceste bonne nouuelle,
> Que par la Foy, IESVS nous renouuelle.
> Par la Foy fait,
> Que nostre Esprit, se nourrit et reffect,
> Que le lyen de peché, est deffaict.
> C'est le uray bien, et le seul bien parfaict,
> Qu'il fault auoir. (ll. 97-104)

The fourth poem is an "Elegie de l'Ame parlante au Corps, et monstrante le proffit de la Mort". The title makes clear some similarity of themes with the preceding elegy, and again we find Sainte-Marthe's contempt for earthly existence:

> Au monde n'a que mal, et tristesse incertaine,
> Labeur perpetuel, pour une chose uaine: (ll. 13-14)

The soul is in constant battle against the body, the temptations of the world and the temptations of the devil. Death removes all three enemies. This monologue of the soul ends in an epitaph which makes a final plea to man that he look upon death as a happy deliverance.

In the last two elegies, Sainte-Marthe reveals himself as a moralist: with his eyes fixed on the finite world, he discusses some of the qualities necessary for a man to be worthy. Both poems are addressed to particular men, but the complimentary element is reduced here to a minimum: in both cases, the compliment simply serves as a graceful conclusion to the poem. The fifth elegy concerns "De la vraye Noblesse", and in defining the term Sainte-Marthe feels constrained to criticize both the debased nobles of his day, who had become mere courtiers, and the new class of bourgeois-nobles, whose virtue resided in their purse. True nobility is to be found in virtue, for it makes the heart noble.[67] The sixth elegy defines wisdom for us. The opening of the poem comes perhaps as something of a surprise:

> Ie m'esbahy d'un tas de personnaiges,
> Qui, pour auoir le tiltre d'estre saiges,
> Veulent user, contre la Verité,
> En tous leurs faicts, d'une seuerité: (ll. 1-4)

One almost had the impression that Sainte-Marthe was one of these sober souls! He is, however, very critical of these severe, harsh characters who, he feels, inevitably fall into the trap of egoism. Wisdom is entirely different. The lessons which Sainte-Marthe disengages from his readings of the philosophers are twofold and are summed up in the title of the poem: "Que le Cueur fort et magnanime, est le seul riche du Monde". Typically for the period, magnanimity is seen as a serenity and strength which are the result of one's detachment from the ambitions of this world. Even philosophy is of no use, for it concerns human wisdom; true wisdom is of God and holds God as the sole good:

> Saigesse dy, de DIEV la cognoissance,
> Laquelle fait de tout bien accroissance.
> Qui tant bonne est, qu'en tout temps, et tout lieu,
> Elle maintient pour souuerain Bien, DIEV.
> Souuerain Bien, car a iamais il dure,
> Et ne permet qu'aulcun Mal on endure. (ll. 62-67)

[67] See Scollen, 89-91, for details regarding the source of this poem.

This résumé of the six elegies of Sainte-Marthe is perhaps suffi-cient to make us completely sceptical once again about Marot's influence. Although Sainte-Marthe referred to Marot as his "Pere d'Alience",[68] it is not easy to see how the twenty-seven elegies of Marot had anything to do with the six of Sainte-Marthe. The sub-ject-matter is entirely different in the two poets; Sainte-Marthe shows some originality in his use of form; the *épître* nature of Marot's poems is considerably less in evidence in Sainte-Marthe. As well, precise sources for the individual elegies of our poet are rarely considered to be Marot: the latter's "Temple de Cupidon", may have had some influence on the Tempe poem,[69] but Ruutz-Rees and Scollen both consider Marguerite de Navarre to be the important source for the elegies.[70]

What does resemble Marot is the arrangement of the whole of the *Poesie Francoise* according to genres. The volume is divided into three main sections: *Epigrammes; Rondeaux, Balades et chant*(s) *Royaulx;*[71] *Epistres et Elegies.* Of all the forms used, and these sec-tions include various forms not mentioned in the general headings, only one appears relatively new to French literature: the elegy. The problem is precisely why Sainte-Marthe decided to call six of his poems elegies.

The problem is all the more difficult to solve since the *épître* sec-tion contains poems which could have been considered elegies according to Sainte-Marthe's use of the word,[72] or else according to Marot's. That is, if Sainte-Marthe had been consciously imitating the elegy of Marot, he could easily have formed a section with such poems as "A Mademoiselle Beringue, De leur honneste, et irrepre-hensible Amour" (X), "Consolation à vne Damoiselle Affligée de ses Parents" (XII), "A vne Dame, soubhaittante la moytié des desirs

---

[68] See *Poesie Francoise*, 55: "A Clement Marot son Pere d'Alience".

[69] Ruutz-Rees, *Charles de Sainte-Marthe*, 134.

[70] Ruutz-Rees, 183, 191-2; Scollen, 96. We do not always find the comparison of texts very convincing as proof of direct influence.

[71] There are in fact no *chants royaux* in this section.

[72] Cf. I "A DIEV, Confession de son infirmite, et Inuocation de sa Grace"; XX "A R. Pere en DIEV, Monseigneur Anne de Grolée, Abbé de S. Pierre de Vienne"; XXI "A noble et puissant Seigneur, Monsieur Antoine de Muillion, Baron de Bressieux, frere de susdict Seigneur de S. Pierre" etc.

de son Amy" (XVII), "Pour vn gentilhomme, A vne Damoiselle" (XIX), "Pour vne Dame, à son Mary, de long temps d'elle absent" (XXX). Our poet not only seems to have ignored Marot's example, but has not clearly distinguished his own use of genres clearly.

Again the problem of the use of the word *élégie* remains insoluble. In the end, it is perhaps simply the result of Marot's having used it for a section of his works: we shall see after 1540 a number of important examples of this new practice of arranging poems according to genre and often as vaguely as Sainte-Marthe has done. The book of elegies itself, however, is not so diverse as the author's preface suggests: except for the first poem about Tempe in France, all the poems deal with serious subjects concerning thought and conduct. The poems are, in effect, *discours*, as even their titles suggest: "Du vray bien, et nourriture de l'Ame", "Que le Cueur fort et magnanime, est le seul riche du Monde, par son contentement". In a clearly reasoned form, Sainte-Marthe sets out to prove his ideas and to convince us of them. If there is something of the "élément émotionnel"[73] of Marguerite's poetry in Sainte-Marthe, there is much more of the logician who plans his arguments and proceeds slowly, step by step, to his demonstration. These poems are not entirely unlike the Vanity elegy of Michel de Tours: the main difference is perhaps to be found simply in the evolution of French poetic style towards 1540.

The history of the elegy until the death of Marot is thus pure anarchy. Any prosodic form, any theme, even any mood seems to be acceptable. Only two firm points can be made: Marot's influence is nil, and all of a sudden after 1534 there is a measure – let us not exaggerate – of popularity in the use of the title elegy. It is surely significant that before 1534 only two poets cared to attach the word to their poems and that in the decade after the *Suite* about ten poets care to do so. If this is the influence of the *Suite*, it is an influence which involves vocabulary only.

[73] Ruutz-Rees, 183.

II

BETWEEN MAROT AND RONSARD: 1544-1560

1. CHARLES FONTAINE

The first clear sign of Marot's influence on the French elegy is an impressive one: there are twenty-two elegies in Charles Fontaine's *La Fontaine d'Amour* of 1545.[1] All of these poems deal with the theme of love. In 1555 Fontaine presents us with two more elegies, both death lamentations.[2] Thematically, then, Fontaine follows in Marot's footsteps. Closer similarities are not difficult to find at least in the case of the love-elegies.

Like Marot's poems, these love-elegies are letters sent to the beloved, letters of complaint that the lady does not keep to her promises (XI), will not write to him (VIII), will not receive him (II), will not give in to his clearly sensual entreaties (V); letters concerning their separations, the inevitable trips (XVI); frequent letters of praise (XII), even more prominent an element in Fontaine's poems than in Marot's; some letters of rebellion (XIII) and criticism of woman's cruel lack of sympathy (XXI). There is a great fund of common themes, then, in the epistolary elegies of Marot and Fontaine, themes which are of course common to all the love-poets of the sixteenth-century.[3]

Fontaine's style is often reminiscent of Marot as well. Just like

---

[1] See Catalogue 17.
[2] See Catalogue 31.
[3] See, for a more detailed description of the contents, Christine M. Scollen, *The Birth of the Elegy in France 1500-1550* (Genève: Droz, 1967), 97 *sqq.* We do not agree with the interpretation of the eighteenth elegy as a love poem; Glatigny regrets the absence of his 'mistress' but the word is used in the sense of 'the wife of the master'.

Marot, Fontaine is downright medieval at times: we find some humourless rhymes like "commandement – qu'on mande ment" (XI, 3-4), and once again we meet *Dame Raison* and *Fol Jugement* (X). However, Marot's influence, or Fontaine's similarity to Marot, is to be found more particularly in the frequent simplicity of the verse. The sixth elegy is remarkably direct and unaffected:

> O meschant sort, o maudite fortune,
> Qui pour auoir aymé ainsi fort vne,
> M'as bien tenu l'espace de deux ans
> Entre tes lacz tant durs, & mal plaisants! (ll. 1-4)

Fontaine's imagery is also often reminiscent of Marot:

> Que n'es sinon qu'un arbre de plaisance,
> Portant un fruict amer de desplaisance.
> Mais quand le feu couuert de ce beau taint,
> Iusques au cueur les regardants ataint,
> Incontinent on iuge que la flamme
> Te monstre auoir un courage de femme,
> Tel que ie quiers. (II, 17-23)

Fontaine's love-elegies are thus generally not easy to distinguish from Marot's: they are *épîtres* in decasyllabic couplets, normally between thirty and eighty lines in length, and they express the same basic themes in a similar style.

Fontaine nevertheless does show some interesting points of originality. His elegies tend towards a more personal, or at least circumstantial, treatment of the popular themes. If the banal theme of separation is the very basis of XVI, the poet entices our interest by his not quite precise enough references to the "cité", "terrain & cloistre", and "palays" that he leaves behind but haunts in his mind because of his beloved:

> Ie suis en lieu, & en rue plus vile,
> Peuplée moins, & sentant mieux ses champs,
> On ne voy tant de sortes de marchants. (ll. 18-20)

One is often thankful for even this much of the seemingly lived experience. XXII is infinitely more biographical in nature. The writer has fallen in love again, and with greater intensity than in the past. The lady is married, has a daughter – but where is the husband? Upon the poet's return from Italy he immediately goes to Paris to see the lady:

> Amour me fist au retour tant oser
> Que vous allay la premiere bayser:
> Sans prendre esgard d'embrasser vostre pere
> Premierement, ou baiser vostre mere. (ll. 78-82)

Is the lady a widow? In any case, from Lyons he sends the elegy to request that she accept him as her *serviteur*.

What is particularly special about Fontaine is the sort of thing that we find, for instance, in the first three elegies. The poems make the expected request, but they are principally devoted to praise of the lady's beauty. In some lines this praise is accomplished in a straight-forward enough way, but Fontaine has often the ability to transform even this type of traditional approach and idea into peculiarly sensual verses:

> Si l'esprit grand, qui tous tes faitz regist,
> Si la beauté (Dame) qui en toy gist
> Ne mentent point, tu es de douceurs pleine
> Comme de fruitz en saison une plaine.
> Si autrement (ce que croire ne puis)
> Apres auoir repeu mes yeux seduitz,
> Ne veux le cueur pareillement repaistre:
> Mieux me voudroit mieux cent fois sans yeux estre. (II, 3-10)

> Mais quand le feu couuert de ce beau taint,
> Iusques au cueur les regardants ataint,
> Incontinent on iuge que la flamme
> Te monstre auoir un courage de femme,
> Tel que ie quiers. (II, 19-23)

Fontaine has still more effective means of heightening the sensual atmosphere of his verse, and he uses them to good advantage in these first poems. First of all is memory of precise moments, a much more vivid way to suggest the lady's beauty than the usual sort of description of her *sub specie aeternitatis:*

> Depuis le iour que vy ton blanc tetin,
> Par l'entrebail d'un collet de satin... (I, 3-4)

The lady of these first elegies captured the poet's heart, shall we say, at a party. The party itself is described in an appropriately atmospheric way:

> O quelle grande chere
> Là on nous fait! Vn chacun met enchere
> A qui mieux mieux, suruiennent metz sur metz,
> ....
> Chacun repeu, nous leuasmes de là,
> Ayants bien veu les iardins, & mesnage.
> Car vous sçauez que cueur amoureux nage
> En nouueautez.   (III, 59-69)

It is the lady's dancing, however, which comes back most obsessively to the poet: she is remembered as a moving, living creature:

> Ie te voyois (i'en ay bien souuenance)
> Rire, & parler en bonne contenance.
> Et quand quelqu'un deuers toy s'adressoit
> Tant saigement le tien corps se dressoit
> Le receuant d'vne façon humaine,
> A celle fin que danser il te meine.
> ....
> Tu sçais si bien en bransle, en basse dance,
> Comment le pied, & comment le corps dance,
> Qu'on te tenoit de la dance le chef,
> Soit à baisser, ou à faire relief.
> ....
> Tantost apres deuers toy ie m'adresse.
> Lors en doux œil d'amoureuse caresse
> Tu m'acceptas, sans delay, ne refus:
> Dont fort ioyeux dedans mon cueur ie fus.
> Non pas doutant que femme me refuse.
> Ie la rendrois trop plus que moy confuse.
> Mais que tant plus auois à toy desir:
> En ta caresse auois plus de plaisir. (III, 23-54)

Memory returns to torment the ambitious desires of the lover, and, as he remembers, his mind goes on to create purely imaginary events, thus adding fuel to his torment:

> Certainement bien souuent m'est auis
> Que deuant moy tu es tout vis à vis,
> Et que le bransle auecques toy ie meine,
> Te contemplant mieux que de la semaine
> Depuis le hault iusqu'en bas: puis souuent
> Pour te donner au bas un peu de vent
> Leve du pied ta cotte bien doublée,
> Sans que la danse en soit en rien troublée. (I, 21-8)

The point of these many quotations is to indicate how far the
first poet to be influenced by Marot also went off in a new direction,
for in poems such as we have just been looking at, we have a spirit
quite different from what we find in the poems of Marot. It is the
spirit almost of the classical elegy – the classical elegy with an Italian accent: the sensuality of the first three elegies is not Gallic.

Nor is the expression in Fontaine's elegies always Gallic. The
image at the end of XVII is the sort of *concetto* which delighted the
strambottists and their audiences:

> Le feu que sens est feu chauld, cler, et beau:
> C'est à sçauoir de Venus le flambeau,
> Qui tousiours luyst, et long temps ne se cache.
> Ah! vostre cueur n'est pas qui ne le sçache.
> Luy plaise doncq' espandre tant soit peu
> De l'eau de grace au milieu de ce feu,
> Dont par vostre œil qui sur moy estincelle,
> M'auez ieté la premiere estincelle. (ll. 71-78)

It is the twenty-first elegy, however, which uses most noticeably
Italianate imagery. Again it involves fires "plus grand que cil
d'Ethna" (l. 15), the fear of being consumed, and "pluye de grace"
(l. 5), but here the images are developed throughout the extent of the
poem and not simply referred to quickly. There is some direct
borrowing from classical poets as well,[4] but both the Italian and the
classical influences are to be found more in spirit and approach rather than precise borrowing.

Fontaine is, therefore, an ambiguous sort of poet – all his writing
is marked by a hesitancy in what direction it will take, and this
has led to his being taxed as a poet lacking in personality.[5] In the
elegies we certainly are confronted with the old and the new in both
treatment of theme and style. We must also point out that Fontaine's
seeming adherence to Marot's formula of *élégie* equals *épître* is
not without its ambiguity as well.

Usually, it must be stressed, the signs of the elegy as an *épître* are

---

[4] Scollen, 100-104.
[5] See Alice Hulubei, *L'Eglogue en France au XVIe siècle, époque des Valois*
(Paris: Droz, 1938), 328-9.

as clear as in Marot. If Fontaine often contents himself with simple references to writing, his terms are often without ambiguity:

> Ly doncq' la lettre, et prens en bonne part
> L'affection du cueur dont elle part. (XV, 45-46)

> Apres que i'ay bien veillé, et n'ay peu
> Aucunement vous trouuer à temps deu
> Pour vous bailler vn petit mot de letre... (XVIII, 1-3)

There are, nevertheless, two poems which are exceptions to Marot's habits. The sixth elegy is addressed to Fortune, not to the lady; and the twenty-first does not have an address at all: the poet ruminates on the lack of pity which his beloved shows towards him and considers how he should react to it. However, these two exceptions out of a total of twenty-two poems can hardly make us hesitate to observe that the Fontaine elegy as a decasyllabic-couplet, epistolary love-complaint does not distinguish itself in any way from the same poet's *épîtres*, nineteen of which follow the elegies in the *Fontaine d'amour*. Just as much as the elegies, these letters deal with the common themes of love along with Fontaine's own special type of remembered and imaginary experiences. A few *épîtres* of a more original nature[6] cannot obscure the fundamental equivalence of the elegy and the *épître* in the writing of Fontaine.

The distinction, then, which Marot made in the *Suite* of 1534, is thus destroyed: there is no literary reason for Fontaine to have given three sections to his *Fontaine d'amour* – *Élégies*, *Epîtres*, and *Epigrammes*. What prompted him to do so was perhaps the feeling that at least an air of variety would not hurt the success of his book: a collection of only *épîtres* (or elegies) and epigrams appears much less interesting than the chosen arrangement. What is important for us to see, however, is that, while greatly influenced by Marot in the arrangement of the *Fontaine d'amour*, in the use of the word *élégie* and in the elegies themselves, Fontaine has not understood the reason behind Marot's use of the genre as a means of limiting the

---

[6] For example, in X, a young woman who has just given birth to a son discusses her experience, which she holds to be greater than that of the nun's dedication to God; XIX, addressed to two sisters, discusses the pleasures of pastimes with women.

épître, which was unlimited in its range, and of giving sharper definition to one type of *épître*.

There is one further point to be stressed, and it is that in neither the elegies nor the *épîtres* of Charles Fontaine do we find the syllogistic structure typical already of an earlier age. For all that he owes to his immediate predecessors and contemporaries, Fontaine's poetry looks ahead in style and also in the freedom of structure essential for the creation of new genres.

2. THE TWO STYLES OF 1551

The two tendencies in Fontaine – a rather strict adherence to the Marot lesson and a more 'modern' style and atmosphere – reappear in exaggerated and purer forms in 1551, the next important date in the history of the elegy. In that year, Bérenger de la Tour d'Albenas reveals himself to be far more clearly a follower of Marot than Fontaine was, while Etienne Forcadel indulges in much more florid expression and a looser form than Fontaine dared. In the elegies of these two poets we see with considerable clarity the extraordinary indecision in French poetry during the 1540's and 1550's, an indecision created by an ever widening culture and a feeling that all was possible without the certainty of what was desirable.

In the case of La Tour himself, rather than appearing in simultaneous confusion, the various possibilities follow each other in a clear evolution. In 1547 he produced for the death of the king a *Chant elegiaque de la Republique*[7] which is virtually a *rhétoriqueur* deploration; after 1551 he is even an initiator of new influences in French poetry;[8] and in 1551,[9] specifically in his elegies, he shows himself to be a dutiful follower of Marot.[10] The elegies are indeed in

[7] *sur la mort de hault et magnanisme Prince, Francoys premier de ce nom Roy de France* (Toulouse: Boudeville, 1547), in-4.
[8] See Hulubei, 331-7; A . Cioranescu, *L'Arioste en France des origines à la fin du XVIII siècle*, 2 vols. (Paris: Editions des Presses Modernes, 1939), I, 127-8.
[9] Catalogue 25. The elegies are found among the *vers divers*.
[10] The genres favoured by our poet are all those of the first half of the century: *chants royaux, cantiques, épîtres, chansons, épigrammes, épitaphes* and *blasons*. V.-L. Saulnier in his article on Bérenger de La Tour in the *Dictionnaire des*

the clearest *élégie-épître amoureuse* style[11] and thus do not require much comment.

The precise themes of La Tour's poems are also not particularly original: he shares most of his themes with Marot and with a host of other poets. It is interesting to consider, however, a poem like IV in which we see how La Tour is on the one hand unoriginal and yet, in the end, able to give his poems a special accent. This elegy is subtitled "D'une ieune Espouse, a son Mari", which reminds us immediately of Marot's *malmariée* (Elégie XX). There is no precise debt of La Tour to Marot, however: both poets simply try their hand at a commonplace theme. In this poem La Tour reveals the dominant characteristics of all his elegies. First their essentially narrative character: he is not always very strong on pure description or analysis of feeling; he much prefers to attach his emotional states to a lengthy account of events, however trivial they may be. Also important to notice in this respect is the frequent lack of clarity that this narrative often has for the 'general' reader: it is only the person addressed in the letter who is, presumably, likely to understand fully the implications of the narrative detail. By an obscurity thus born of incomplete revelation, these epistolary elegies take on a heightened degree of realism: one almost feels one is snooping into a correspondence intended to remain private.

In the fourth elegy we have as well the themes which recur most insistently in La Tour's poems. The very basis of the poor woman's complaint is the change in her husband's attitude. His attentions, his devotion to her began to wane as soon as she fell in love with him:

> Mais tost apres que mon feu ietta flamme,
> Ton cœur malin fut autheur de mon blasme,
> Sans toutesfois iuste cause et raison. (ll. 25-7)

This emotional fickleness is not exclusive to men: in the first three

---

lettres françaises: Le seizième siècle, sees an influence of Scève in the poem entitled *Le Siècle d'Or*, because of its obscurity.

[11] Elegies IV and V even have the old-fashioned subscription. Only VII is not a letter, but the lament of a young lady before she is to be executed for some unspecified crime. In the other poems the epistolary nature is usually unambiguous, and the theme of letter-writing is itself prominent (V, XI, XIII).

elegies the poet makes the same complaint about the lady. The lady was the first to speak of love, but once he became enamoured in return she changes:

> Je ne voy plus, en toy, qu'une rudesse,
> Vn oeil iré, vn sourcil qui m'estonne (II, 6-7)

The old theme of reciprocity in love thus receives a special bias in the poet's emphasis that the problem is the simultaneity of the feeling of love in two people.

The sixteenth-century poetic conventions of love poetry always give some importance to the theme of death: life without love is more often than not seen as a virtual impossibility. In La Tour the theme of death takes on a peculiarly vivid character, no doubt because his poetry generally avoids the usual clichés and conventional expression of the death theme. In the fourth elegy again, it is striking, even upsetting, to read that the lady almost hopes for the death of her still unborn child. In VIII the hope for death on the part of the poet is more of the conventional type, but even in V, which is basically a poem of happiness, his apprehension before he knows the content of his lady's letter leads him to the threshold of suicide. The fire of love is too slow a way to die; he contemplates a faster method:

> L'espee en main, par grand fureur tendue
> Droit vers le cœur ay responce attendue
> De vous Madame: à fin de me sousmettre
> A dure mort, la et quand vostre lettre
> M'eut denié l'esperé traitement. (ll. 1-5)

The seventh elegy gives the final complaint of a woman before her public execution. The ninth elegy, a poem of departure, is filled with the fear of death through plague. The theme of death in these poems is varied, therefore, and its constant presence contributes to a strangely dark and violent note in La Tour's verse.

As we have suggested, the effectiveness of these themes is increased by the realistic simplicity of the style. La Tour's pen is even more natural than Marot's in his elegies. Indeed, in La Tour the directness and the simplicity of the style almost remove the poems from the domain of poetry. Even when mythological ornamentation appears, how bare the poetry of the fourth elegy remains:

Bien que Iason en mon endroit tu soyes,
Et, comme luy, prennes ailleurs tes voyes,
Tant est ma foy sus fermeté fondee,
Qu'on te dira, vn Iason, sans Medee,
Amour m'incite auec soin & esmoy,
Garder le fruit commun à toy & moy. (ll. 31-6)

La Tour is thus the most dramatic example of the simple, natural style which came as a reaction to the *rhétoriqueurs* after 1525. In his elegies he presents us with a surprisingly realistic and personal series of poems describing the *malheurs* of love.[12] Unfortunately, they risk sometimes being as uninteresting as other people's correspondence tends to be in real life.

The elegies of Etienne Forcadel present the opposite extreme. If in a very general way they might be said to resemble Marot's poems, the style adopted represents the artificial and ornamented stream of pre-Pléiade poetry which we found in Le Blond and to a certain extent in Fontaine and which prepared the 'revolution' of the odes and sonnets of the 1550's. This increasing tendency towards learned allusion and mythological development in French poetry is interestingly illustrated by Forcadel's elegies themselves. In *Le Chant des Sereines* of 1548[13] two elegies appear which become *Elégies* II and III in 1551.[14] Eight new elegies are added, and these ten appear again in the posthumous edition of 1579,[15] prepared by the author just before his death. In each successive version of the elegies, the poems are lengthened as the embroidery of the theme becomes more complicated. *Elégie* II is first only sixty-two lines in length, then sixty-eight and finally eighty-six; III goes from seventy-four lines to

---

[12] Unlike Fontaine, La Tour seems to follow Marot's lead in naming these poems elegies in order to separate a particular type of *épître* from the others, for if we read through the *épîtres* contained in *Le Siecle d'Or*, we do not find any which could be placed satisfactorily among the elegies. Only two ("A ma Damoiselle du Besset" and "Pour vn Gentilhomme, à Mademoiselle Olimpie de la Val, sa Maistresse d'alliance") deal with love, but neither is of the essentially sad nature to be found in the elegies: both are poems of praise and offers of servitude.

[13] See Catalogue 21.

[14] This is the edition which we shall use for our discussion. See Catalogue 26.

[15] See Catalogue 26.

eighty lines and then to 102 lines. The additions and revisions are never important: they show a will simply to decorate.[16]

The outer garb of these poems is somewhat different, then, from that of Marot's or La Tour's elegies. It must be pointed out immediately that there is also an important aspect of form which is different. When comparing the elegies and *épîtres* which appear in Forcadel's 1551 volume, one immediately thinks back to Marot as it is noticed that the elegies all deal with love and that the *épîtres* all address men and treat a variety of subjects excluding love. The elegies are not, however, self-consciously epistolary in nature and five of the ten do not contain a personal address:[17] four of the poems develop for the reader the history of the poet's love, its origin and its effects (I, V, VII) and comment on the sad state of love in the world since the passing of the Golden Age (VIII), and the third elegy expresses his devotion to women despite the evil tongue of a slanderer.

This weakening of the epistolary type of personal communication between two people is symptomatic of the approach to content in these elegies, and again one thinks back especially to Le Blond as an earlier exponent of this type of elegy. Forcadel generalizes his themes in such a way that they finally become impersonal. It is perhaps only the eighth which is blatantly general: here the poet in lamenting the passing of the Golden Age even weakens the precise application of his lament to the sixteenth-century world by too great an emphasis on remote mythological examples. What is particularly significant, however, is that poems which have a basis of personal (or pseudo-personal) content invariably seem to end up speaking of *Amour* and *la Femme*. Thus I, which tells of the poet's awakening to love, also contains Cupid's rhetoric concerning the beneficent effects of love. Elegy V, which sums up the poet's experience of love after a certain length of time, is principally a statement of what love does to all humans. Despite the great misery he claims to have found in loving, elegies VI and X argue the case for loving – addressed to a lady who stubbornly refuses him but applicable to all the stubborn of this world.

---

[16] See Charles Oulmont, *Estienne Forcadel* (Toulouse: Edouard Privat, 1907), 27 *sqq.* for a discussion of the poet's revisions.
[17] VII addresses the lady directly during the final third of the poem.

One must conclude, then, that Forcadel is not the circumstantial poet that we found in La Tour. From a vague, pseudo-personal idea, he constantly applies his theme to the experience of all men. Since he is not a creative analyst of the experience of love, his energies go especially into the poetic elaboration of his commonplaces. There is perhaps no better example of his style than the fourth elegy. The inspiration for the poem is the poet's receiving a gift of three violets from his lady. The emphasis throughout the poem, however, is on the symbolic interpretation of this present, and his many thoughts are only sometimes personal in nature. The colours of the flowers, yellow, white and blue, are indeed reminiscent of the colours which love causes his face to take on, but the fact that there are three flowers cheers him because three is a sacred number. The 'filet d'or' which binds the flowers together reminds him of his lady's hair (which is "longs & luisans, ie dy luisans & longs") but the garden in which she picked the flowers must be Venus's or Cupid's. This bit of fancy causes the poem to veer off into the world of the gods, a development which leaves the three humble violets rather far behind. And so the poem meanders throughout its fifty-eight lines, the supposedly personal details losing in the context all possible suggestion of reality. The poem is simply a poetic tribute to the violet.

This symbolic analysis of the bouquet of violets seems particularly French in its origins: for a good many years before Forcadel's poem, French poets had given elaborate interpretations to the material world. Indeed, Forcadel sometimes appears even slightly old-fashioned in the sources of his poetic elaborations since a number of poems show his fondness for the lore of the old lapidaries and bestiaries (II, VIII, X). His mania for decorative detail fed on a great variety of sources, however, and it is curious that he should have presumed to give a poet friend a warning about using too elaborate and erudite a style.[18]

Of all his poetic habits it is perhaps especially his fondness for decorative myths which strikes us. This is increasingly the case in French poetry during the 1540's, and Forcadel's own humanistic culture must have been broad. It is possible that he also had the

[18] "Epistre VII à Tomas Amerin".

encouragement of Jacques Peletier du Mans, as Pierre de Nolhac has suggested,[19] and he was by 1551[20] already familiar with Ronsard and Du Bellay: in the "Epistre V, au seigneur Henri de Mesmes, parisien, Iurisconsulte", we learn that Ronsard has read Forcadel's poetry,[21] and in "Epistre VII. à Thomas Amerin" we find the following lines:

> Tu suis Dubelay de si pres
> Que fais vers dignes de Cypres. (ll. 13-4)

At a very early date, then, our poet was in contact with the poetry which made a cult of antiquity. The signs of Forcadel's adhesion to this cult are evident in his treatment of classical themes throughout a whole poem (VIII, on love after the Golden Age); his lengthy (Prometheus in V, ll. 33 *sqq.*) and abundant (IV, ll. 23 *sqq.*) use of mythology; a number of sentiments and images (poetry as sacred in I, 46; the idolator and not the sculptor lending deity to the image, in VI; the beauty of combat between man and woman only when they are beautiful and naked, in III, 36-40). The first elegy as an introduction to the whole group is also a classical practice not found so far in France. Some habits of expression suggest more precisely the influence of the *Greek Anthology*, although Hutton is inclined to believe that this influence was transmitted to Forcadel by Renaissance-Latin sources or else by Ausonius.[22] Whatever the case, we have a certain flavour of the *Anthology* in the rather frequent use of adynaton, as in III:

> Quand est à moy, auant, que là m'espreuue,
> Verrons secher Garonne le cler fleuue
> Au froid Ianuier, ou couler au rebours.

[19] Pierre de Nolhac, *Ronsard et l'humanisme* (Paris: Champion, 1921), 192.

[20] Or even earlier, for the licence of the 1551 *Œuvres* is dated December 14, 1550.

[21] Vray que tu m'escris, que Ronsard
Est riche tesmoing de ta part:
Et qu'il ha noz vers estimez,
Que puis peu de temps i'ay limez.
Celuy donques m'ha daigné lire,
Qui seul peult à prouuer suffire. (ll. 35-40)

[22] James Hutton, *The Greek Anthology in France and in the Latin Writers of the Netherlands to the year 1880* (Ithaca: Cornell University Press, 1946), 329-330.

Auant paistront la Mer Dains et Ours
Fuyans les bois, que ie tache de poindre. (ll. 41-45)

The bitter-sweet idea of love is not exclusive to any one poetic tradition, but again the absinth-honey comparison in the first elegy recalls the *Anthology* rather than Italian or French expressions of the idea.

It is not Forcadel, however, whom we would choose as the important representative during these years of the attempt, hitherto not apparent, to create in French a new type of poem which would be a counterpart to the classical elegy. As far as the weight of the experiment is concerned, that distinction belongs more justly to Jean Doublet.

3. THE FRENCH OVID

It is a curiosity of the history of the elegy in France that it is not until 1559 that we have a significant attempt to recreate the classical elegy, and it is also curious that when that experiment is made it is thanks to an obscure poet from Dieppe and not to the poets whose names are most usually associated with the renovation of French poetry.

We have said that Doublet's is the first 'significant' attempt, because it must be recognized that there were a few very slight experiments before him. As we shall see in the next chapter, Ronsard tried in two of his earliest elegies (1553) to imitate the classical distich and, in one case, to use freely the themes of a particular classical elegy. Also in 1553, Guillaume des Autels obviously is thinking of the classical elegy in his own single example of the genre, the "Elegie à la Toute Divine de Pontus de Tyard".[23] He begins his poem by asking the "Manes sainctz de Philette / Et Callimach", who inspired Propertius and Tibullus, to teach him the ways of the elegy:

Enseignez moy, pour mieux flatter l'oreille,
Mes nombres ioindre en façon non pareille:
　　Bien que leurs pas, par piedz tant assurez,
　　A vostre loy ne soyent pas mesurez.

[23] See Catalogue 28.

> Mais toutefoys notre matiere est mesme,
> l'écry d'Amour, Amour est votre theme: (ll. 5-10)

These lines show his awareness of the two essential characteristics of the vast majority of Alexandrine and Latin elegies: a distinct prosodic form and the subject of love. He claims not to satisfy the first of these, but it is interesting to see that he arranges his decasyllabic couplets in such a way that the couplet structure is emphasized upon the eye, and he allows himself only three cases of enjambment between the couplets. He does think that he satisfies the classical use of theme. However, if his subject is love, it is not the sort of handling of the subject that we usually find in the classical writers. The address is not to the beloved, but to another woman, and the complaint is not about difficulties in love but rather to affirm the strength of the mutual love which the poet and his lady experience.

A more curious example of a classical-type elegy is provided by Etienne Pasquier in his *Recherches*.[24] In the chapter devoted to the experiments that were made in writing *vers mesurés* in French, Pasquier mentions and quotes writers such as Jodelle and Nicolas Denisot before going on to present his own experiment, which was encouraged by Ramus:

> Quelques annees aprés[25] devisant avecques Ramus, personnage de singuliere recommandation, mais aussi grandement desireux de nouveautez, il me somma d'en faire un autre essay de plus longue haleine que les deux precedens. Pour luy complaire je fis en l'an 1556. cette Elegie en vers Hexametres & Pentametres.[26]

Pasquier's elegy in *vers mesurés* predates, then, the few other examples that we will find. Formally, the poem is obviously the most classical produced during the 1550's; its content is also quite close to classical traditions. It is a love-poem, it addresses the beloved, and it gives voice to the unhappiness of the writer:

---

[24] See Catalogue 146.
[25] These words add confusion to the dating of the poem because the poem is dated 1556, and it was supposedly written a few years after Denisot had graced an edition of Pasquier's *Monophile* with a few *vers mesurés* of his own: the edition spoken of is that of 1555. See *Les Œuvres d'Estienne Pasquier...*, 2 vols. (Amsterdam: la compagnie des libraires associés, 1723), in-fol., I, col. 732.
[26] *Ibid.* The elegy itself is on cols. 732-3.

> Rien ne me plaist sinon de te chanter, & servir & orner
> Rien ne te plaist mon bien, rien ne te plaist que ma mort. (ll. 1-2)

There is very little imagery in the poem's twenty-eight lines, but the references to chaos and the elements help give the poem a more classical atmosphere than we have usually found in the elegies of this period. Pasquier's attempt at writing an elegy in the classical style is, of course, slight, but it provides us with evidence of the awareness which some poets at least had of the elegy as a classical genre.

Similar evidence is provided in the book of elegies by Jean Doublet.[27] There could be no doubt about Doublet's intentions on the strength of the poems themselves, but he gives us as well a very clear explanation of his purpose and attitude in an important preface.

Doublet's first concern is to justify his choice of love as a theme in his verse. As well as the usual excuse of ardent youth, he goes on to point out that, if he has treated love, he has done so with more modesty than the Ancients showed:

> ...je ne crein avoir beaucoup transgressé les bornes de modestie, ayant tousjours evité comme un rocher toute cete deshonneste lasciveté, laquelle usurpée impudemment par quelques antiques Elegiaques, les a rendus moins recommendables aus chastes oreilles, et a fait grand tort au reste de leurs doctes et ingenieuses inventions... (4)

We are warned, then, from the beginning that although the poet definitely has the classical poets in mind, he has not gone so far in his imitation as to recreate their characteristically erotic atmosphere.

Doublet, next deals with the question of form:

> Quand à cette nouvelle composition de Françoises Elegies, à la mienne volontée que quelque esprit plus eureux s'y fut bien employée devant moy, lequel auroit peut-estre inventé quelque vers et nombre plus propre et mieux raportant au disthique elegiaque. Car, quant à moy, voyant la façon vulgaire de nos vers estre plus courte que l'exametre et pentametre,

---

[27] See Catalogue 42. There have been two modern reprints of this work, by Prosper Blanchemain in 1869 for the Société des Bibliophiles normands in Rouen, and by an unnamed editor in 1871 for the Librairie des Bibliophiles in Paris. Since it is the latter which is more complete than Blanchemain and the most readily available of the three, we shall refer to it, but Blanchemain's notes and the text of the original have been consulted.

et la difficulté de mesurer deux lignes Françoises capables de sentence entière et parfaite, ainsi que se trouve ordinairement en un distique: je confesse que mes dois n'ont sceu, pour cete heure, tordre fil plus propre à lier et assembler fleurs elegiaques que ces petits quatreins de vers inegaus. N'ayant toutefois deliberé me tant complaire ny ostiner en ma propre invention, que je ne la laisse et quite tres-volontiers si tot qu'il en sortira d'autre main quelcune meilleure. (4-5)

With all humility, Doublet claims to be the first to attempt seriously a recreation of the classical form in French verse. Indeed, our study has not proved him wrong: the feeble attempts immediately abandoned, by Ronsard, by Des Autels and by Pasquier do not give the lie to the words of Doublet, and the various other strophic forms that can be occasionally found in the French elegy before 1559 do not indicate clearly an attempt at creating something to take the place of the classical distich. It is Doublet alone who has composed a book of elegies, twenty-six in all, with one form which was a conscious and not ineffective attempt to imitate a foreign prosodic form. At least twice in the elegies themselves, he reminds us of this fact: in the first of his poems, he tells us what happened when he attempted to write heroic verse:

> Tout alloit bien: Amour s'en prit à rire.
> Et de mes vers, qu'egaux il vit marcher,
>> Leur coupant un pié sans mot dire,
>> Toute une moitié fit clocher. (11. 13-16)

The idea is the same found at the beginning of Ovid's *Amores* (I, i, 1-4) and the quotation just given may serve as a concrete example of Doublet's solution to the problem of elegiac form, a solution which causes him to say in his fourth elegy "je cloche en ces quatreins boiteux" (l. 6), another reminder of the Ovidian idea.

We have a fixed 'elegiac' form then, and presumably the usual classical subject-matter of love. Is this entirely the case? When we read through Doublet's poems, we are somewhat surprised that he should have been so apologetic about his love-theme. In fact, only fourteen of the twenty-six poems deal with love in any way, and three of these are far from any trace of eroticism: I is a general introduction which prepares us for a series of love-poems; IV is another defence of treating love in poetry; X is a prayer which explains that his love for Sibille has become a spiritual one. There are only eleven poems, then, which recount the course of his love.

It must be noted immediately that, although these eleven poems are interrupted by elegies on other themes, they nevertheless appear to follow in a chronological sequence the main events of the poet's love for his lady Sibille. There is considerable unity, therefore, in this volume of elegies despite the presence of the non-amatory poems. Briefly, Doublet's story is this:

II: he succumbs finally to Cupid's arrows
III: he promises fidelity to his lady and mentions points in his favour (the old principle of capturing 'bénivolence')
V: the poet expresses his bitterness over Sibille's marriage to an old and wealthy man
VI: in addition to the problem of her marriage, Sibille has never shown pity for the poet in any case
IX: a change in Sibille's attitude makes her marriage the principal problem, and the poet pleads the hedonist cause
XII: Sibille is the real name of the lady, and she is preferred by the poet to the ten Sybillæ: a poem of praise
XIII: while on an official mission to Fontainebleau a pictorial representation of the Sybillæ reminds him of his lady
XV: he thinks about the ring that he intends to give to his lady
XVII: he calls on Apollo to cure his lady's fever
XVIII: Sibille's husband has died! An old hag is trying to arrange a new marriage for Sibille to another old man
XX: Sibille has so far resisted a new marriage but people try to dissuade her from the trip Rouen-Dieppe to be with the poet. The poet argues the charms of Dieppe.

At this point Doublet leaves his story, perhaps because it had gone no further by 1559. We can perhaps assume, however, that he failed to convince his Sibille to marry him inasmuch as he seems to have become a monk.[28]

More interesting for us than the simple story of Doublet's love for Sibille is the fact that, in recounting the events, Doublet uses a number of themes which are common to the Latin love-elegies. We have already mentioned the similarity between Doublet's first elegy and the first elegy in Ovid's *Amores*. In this case, as in the others that will be cited, the similarity is not to be found so much in a

[28] See "Préface", viii.

precise textual imitation but in the theme and general movement of the ideas. For the detail, Doublet was as much inclined to pillage the works of Horace or Anacreon as the elegists. However, in the first elegy, it is obviously Ovid who was in Doublet's mind when he described his intention to write an epic and the prosodic mischief which *Amour* caused him. Similarly Doublet's third elegy reminds us of the *Amores* I, iii. Both Doublet and Ovid offer themselves as slaves to their ladies, mention their humble estate, their fidelity and their poetic gifts which will render them immortal. Doublet's poem is somewhat more highly developed, but the ideas – even the order of the ideas – follow the poem by Ovid. In Doublet's fifth elegy, less precise parallels can be pointed out. The two main themes of the poem are common ones in classical elegies: the beloved's marrying a rich but elderly man and the power of wealth. Two poems that come to mind are Ovid III, iv and Tibullus I, v, but the themes are developed somewhat differently in these poems. On the other hand, Doublet's XVIII resembles closely Ovid's I, viii. In both poems we have a portrait of the old hag who tries to influence the young lady against the poet. While in Doublet's poem she is really nothing more than a marriage-arranger, he begins, like Ovid, by recounting her reputation as something of a sorceress:

> Plusieurs ont creu qu'a ses charmes arrive
> Humble et tremblant le noir peuple d'Enfer,
>   Et que d'humain sang elle écrive
>   Ne sai quels mots à Lucifer. (ll. 9-12)

Again Doublet follows the general idea of Ovid rather than the precise details which he gives. In both poems the descriptive information is followed by the old woman's words to the beloved, overheard by the lover in exactly the same way: "me duplices occuluere fores" (l. 22), "j'ai ouï toute la harengue, / Entre deux huis sur moy poussés" (ll. 55-56). The speeches are not similar in their details since each is made to fit its own context, but in both the poet and poets in general are held in contempt.

Other similarities could be pointed out, although themes such as the lady untouched by love (VI) and the licence which is permitted youth (IX) are perhaps not so exclusively elegiac as to permit our dwelling on them. What remains true is that Doublet appears to have made a serious attempt in his subject matter as well as in his form to recreate in French literature the Latin love-elegy. And even though his preface warns us of his desire to keep away from his poems the erotic character of the classical models, the reader is not likely to quibble with the line which ends the dedicatory poem to these elegies, the line which credits Doublet as France's "premier Ovide François" (l. 64).

Doublet's elegies are not all about love, however. Twelve of them – almost half the total number – deal with a variety of other subjects. XXII is about the death of Jan de Bourbon, comte d'Enghien, killed in battle in 1557. If the subject of the poem is still elegiac, its form is not particularly so since it belongs more properly to the literary epitaph:

> Le noble cors qui ci dessous s'empoudre,
> François passans, ne mourut pas ici... (ll. 1-2)

The other eleven poems, however, are considerably less elegiac. In three poems, Doublet talks about himself, about his simple life on his farm and his contempt for money and honour in XVI, and he gives a defence against the critics of this mode of living in XIX. Much of the happiness which the poet managed to find in his quiet life was the result of his interest in reading and writing poetry, and in XXIV he tells his teacher, Jan Fourdin, of his gratitude. XIV develops similar themes, but this time they are in the form of advice to a cousin who is interested in poetry but tempted to enter the Palais de Justice; on the other hand, in VIII he belittles poetry in favour of medicine as he addresses the doctor Pierre Desmireurs. Other poems are more particularly adapted to a precise event. XI welcomes the archbishop of Rouen (Charles, cardinal de Bourbon) back to Normandy; XXIII is an epithalamium in honour of the union of the dauphin and Mary Stuart; XXI is a call to poets to take part in the 1556 *puy* at Dieppe. This last poem is interesting in some of its details. We learn that prizes were now to be given for the best odes and sonnets as well as for the older forms, an interesting indication of the progress of the new poetry in the provinces, and Doublet's own awareness of new poetry comes out again clearly when he refers to Ronsard's "Hercule Chrestien", which was pub-

lished only a year before this elegy. The remaining few elegies add
further confusing variety to Doublet's use of the elegy.

Apart from the twenty-six poems just considered, there is one
more elegy in this book, an introductory poem called "Elégie de
I. D. A Jan Doublet, Dieppoys". The form of this poem is identical
to the other elegies, and since the initials of the writer are the same
as our poet's one is almost tempted to think that the poet wrote his
own flattering introduction. As well as ending with the claim that
Doublet is the first French Ovid, the poem abounds in such lines as:

> Or ta douceur à nulle autre seconde,
> En mille vers attiquement sucrés
> Nous redonne la grand'faconde
> Et des vieus Latins et des Grécs. (ll. 17-20)

The two references to the Greeks in these lines must not deceive
us: they do not refer to Greek elegies but to the considerable influence of Anacreon on Doublet's choice of image and theme. As
far as a major elegiac influence is concerned, there is no doubt that
it is Latin and more particularly Ovid. There is no doubt either that
Doublet is the first French poet to attempt to compose a book of
elegies which would resemble the classical writers. To what extent
did he succeed? Our discussion has pointed out quite a number of
themes which were common to the Latin elegists; we have shown
that in some cases he has followed the general structure of some
of Ovid's poems. Also stylistically, Doublet's writing resembles that
of the elegists by its frequent embroidering of the themes by mythological references. Formally, there is the attempt to create a French
verse structure which would correspond to the classical distich.

Ovid, like the other Latin elegists, wrote in his *Amores* almost
exclusively of love, love of an erotic nature, and the poems were
addressed either to the woman directly or to a friend, However,
Doublet, as we have seen, did not choose to write only of love. This
in itself is not enough for us to discredit his attempt at imitating his
models since they did include poems on various themes, but Doublet's poems on themes not connected with love number almost
half his poems, and so the total effect of his book is somewhat different from what we find in Ovid or Propertius. Also, Doublet's
avowed intention not to emulate the eroticism of his models con-

tributed to a different atmosphere in the love-poems themselves. This is a characteristic about which Doublet chooses to be most indifferent. Eleven of his poems do address a precise person, two are prayers to God, one apostrophizes a ring and two are general addresses. But ten elegies have no precise address and seven of these involve the love-poems, half of them.

Doublet's attempt, then, at naturalizing the classical elegy is only a partial success. We must nevertheless not belittle it too much. Doublet shows great development in the small amount of poetry that he has left behind him. Some unpublished early works included in the 1871 edition of the *Elégies* clearly demonstrate that he jumped from the *rhétoriqueur* style to that of the modern 1550's.[29] And if the *Elégies* do not have everything that we might expect in a recreation of the classical elegy in French literature, Doublet nevertheless succeeded to a much greater extent than any other poet that we have studied so far. Unfortunately Doublet was not eminent enough in his own time to influence the course of French letters. His experiment was to bear no fruit.

4. THE CASUAL ELEGISTS

It is now clear that, in the period that goes from the *Fontaine d'Amour* to the year of Ronsard's first collective edition, the important poets in the history of the elegy show whatever originality they have in style rather than in the use to which they put the elegy. Doublet, it is true, tackles a certain variety of themes, but considering as a whole the production of the four poets just studied it is certainly the elegy as a love-poem that is striking. It is not always precisely in the

---

[29] See xij-xv. The forms are *ballade* and *rondeau*. The *ballade* begins with the following lines:

Marie non subjecte gecte
Ondeur influente fluente,
Que véois si parfaicte faicte
Que Dieu l'eslit regente gente

The use of *rime couronnée* is constant throughout the poem.

épître amoureuse tradition, but more often than not it is; it is not always a poem in couplets, but one expects it to be.

What is true of these four poets is true of the bulk of the other elegies written during this period. A number of poems resemble rather closely the sort of elegy that La Tour wrote, that is, a rather 'old-fashioned', Marot type of *épître amoureuse*. This style is not always found where one most expects it. For instance, it is curious that a poet of the avant-garde like Du Bellay should write in so clear a marotique vein,[30] but that is precisely what he does in his three elegies, simple *épîtres amoureuses* in couplets proclaiming fidelity, praising his lady and asking for her love in return. Du Bellay's poems belong to his platonist period, and so the tone is not overly plangent; in all other respects it is hard to distinguish his poems from the Marot-Fontaine-La Tour stream.

The Le Blond-Fontaine-Forcadel group also have their minor representatives. It is curious that this style should almost always bring about a certain weakening of the *épître*-elegy association: this was clear in Le Blond and in Forcadel, and in Gilles d'Aurigny the elegy is not an *épître* at all.[31] Whereas Marot separated his elegies from his *épîtres* because of the subject matter, d'Aurigny does so because of form: he wrote letters dealing with love but his three elegies, on amorous themes, are not letters. The first elegy, "d'une fille se complaignant d'auoir aymé homme de trop grande qualité, sans pouoir estre aymé", consists of the lengthy, unhappy reflexions of the girl without any realistic personal address such as we find in letters. The numerous rhetorical apostrophes do not completely rob the poem of a certain touching naivety. The other two elegies are quite exaggerated examples of Petrarchan preciosity, and they are directed to a sort of general audience never defined.[32]

A number of other poets show greater independence in a variety of ways. Louis Le Caron, Mellin de Saint-Gelais and Jean La Péruse[33] add to our list of experiments in stanza forms as an alter-

[30] Catalogue 27 and 40.

[31] See Catalogue 19.

[32] See Scollen, 135-141 for a discussion of the content. The second elegy with its strange narrative concerning Monsieur de La Clayette's horse is unique in the history of the elegy.

[33] See Catalogue 30, 60, and 34.

native to the usual couplets. It is also during the 1550's that the alexandrine couplet begins sometimes to replace the decasyllable. The elegy is not invariably about love either. Habert[34] writes a poem of fulsome praise, a type of elegy that will be met with frequently after 1560; Tahureau,[35] before Ronsard, writes a prefatory elegy dealing with themes of literary interest;[36] Ferry Julyot, in the words of his "belle fille, lamentant sa virginité perdue",[37] gives us a sermon of eight elegies on filial obedience and the proper clothing, education, and deportment of young girls. The poetesses of Lyons remain much more clearly within the normal patterns that we have seen, but they are not without their own very special talent. Two of Louise Labé's three elegies[38] are *épîtres artificielles*, laments addressing the women of Lyons. Nor upon examination is the style without its artifices. But Labé manages the apparently impossible, and in these two poems as well as in *Elégie* II, an *épître naturelle* to her beloved, she gives us the impression of absolutely spontaneous expression with all its hesitations, contradictions, and repetitions. Pernette du Guillet[39] is even more original in her elegy "Combien de fois ay-je en moi souhaicté". The poem addresses no one; it seems to exist simply because of the writer's need to express her thoughts and dreams. It is extraordinary how skilfully Pernette is able to suggest in this poem her ever deepening day-dream by going from realistic description to idyll and then to the world of the gods. One is thankful to come across elegies as fine as this one, but they are, alas, the exceptions in the history of the elegy.

The elegies on death are rare during these years but they nevertheless form the second most important group of elegies. Seven

[34] See Catalogue 44.
[35] See Catalogue 36.
[36] Tahureau's elegy is further proof of his artistic independence and criticism of the excesses of the new 'Pléiade' style: see Marcel Raymond, *L'Influence de Ronsard*, 2 vols. (Paris: Champion, 1927), I, 199-202. Tahureau's poem defends love-poetry, praises the work to which it is a preface for the author's great knowledge of the French language, goes on to define existing good usage as the ideal in language and finishes by criticizing the misguided zealots of eccentric language enrichment.
[37] See Catalogue 41.
[38] See Catalogue 32.
[39] See Catalogue 18.

poets are involved and a total of eleven poems. They are not poems about which it is easy to generalize. It is true that the same basic ideas about death reappear in almost all deplorative elegies, but the final appearance of the poem containing the commonplaces is sometimes original to a certain degree. Three of our ten examples deplore the death of children, and inevitably these poems are to be distinguished by a simplicity of style and approach suitable to the youth of the defunct. What is less suitable, and certainly less usual in death-elegies, is the fact that Fontaine's poem on the death of his week-old son[40] and La Péruse's poem on the death of a friend's son almost at birth[41] both address the dead infants. The youth, Henry du Bellay, comte de Tonnerre, lamented by Tahureau[42] is already too grown up to receive this special attention.

Tahureau's poem is also a little more grown-up in its reminiscence of the "Lament for Bion" at the beginning:

> Pleurés, Muses! pleurés, Caliope et ta bande!
> Pleurés, Muses, pleurés la perte la plus grande
> Que vous sçauriés sentir, et le plus grand malheur
> Que arriva jamais pour troubler vôtre cueur!
> Pleurés, Muses, pleurés, et d'un son pitoyable
> Faites ouyr partout vôtre cri lamentable,
> Et sus vos instruments d'un lamentable accord
> Trainés des chants piteux des horreurs de la mort!
> Pleurés, Muses, pleurés, et vos larmes coulantes
> Tombent en vostre sein à l'envi devalentes! (ll. 1-10)

More so than in the love-elegies, death inspires a certain classicism in our poets. In another Tahureau poem[43] the highly circumstantial account of the drowning of Françoise Belot is decorated by the introduction of Naiades in the waters of the Huisne and the delightful idea at the end of the poem concerning the grief of the river itself:

> La (Françoise) plaignant à jamais du son d'un piteux flot
> A ses bords ne dira rien que: BELOT! BELOT!
> Ainsi que de la mer le resonant rivage,
> Après le sort cruel du malheureux naufrage

[40] See Catalogue 31.
[41] See Catalogue 34.
[42] See Catalogue 33.
[43] See Catalogue 29.

D'Hylas, aimé d'Hercule, émeu des criz, helas!
D'Hercule, ne disoit sinon: Hylas! Hylas! (ll. 139-144)

The debt to Antiquity is honestly indicated.[44] La Péruse owes a similar debt for the opening of his elegy on the death of F. Clermont, seigneur de Dampierre. Ovid inspired both La Péruse and Ronsard to introduce their lamentations by an apostrophe to the muse *Elégie*, and the idea led La Péruse to a development of twenty-six lines which is largely original in its details.[45] Of interest in La Péruse's exordium is the indication that he knows that the elegy has come to be a love-poem; his intention is to convert *Elégie* back to her original song:

Pleure, pleure, Elegie, Elegie pleureuse
Repran à cette fois ta face douloureuse,
Repran ton premier dueil, repran l'état premier,
Qui a des premiers ans te fut plus coutumier... (ll. 7-10)

Fontaine's lament on the death of his sister[46] not only uses the elegy in this supposedly authentic way but speaks of the funeral in pagan terms:

Allons offrir à Pluton l'ancien,
Vin auec laict, noirs moutons, et brebis,
Allons en deuil et de cœurs et d'habitz
Ses beaux os blanc recueillir tous ensemble,
Auec la main qui toute de dueil tremble:
Puis les mettans en beau coffre de marbre,
Pres d'vn cypres, qui est douloureux arbre,
Les baignerons en pleurs, en laict, et vin,
Entremeslans ce seruice diuin
De telz regretz: (ll. 44-53)

Lines such as these are remarkable especially if they were written at the time that Catherine Fontaine died, that is, about 1540:[47] such 'paganization' of a religious ceremony would not be acceptable to many sixteenth-century readers. Even the emphasis on earthly glory after death in La Péruse's elegies would be suspect for the majority in the 1550's. It is a curious fact, however, that poets felt

[44] The lines are somewhat distantly inspired by Propertius I, xx, 48-50.
[45] Ovid, *Amores*, III, ix, 1-28; La Péruse, Catalogue 34; Ronsard, *Elégie* 2.
[46] See Catalogue 31.
[47] She died while the poet was in Italy (see ll. 74 *sqq.*).

freer to draw upon classical ideas and motives when speaking o death than when dealing with love. The eroticism of Antiquity appears to have been largely either meaningless or forbidden to our poets.

The years 1545-1560 have yielded for our study a fairly large number of elegies. It is interesting to remind ourselves, however, of the areas of poetic activity which proved to be barren. The Marguerite de Navarre circle, the feminist and neo-Platonist literature, the religious and moral poetry – all these currents virtually shunned the elegy. The Petrarchan and strambottist influence encouraged mainly the sonnet or the epigrammatic forms (as among the Lyons poets). The anthologies of these years, devoted to a rather popular conception of poetry, are almost completely devoid of examples of the elegy: the poets whose names were cited by Ronsard as forming a sort of Pléiade of divine and learned poets[48] were hardly very assiduous in cultivating a genre whose origin should have seemed glamorously classical. Nevertheless, it is clear that after 1550 the elegy begins at last to attract the attention of a fairly large number of poets. Curiously, the important writers of elegies are not those poets otherwise considered as important.

The elegies written over this sixteen-year period include a fair number of poems which are difficult to put into representative groups. Love and death are not the only themes to find expression in the elegy; the couplet gives way to experiments in more obviously lyrical forms. All this experimenting shows a certain indecision on the part of the poets as to the nature of the French elegy. It is interesting to note how small a number of poets attempted in their experiments to recreate an obviously classical type of elegy. Nevertheless, such experiments do make their appearance for the first time during the 1550's.

Despite the appearance of these various experiments, there is a good deal less anarchy in this post-Marot period than we found before 1545. Without there necessarily being a direct influence, the

---

[48] Concerning the idea of the Pléiade, see R. Lebègue, "De la Brigade à la Pléiade", in Lumières de la Pléiade, Neuvième Stage International d'Etudes Humanistes, Tours, 1965 (Paris: Vrin, 1966), 13-20.

writers of the largest numbers of elegies tend to suggest that these years are best characterized as a continuation of Marot's limitation of the boundless *épître* by the exclusion of one of its important varieties. By calling the *épître amoureuse* an *élégie*, already some poets see little reason to adhere in any clear way to the narrow confines of the *épître* conventions. The elegy thus comes a little closer to being a new and quite individual genre. We have not yet spoken of Ronsard, however, and during the years 1553-1560 he wrote twenty-four elegies which show a somewhat different intention.

III

RONSARD, *Prince des Poètes Élégiaques*

Ronsard, is, of course, a far from neglected poet, and in the numerous studies of his works there are many of his elegies which come
in for analysis and discussion. Indeed general studies of sixteenth-
century poetry often draw upon his elegies to illustrate the themes
and style of the poetry of their period: one thinks especially of such
a rich work as Henri Weber's *La Création poétique au XVIe siècle
en France.*[1] In addition, some scholars have specialized in a study
of the elegies themselves. In 1907, Constantin Bauer produced a
thesis on them,[2] but it is a work of a somewhat sketchy character. It
discusses some themes and sources, considers matters of prosody
and vocabulary, and it offers some corrective comment on Blanchemain's edition of Ronsard. In 1939, D. E. Frey turned out a much
richer study,[3] but the author finally opts for a modern definition of
the word elegy and thus does not necessarily always deal with the
poems called elegy by Ronsard. Still more recently there has been
Robert E. Hallowell's study of the influence of the Roman elegy on
Ronsard's poetry.[4] This influence permeates the whole of the poet's
writing and is not significantly more noticeable in the elegies.

There is not yet a study of Ronsard's elegies which deals only with
them and as Ronsard himself defined them. This is the particular
task that we have decided to undertake here, and as a necessary
preliminary we have drawn up in an Appendix a catalogue of Ron-

[1] Paris: Nizet, 1956 (2 vols.).
[2] Constantin Bauer, *Die Elegien Pierre de Ronsarts* (Leipzig: Dr. Seele & Co.,
1907).
[3] *Le Genre élégiaque dans l'œuvre de Ronsard* (Liège: Georges Thone, 1939).
[4] *Ronsard and the Conventional Roman Elegy* (Urbana Illinois: University of
Illinois Press, 1954).

sard's elegies with all the pertinent information concerning changes of title in the various editions.[5] A quick glance at this catalogue will first of all impress on the reader how rich a vein the elegy is in the works of the Prince of Poets: no other sixteenth-century writer produced anywhere near the same number of elegies. Secondly, one is somewhat startled to see the constant hesitation over the titles of these poems. It would appear that while the title elegy was attractive to Ronsard, he was not always of the same mind about its meaning. Specifically, we shall trace the course of these title changes in order to determine the *various* definitions of the elegy that Ronsard seems to have entertained.[6]

1. 1553-1560

It is usual for critics to say that the elegy did not tempt Ronsard at the beginning of his career and that it was therefore the last classical genre that he was to imitate.[7] This is hardly an adequate description of the situation. Ronsard's first three elegies were published in 1553, early in his career then, and by 1553 he had experimented with few forms. Almost all his poems before that date were either odes or sonnets; a very few poems were given no generic title;[8] and we find only two *hymnes* and one *chanson*.[9] The elegy, then, comes near the beginning of Ronsard's writing career and marks the beginning of a period of greater experimentation in form. His interest in the elegy resulted as well in his writing twenty-four of them – and not "une quinzaine"[10] – by the time that he published his first collective edi-

[5] See p. 239. Since Ronsard's case is so complicated, we thought it advisable to keep his elegies separate from our general Catalogue of Elegies. Henceforth in our discussion of Ronsard the number of each elegy is that of our catalogue of his poems.
[6] We are using the Ronsard edition prepared for the S. T. F. M. by P. Laumonier, completed by I. Silver and R. Lebègue, 18 vols. (Paris: Hachette-Droz-Didier, 1914-1967).
[7] An idea still held by Miss Frey, *Le genre élégiaque dans l'œuvre de Ronsard*, 15.
[8] See I, 9, 17, 35; IV, 177. The poems in the *Bocage* of 1550 do not have generic titles but they resemble the ode forms used by Ronsard at this time.
[9] I, 24; III, 54; IV, 173.
[10] Henri Chamard, *Histoire de la Pléiade*, 4 vols. (Paris: Didier, 1939-1940), III, 29.

tion in 1560, a considerable number compared with other poets and when one considers that they are, in almost every case, poems of some length.[11]

What the elegy illustrates first of all in the poetry of Ronsard is the awakening of interest in the use of decasyllabic and alexandrine couplets. Before the elegy of 1553, there are only three such couplet poems to be found in his works, all of them written before 1550.[12] On the other hand, among the first twenty-four elegies which we shall consider, only three are not in either decasyllabic (seven poems) or alexandrine (fourteen poems) couplets. Elegy 10 is written in sextains and was quickly renamed a *chanson* the year following its first appearance. Elegy 15 is in octosyllabic couplets and has perhaps the most complicated history of any poem of Ronsard (it was first written as an ode and it finally becomes a *chanson*). Elegy 2 is the most interesting departure from the regular couplet form, for it is an attempt to imitate the classical distich in its use of a couplet made up of an alexandrine followed by a line of ten syllables. Elegy 1 also shows some desire to imitate the classical form. Although it is simply made up of decasyllabic couplets, Ronsard has made an appeal to the eye by having the second line of each couplet slightly indented.[13]

Along with this attempt – albeit slight – to imitate the classical form of the elegy, we might expect to find a corresponding imitation of the classical style and subject-matter. Indeed, in elegy 2 (on the death of Chateignier) we have the imitation not only of the distich but also of the opening lines of Ovid's elegy on the death of Tibullus (*Amores*, III, ix).[14] In elegy 17, the well-known "A son Livre" written for the *Nouvelle Continuation des Amours* (1556), Ronsard talks of his new "stille bas" in imitation of Tibullus, Ovid, and

---

[11] Only four have fewer than sixty lines; fourteen have more than one hundred.
[12] I, 17, 24 and 35. In the *Odes* and *Bocage* of 1550, six poems are written in couplets of seven or eight syllables.
[13] This pretence is dropped after 1560.
[14] Concerning this poem and the elegy on the death of Marie (number 71), see the interesting article by Françoise Joukovsky-Micha, "Tombeaux et offrandes rustiques chez les poètes français et néo-latins du XVIe siècle", *Bibliothèque d'humanisme et renaissance*, XXVII (1965), 226-247. In connection with this article it is also interesting to recall Fontaine's elegy on the death of his sister.

Catullus (ll. 174-6), and in elegy 4 (to Cassandre) he assures us of having much studied the classical elegists (ll. 13-14). But we are surprised to read a few lines later in the same poem that our poet had

> ...desja commancé de trasser
> Mainte Elegie à la façon antique, (ll. 24-25)

We are surprised because, apart from the opening lines of elegy 2 and occasional scattered details in other elegies, Ronsard's first twenty-four elegies do not imitate his classical models to any particularly significant degree. Unlike the odes and the sonnets, the elegies are fundamentally original poems, original despite their frequent borrowing of details and images from a great variety of sources and not simply from his elegist predecessors.

If we try to find any particular pattern in these first elegies of Ronsard, we are faced with a considerable problem. In subject-matter alone these poems fall into several categories. From our knowledge of the elegy as it has been established at this point, we would expect to find mainly poems on love and on death. Elegy 2 does treat the theme of death, a subject which Ronsard will not later favour in his elegies: there is only one other example (elegy 71) and the poem under discussion here underwent a title change in 1567 and remained an "Epitaphe" until 1584, when the poet compromised and called his poem an "Elégie en forme d'Epitaphe". Death, then, does appear as a theme in these early elegies, but the significance of this poem in indicating Ronsard's attitude toward the genre can hardly be under-estimated. And this is interesting because the poem is one of the most classical of Ronsard's elegies.

Only eight poems can be termed love-elegies, and these poems belong to two types. First of all, and quite different from the sort of elegy that we found to be typical among either the classical writers or Ronsard's French predecessors, it is a *discours* sort of poem which is only incidentally personal. In elegy 1, Ronsard comforts Muret by recounting how the greatest heroes, especially Hercules, were conquered by Love, which means that the two poets need not feel ashamed for succumbing to Love's great power. Then, in elegy 5, Ronsard argues that love is really a strengthening experience and that Brinon should fall in love if he wants courage. Elegy 9 addresses *Amour*: the poet complains of never being allowed any peace, but he intends to remain the servant of the god. In elegies 14 and 15 we are closer to the typical love-elegy, but there is no address involved. Number 15 is the poem that was first called *Ode* and later *Chanson*, but elegy 14 remained an elegy throughout all the editions published during Ronsard's life. In it the poet complains of his lady's having been stolen from him, and this causes him to reflect on the wisdom of loving women of exalted station. Only three poems address a lady directly about his love. In elegy 10 (published in 1556 and after 1557 always entitled *Chanson*) Ronsard complains of having lost his freedom; in elegy 16 he complains to Cassandre that he has lost his youth foolishly since she has not satisfied his desires; and in elegy 18 he sings, without complaint of any sort, the praises of Marie and tells her that his poems will immortalize their love.

Another elegy (number 6), addressing Janet (François Clouet), perhaps belongs to this group of love poems, but, in its detailed description of the physical charms of Cassandre, the poem is really a sort of *blason*, a compendium of what Marot and his friends created in the *Blasons du corps féminin*.[15] The "Elegie du Verre à Jan Brinon" (number 7) is more clearly a *blason* written in an extremely learned style.

This elegy to Brinon is rather typical of a number of elegies already quite prominent before 1560. In these elegies, it is very difficult to decide whether the poem should be classified according to its general intention, which is praise and flattery of the person addressed, or according to the often interesting themes which Ronsard develops for his praise. One forgets Brinon in favour of the *verre*; in elegy 21 one forgets La Haye and thinks about the theme of the possible superiority of animals over man and the vanity of our human ambitions. The elegy can thus become a sort of *discours*, and it does so quite clearly in elegies like 13 and 21. It can also deal with

[15] See R. A. Sayce, "Ronsard and Mannerism: The *Elégie à Janet*", *Esprit Créateur*, IV, 4 (Winter 1966), 234-247. There is a striking similarity between the poem and feminine beauty as painted by Clouet. See also D. B. Wilson, *Descriptive Poetry in France from Blason to Baroque* (Manchester: Manchester University Press, 1967), 57 *sqq.*

history, but only one elegy, 23, mentions significantly France's religious problems (24 refers briefly to them).

Ronsard also likes to use the elegy in a very personal way in these early years. In elegy 20 the theme of praise (of Henri II and the architect Lescot) is again forgotten, in favour this time of an account of the writer's own youth, studies, and choice of becoming a poet against his father's wishes. Elegy 22 gives a somewhat different version; elegy 19 expresses regret over the quickly passing years: loss of youth means a noticeable loss of inspiration, It is indeed poetry that obsesses Ronsard in these personal elegies: at least six poems can be placed in this important group (3, 4, 8, 11, 17, 24). These poems deal both with Ronsard's own choices as a writer and with the literary activity of the 1550's. This tendency to link literary themes with the elegy, a curious and original union it seems, no doubt accounts for four poems (8, 11, 13, 17) serving as prefaces to whole works or distinct sections of a work. Found before Ronsard only in a poem by Tahureau (Catalogue 36), it is a type of elegy that will increase in frequency after 1560.

If we try to resume now whatever general characteristics there are in these elegies, we can first mention a point already touched on: all these poems are either in decasyllabic or alexandrine couplets except for three: number 10 (quickly renamed a *chanson*), number 15 (originally an ode and to become a *chanson*), and number 2 (which imitates the classical distich).[16] There is, then, a definite tendency to adopt couplet form.

Another general characteristic is the use of address in these poems. There are only two exceptions, again elegy 15, and as well elegy 14, which is supposed to be a translation of an unidentified poet, Ergasto. The fact that the address is not always to a living person (number 9 addresses *Amour*, number 17, Ronsard's book) or one precise person (number 13 addresses the reader) results in no change of style or significance, and indeed, perhaps the separation of these elegies into the two divisions which Henri Guy created for the

---

[16] See F. Desonay, "Les Variations métriques de Ronsard, poète de l'amour", in *Lumières de la Pléiade* (Paris: Vrin, 1966), 363-390.

French *épître* at the beginning of the sixteenth century,[17] *artificielle* and *naturelle*, is particularly significant.

The two characteristics, couplets and address, which have just been mentioned here are, of course, characteristics as well of the French *épître*. Another characteristic of the *épître* is its capacity to treat any subject, and, as we have seen, the variety of subjects treated in Ronsard's first elegies is considerable. Ronsard's elegies do, in fact, resemble the old French *épître*, and it is an awareness of this which removes any surprise that we might have at the frequent lack of any sadness or complaint in these elegies.

These elegies are both original and traditional. They are traditional in that they strongly resemble and do very little more than the French *épîtres* written before 1550; they are original insofar as the French elegy before 1553, tended to be one particular type of *épître*, that dealing with a plaint to the beloved. By 1560, Ronsard had written only one poem (elegy 16) which can be properly termed an *épître amoureuse*.[18]

In a sense, it is not surprising that Ronsard's elegies depart from either the classical or preceding French elegies. By 1553 when he wrote his first elegies, Ronsard had already developed the ode and the sonnet for his love-poetry; in the *Tombeau de Marguerite de Valois* of 1551 he used the ode and the *hymne* for death, and after 1553 he prefers to call his death poems more precisely *épitaphes*, which accounts for the change of title that elegy 2 later underwent. What Ronsard felt the need for in 1553 was simply a less rigid, less lyrical poetic form than the ode or sonnet, a form that could be used for a diversity of subject, and ideas rather than lyrical treatments either of love or of praise of the powerful. Chamard's claim that the first "élégie d'idée" is the one written to Baillon in 1563 is manifestly wrong.[19] As we pointed out earlier, the appearance of the elegy in Ronsard's works coincides with the first significant use of couplets, either decasyllabic or alexandrine, and the adoption of this form is motivated by the same reasons – as we can see from the results –

---

[17] Henry Guy, *Histoire de la poésie française au XVI siècle*, 2 vols. (Paris: Champion, 1910-1926), I, 105 *sqq*.

[18] We are not including elegy 10, renamed *Chanson* a year after its publication.

[19] Chamard, *Histoire de la Pléiade*, III, 30.

which occasioned the great popularity of the *épître* before Ronsard.

Why did Ronsard not write *épîtres* then? He did in fact write three during his whole career, and all three belong to the years under discussion: in the *Bocage* of 1554 there is one to Ambroise de la Porte,[20] in the *Hymnes* of 1555, one to Charles de Pisseleu and, in the *Hymnes* of 1556, one to the cardinal de Lorraine.[21] When one remembers the unpleasant quarrel aroused by Du Bellay's *Deffence* concerning the elegy and the *épître* and the violent reply of the *Quintil Horatian*, we should perhaps ask instead why Ronsard wrote these three *épîtres*.[22] It is obviously the sort of question that can never be answered, and we have to remain content with the fact that while these three *épîtres* do exist, Ronsard preferred to call his *épîtres* *élégies* and after 1556, always did so.

If we look carefully to find any differences between the elegies of Ronsard and the typical *épître*, we discover that there is less insistence – at this particular time at least – on the epistolary nature of the poems by references to writing and to the intention of sending the missive, to the adding of super- or subscriptions. Perhaps more noteworthy, however, is the use of a less familiar style. Most of the elegies of this period are extremely learned poems in their wealth of mythological adornment, a characteristic of the classical elegy which Du Bellay, as we saw, recommended.

2. 1561-1567

Once Ronsard had begun to experiment with the possibilities of couplets, he seems to have had little inclination to use strophic forms. This tendency is particularly noticeable after 1560, and as a

[20] VI, 10.

[21] VIII, 224 and 328.

[22] Miss Frey, 25-27, offers two theories to explain the *épître* title in these three cases. For the first one she points to its very personal nature, and it is true that by 1554, the four elegies written by Ronsard are not particularly personal. In the case of the other two *épîtres*, Miss Frey points to the fact that they are dedicated to men of the Church and that the elegy was a profane genre. This explanation can hardly be credited since appearing in the 1556 *Hymnes* along with the third *épître* is the elegy (11) to Chretophle de Choiseul, Abbé de Mureaux. A few years later in 1559 and 1560, several elegies are addressed to ecclesiastics.

result we find an increase in the number of elegies. Between 1553 and 1560 Ronsard gave that title to twenty-four poems, of which twenty-one appeared as such in the *Oeuvres* of 1560;[23] between 1561 and 1567 we find thirty-one new poems bearing the title elegy. This increase has been somewhat overly exaggerated by some critics.[24] Let us be satisfied to say that the years of Ronsard as court poet present us with a heightened interest in the writing of elegies. Furthermore, it is more logical to see this interest stemming from Ronsard's concern for couplet-form rather than in the fact that the poetry of this period is courtly in inspiration: the early odes of Ronsard give ample proof that he was able to use lyric forms for the sort of subject-matter which comes in the elegies of the period under discussion.

Critics have also tended to emphasize the difference between the elegies before 1560 and those which come after the first collective edition. The difference is there but here again it is easy to exaggerate. After 1560 we mainly find the development of two types of elegy that Ronsard had already touched upon.

First of all there is the love-elegy, found principally in the *Recueil des Nouvelles Poésies* of 1564: of the eleven elegies in this collection, nine are love-poems and seven of these are particularly interesting to us because they show us Ronsard's interest – hardly noticeable before – in the Marot type of elegy. This characteristic has already been dealt with by Miss Frey,[25] and so it is not necessary for us to dwell on the point. Suffice it to recall that these seven elegies (numbers 29, 30, 31, 32, 33, 35, 36) all present a lover writing to his beloved (and apart from these poems,[26] the epistolary character of Ronsard's elegies is rarely particularly explicit), that we see the poet

[23] In 1560 elegy 8 has no generic title; elegy 9 is rejected altogether; elegy 10 has become a *Chanson* (so named since 1557).

[24] Hallowell, *Ronsard and the Conventional Roman Elegy*, 44, gives the number as 40, as does Frey, 34. They both are counting the number of the elegies produced between 1563-1569, but I find it impossible to arrive at this number. They both also give 84 as the total number of elegies, which our catalogue shows to be other. According to their counting, it would indeed seem that the 1560's were the vital ones in Ronsard's career as an elegist.

[25] Hallowell, 46, 55-57.

[26] Elegy 29, l. 9 and l. 61; elegy 30, ll. 155-157 (variant of 1567); elegy 32, l. 84 and l. 87; elegy 36, l. 20.

complaining of her absence (elegies 29 and 33), of the effects of his love (elegy 30), of his unsuccessful attempts to destroy it (elegy 32), of her cruelty (elegies 32 and 35), of the hopelessness of the situation because of her exalted rank (elegy 31) – in other words, themes typical of the elegy before 1550. The fact that these poems are not simply literary creations but were presumably written on command and deal with actual situations[27] is of secondary interest to us: more interesting is their similarity to the early French elegy, not only in form and theme, but often in expression. Elegy 36 can serve as an example. Gone are the elaborate and learned allusions to myths and antiquity: the poem is a letter of explanation that the writer's sighs and sadness are not the result of a new love but the continuation of his love for the lady to whom he is writing. In developing this theme Ronsard's images do not go beyond the stock idea, common before the Pléiade, of the mistress's heart being as hard as a rock (l. 34) and her indifference the result of "la glace/De vostre coeur" (ll. 99-100). On the other hand, he honours her "vertus" (l. 25), her "graces parfaites" (l. 24), and her various charms (l. 51 *sqq.*), all of them vague and general and more on the moral plane than on the physical. His desire – as was Marot's – is to become recognized as her "serviteur" (ll. 41-4; ll. 71-6). Altogether we are right back to the naïve tone of Marot's poetry, and indeed, Ronsard even imitates a *chanson* of Marot ("Secourez moy, Madame, par amours") in lines 101-110.

Seven elegies, then, of personal (affected, at least) love-plaint to the beloved, a type of elegy hardly touched by Ronsard before

[27] All critics presume that the poems were written either as personal poems or on command. There are considerable differences of opinion, however, as to the identification of the lover and the beloved in each poem since no names are at any time mentioned. The general opinion for most of them is that Isabeau de Limeul and Louis de Condé are involved. For a résumé of the attributions, see the footnotes of Laumonier's edition and also Fernand Desonay, *Ronsard Poète de l'Amour*, 3 vols. (Bruxelles: Duculot, 1952-1959), II, chapter IV. The only really important dispute of Desonay concerns elegy 29, which he claims was written for Mary Stuart and forms with elegies 25 and 28 a sort of triptich (the poems were published consecutively in 1564). Perhaps a significant argument against such an interpretation of elegy 29 is the fact that it remains with the other elegies addressed to Isabeau (or to other women receiving letters from their lovers) in the book of *Elégies* of the *Œuvres* in 1584 and 1587 while the other elegies addressed to Mary Stuart are taken from the *Elégies* and placed in the *Poëmes*.

1564.[28] Also in the *Nouvelles Poésies* of 1564 are two poems to Genèvre (elegies 50 and 38). These are definitely personal poems, but they do not resemble the seven elegies just discussed. The first of these poems was, indeed, called a "Discours" in 1564 and did not become an elegy until the *Œuvres* of 1567, the change then probably being the influence of the other poem to Genèvre, which was entitled elegy in 1564. The two poems caused Ronsard some difficulty, however: he realized that they departed from the usual pattern, and in 1584 he called them both "Discours en forme d'Elegie".[29] The variant in the first line of elegy 50 in 1578 prepared for this new change: instead of the first "escoute par pitié", he put "escoute ce discours". The other poem, however, is a letter, as is made clear in the opening lines.

The second poem is, in fact, not too different from the love-elegies discussed. It resembles more, however, a long elegy by Pontus de Tyard to Ronsard than it does the Marot type of poem in its very lengthy development of the effects of his love and the absence of his lady. The other elegy to Genèvre, however, is an extremely long (488 lines) narrative poem full of direct quotations as the poet recounts his meetings with Genèvre, her unfortunate love-affair before their meeting and his arguments in favour of her forgetting the past. After recalling all this, the poem ends with the poet's going to bed, full of hope for the future. It is a curious poem, supposedly from beginning to end his words directly spoken to Genèvre but in fact a narrative poem recounting the birth of his love for her.

Between 1564 and 1567 there are five more elegies which deal in some way with love. In the *Œuvres* of 1567 we find another long (434 lines) narrative elegy (number 55), an *épître* to the beloved but containing at the beginning and the end long apostrophes. Although the problem is not the same, as a type of poem it resembles Héroët's "Complainte d'vne Dame",[30] another long narrative epistle. Ronsard's poem became a "Discours" in 1578: he obviously did not

[28] Only one elegy (number 26) before 1560 is really of this type.

[29] Was it Ronsard who changed the title again to "Elégie" for the edition of 1587?

[30] Antoine Héroët, *Œuvres Poétiques*, edited by F. Gohin (Paris: Droz, 1943), 94.

feel, later at least, that these narratives of great length were proper elegies.

Three more elegies, two from the *Elegies, Mascarades et Bergerie* of 1565 (numbers 44 and 46) and one from the *Œuvres* of 1567 (number 53) deal in some way with the presenting of gifts, a type of poem of which Marot gave us one example as an elegy but which has not been seen to be typical of the pre-Pléiade poets. Elegy 44 concerns two women, Anne who presents to Diane both her portrait and the poem, which deals with their friendship. In elegy 46, a *chevalier* presents a diamond ring to his lady and improvises on the ways in which he resembles the diamond and in what ways he does not want her to resemble it. Finally, in elegy 53, the gift is a bouquet of flowers, which prompts the recalling of the various myths which prove that maidens are punished for not heeding love.

The one remaining elegy concerning love (number 47) is the only one of this period which resembles the largest number of love-elegies written by Ronsard before 1560. The poet here addresses his friend and companion Amadis Jamyn on a general theme of love: just as Ulysses avoided the Sirens, Jamyn should see to it that he avoids the snares of love.

The other large group of elegies of this period belongs to Ronsard's work as a court poet, although, as we have seen, the bulk of the love-elegies are hardly less the work of a professional writer. The difference is that in the love-poems he lends his pen to express the feelings of others while, in the group of fourteen poems which we are to look at now, Ronsard writes almost always for himself. Indeed these so-called court poems are infinitely more personal than the preceding elegies (apart from the Genèvre poems) since Ronsard's own self-interest is involved in these poems of praise. This is the case in elegy 27 (to Baillon), published first in *Les Quatre saisons...* of 1563. The purpose of the poem is to ask for money; the method is not so much one of praise in this poem as the development of the idea of the evils of money which have plagued the world since the Golden Age. This poem illustrates another interesting fact about this type of poetry: while the purpose of the poem is usually without interest for us, Ronsard manages frequently to lend interest by his development of an idea or a myth. As we have seen, Chamard claimed that this was the first "élégie d'idée" of our poet, a false claim but one that points to the fact that the poem remains interesting despite the prime intention of the poet when he wrote it. Elegy 51, published in 1565 but not entitled elegy until 1567, was meant to praise "Seigneur Cecille Secrétaire de la Royne d'Angleterre" (William Cecil), but in so doing it develops at great length the Giant myth, the creation of kings by Jupiter and the importance of the king's favourites and intimates. Elegy 43 takes on interest by referring to the religious troubles in France and in England. Elegy 45, addressed to Claude de Beaune, is only slightly developed and is of little interest as a result.

Most of the elegies of this group are connected with royalty. The *Elegies, Mascarades et Bergerie* of 1565 was dedicated to Queen Elizabeth of England, and so it is not surprising that six of its eight elegies are works of our court poet.[31] Elegies 43 and 51 were published with this collection, and both of them were addressed to people connected with the court of Elizabeth. Elegy 39 addresses the English monarch directly and recounts at length (522 lines) the origin of England as a moving island finally fixed by Neptune. The prophecy of its great future especially during the reign of Queen Elizabeth is given by Proteus. Elegy 40 is dedicated to Lord Dudley, but there is no direct address to him in the poem – the only elegy of the 1561-1567 period not to address directly. The poem is, again, one of praise, of Dudley and of England and its future.

In this 1565 collection, Ronsard does not forget French royalty. Elegy 42 asks Catherine de Médicis to return quickly from her tour of pacification in the south of France, although he does not fail to compliment her on her great success. Elegy 41 incites Charles to fight the Turks, and elegy 49 (published in the *Œuvres* of 1567) contains the most fulsome praise of Charles, but with a purpose: Ronsard asks to be given the order and support to write the *Franciade*.

By far the best of the poems addressed to royalty are the five elegies concerning Mary Stuart. Court poems though they may be, the poet's feelings seem to be very much involved as well. The first

[31] About this collection, see M. C. Smith, "Ronsard and Queen Elizabeth I", *Bibliothèque d'humanisme et renaissance*, XXIX (1967), 93-119.

of these poems (elegy 25) was published anonymously in 1561, addresses Fortune and gives a résumé of her unhappy life; elegy 28, which addresses L'Huillier, is again about her departure. Elegies 37, 54, and 56 speak directly to Mary. The first of these poems, learned and formal in tone, praises her beauty while it laments her departure. Elegy 56 is a letter sent with his book (the *Elegies, Mascarades et Bergerie*) in which he again laments her departure. Most moving of all is elegy 54 in which the poet creates a vision of the queen in white at Fontainebleau as she awaits the time for her departure.[32] Ronsard unfortunately continues with a highly imaginative treatment of Charles's grief, but the poem on the whole remains one of the best of the poet's works of this period.

After these two large groups of elegies only four poems remain to be discussed. Elegies 48 and 52 were first written in 1554 but did not receive the elegy title until 1567. Elegy 52 recounts the myth of Narcissus and resembles somewhat the *Hymnes*; elegy 48 is an interesting poem and belongs to the group of autobiographical elegies. It traces the poet's ancestry and life up to the time of his studies at Coqueret. Elegies 26 and 34 are both preface poems. The first of these, written for an edition of Grévin's theatre in 1561, deals with poetic inspiration and more precisely with tragedy. The second poem was intended as a preface to a genealogy of the Sanzay family which was never published. The poem is essentially one of praise and flattery, but again Ronsard manages to extend the interest of his subject by tracing the history of mankind and the origin of coats of arms.

By 1567, Ronsard had written quite a large number of elegies, and in preparing the collective edition of that year he came to the conclusion that there were too many to be scattered through the sections which he had established for the 1560 edition. In 1567, we have for the first time, then, a section devoted to the elegies, divided into four books. Ronsard had another problem in 1567, however. During the preceding years he had also been experimenting with pastoral poetry but not sufficiently to warrant a separate section for these poems. He

---

[32] See Marcel Raymond, *Baroque et renaissance poétique* (Paris: Corti, 1955), 140-5, for an excellent analysis of the opening part of this elegy.

therefore places these poems, along with a few sonnets, in his books of elegies.

The latter do not include all the elegies written by 1567. Of the pre-1560 elegies which remain elegies in 1567, only four are found in the new section of elegies (numbers 7, 14, 21, 19): the others remain in the *Amours* or *Poèmes* sections where they were placed in 1560, with elegy 2 finding its natural place in the *Epitaphes* and elegy 23 in the *Discours des Miseres de ce temps*. Of the post-1560 elegies only three are *not* put in the books devoted to that form: elegy 26 is never at any time included in the collective editions of Ronsard, elegy 46 retains its place with the *Mascarades* and elegy 47 goes in with the poems of the second book of *Amours*. The four books of elegies of 1567, then, are mainly a catch-all for the new poems, an impression that is only confirmed by any attempt at seeing a guiding hand in their arrangement into four books: the love-poems and those addressed to the great are mixed together without any discernible attempt at order.

If the arrangement of elegies suggests nothing, is it possible to see a clearer conception of the elegy in 1567? The title-changes which occur by 1567 reveal a little. Of the twenty-one elegies to be found in 1560, only sixteen remain elegies in 1567. The elegy on the death of Chateignier is now named an *épitaphe*, which confirms the fact that the elegy was not thought by Ronsard to be particularly concerned with death. Elegy 12, a long moral discourse on friendship, assumes the title *discours*, the sort of title-change which will become more frequent later on. Elegies 3, 11, and 13 lose their generic title for one that is simply a dedication. One wonders why this happened to elegies 11 and 13, because they are preface poems, and we have seen that Ronsard wrote two more elegies of this type after 1560. Elegy 3 is one of the poems dealing with poetry. On the other hand, two pre-1560 poems become elegies in 1567, number 48 dealing with his childhood and his friendship with Dorat at Coqueret and number 52 developing the Narcissus myth.

Otherwise the great variety in the elegies of 1560 remains. We have seen, however, that the bulk of the thirty-one new elegies after 1560 fall into two main categories: the personal love complaint to the beloved, almost a new type in Ronsard, and the court elegy, which

Chamard rightly finds as original in Ronsard.[33] We have seen, however, that this type of elegy admits of great variety, which will cause the poet later to separate them into various sections of his later collective editions, very often with title-changes.

As for form, there are no surprises. The poems are all in couplets, eighteen in decasyllabic lines, thirteen in alexandrines; only one does not directly address a precise person. Perhaps the length of some of the poems is unexpected. In their original forms, elegy 39 has 522 lines and elegy 50 has 488. The bulk of the poems, however, are just slightly longer than those before 1560.

3. 1568-1573

In the six years following the edition of 1567, two more collective editions appeared, but our concern with the elegy takes us only as far as the first of these in 1571 since the few changes in the 1572-3 edition do not affect the elegies in any way. We have only four years of writing to consider, then, and, as well, we need not look backward at all, for Ronsard did not touch the titles of the elegies which appeared in 1567.

In 1568 we find Ronsard writing another preface elegy (number 57), and, like the one which appeared with Grévin's theatre, this poem never appeared in any of the collective editions. Dedicated to Nicolas de Nicolay for the book on his travels, the poem, in addition to praising the writer, discourses on the diversity of man and defines the happiest man as the one whose deeds remain as a memorial after death.

Of the ten remaining poems which we have to discuss, eight were published in the *Sixiesme et Septiesme Livres des Poëmes* of 1569. Of these eight, two (numbers 60 and 65) are clearly of the type that we have called court poems. Elegy 60 has the ulterior motive of flattering Du Lac into handling a lawsuit; elegy 65, found at the end of the *Septiesme Livre*, is a very short (28 lines) poem flattering Belot, to whom the *Sixiesme Livre* is dedicated.

[33] Chamard, IV, 162-3.

Another elegy, number 61, might also be included with the above, but in its lengthy development of a love-theme, it is perhaps preferable to see it as one of the elegies which deal with general themes of love. It is a very curious poem in its elaboration of an image of love as a bird which inhabits and torments the body. Elegy 63 to Jamyn is a little more conventional: Ronsard wants to forget his mistress with the aid of poppies. The three other love-poems are all addressed directly to a lady. Elegy 58 is similar to the 1564 love-poems, which we said resemble the Marot type. Elegy 64 is very much the same with its simple description of the power of the eyes of the lady, the affirmation of the lover's fidelity, sincerity, and discretion. Elegie 62 is, on the other hand, a much more learned poem with several mythological references and allusions to antiquity. Its theme is also more openly pagan in its rhetorical attempt to convince the lady that she should give in to the lover's desires.

The remaining elegy published in 1569 (number 59) is somewhat unusual. It is a very strong reply to a young fop who had ridiculed Ronsard's poetry in public. Along with a terrible curse, Ronsard works in a passage on the divinity of the poet.

In the 1571 *Œuvres*, two more elegies appear, only one of which is a new poem. Very oddly Ronsard now gives the title elegy to a poem which appeared by itself in 1564 and which was dedicated to Catherine de Médicis. The poem has no direct address and, indeed, in its technique is hardly different from the sort of poem so frequently found in the works of the *rhétoriqueurs*. The poet is visited in his sleep by *Promesse*, who engages him in a long conversation centering on the theme of praise of the queen. If the technique is unexpected, the poem nevertheless belongs to the court elegies. The new poem in 1571 is another long (316 lines) poem to Genèvre. Curious that Genèvre should always inspire such long poems! Curious, too, that he should take the trouble to tell her how completely dead his love now is for her. His description of how his career as courtier suffered during his passion leads us to suspect that he regretted the whole affair. In any case, he ends his poem with the observation that all love is inconstant, and Venus serves as a convenient symbol to prove the point.

Ten of these eleven elegies appeared in the edition of 1571, and nine of them were added to the section of *Elégies* (to which a fifth book was added). The elegy to Du Lac was put with the *Poëmes*.

As we have seen, these poems carry on the tendencies that we found in the 1561-1567 period. Only the poem of invective is of a new type and the style of the *Promesse* poem strange among the elegies. Again all the poems are in couplets, all but three in decasyllabic lines.

4. 1575-1578

The first two poems that we have to consider were published in 1575 in the little book *Les Estoilles A Monsieur de Pibrac*...[34] After the first poem which gave its title to the whole volume, we have two poems by Charles IX to Ronsard and a reply to each one by the poet. The poems by the king are short (twelve and eighteen lines) and are simply called "Vers du Roy...". The replies by Ronsard, however, are entitled "Response à vne Elegie de feu Roy..." and "Response à vne autre Elegie...", and, in the title of the book itself, the poems by Charles are referred to as elegies: *Les Estoilles A Monsieur de Pibrac, Et Deux Responses a Deux Elegies ennuoyées par le feu Roy Charles...* In the 1578 collective edition, all mention of the word elegy is dropped.

We have included these two poems of Ronsard in our list of elegies (numbers 68 and 69) since, at least in 1575, if not later, he probably imagined his "responses" to be as elegiac as the poems by Charles. Indeed, they seem even more so to us. In the first of the king's poems, he simply asks Ronsard to join him at Amboise; in the second, he compares his youth with Ronsard's advanced years but points out that his youth is only physical: "Ton esprit est, Ronsard, plus gaillard que le mien" (l. 15). The replies by Ronsard are typical of other elegies that he had written by this time. The first (46 lines) is simply praise of the king and of his writing; the second becomes a sort of *discours* on the virtues of youth and inevitable age and again encourages the king in his literary efforts.

[34] XVII, 35-62.

Nine new elegies appear in the collective edition of 1578, almost all of them showing us a Ronsard still writing for others or in praise of them. Two poems, written in 1567 and 1569, become elegies now (numbers 76 and 78). Number 78 retains a certain interest since, in addition to its flattery of Montmorency, Ronsard goes on to discourse on the proper way to govern. Number 76 is still more interesting since Ronsard here speaks at length of his poetic inspiration and of how he composes his works. Elegy 77 is of the same type: it is essentially a poem intended to please and flatter but again develops a general theme, this time the hedonistic idea that spring and love are to be enjoyed before life is finished.

Elegy 70, published for the first time in 1575,[35] shows the ageing Ronsard's attempt to ingratiate himself with the new king, Henri III, while elegy 72 is a reminder of his great poetic services to Charles IX. In celebrating the love of Charles for Anne d'Aquaviva under the names Eurymedon and Callirée, Ronsard develops ideas on the nature and invincibility of love. Elegy 73, to Marguerite, wife of the future Henri IV, praises her beauty by developing the myth of Amour's transferring his power to her eyes by going to lodge in them through love of her. Elegy 74 is another poem which develops a myth in order to praise the sister of Astrée (Isabeau Babou de la Bourdaisière). Since the lady has all the beauty of Spring, Spring is afraid to return. The poem therefore makes a plea for a marriage between Spring and the lady.

Elegy 75 is the only real love-elegy of this group, and it is not thought to be a personal poem.[36] The man involved explains to his lady in rather harsh terms how fragile love is, how it can be destroyed by a new experience, by a break in continuity caused by a trip, for instance. Orpheus is remembered to give weight to the threat that sin is always punished. A somewhat grim elegy.

The last new poem to appear in 1578 is the second of the two elegies which Ronsard devoted to the theme of death (number 71). Appearing in a new section of the 1578 *Œuvres*, the second part of the second book of *Amours*, *Sur la Mort de Marie*, the poem, unlike all the others except for one, is thought to concern the death of

---

[35] In the *Estreines au Roy Henry III...*, now lost. See XVII, 85.
[36] See Desonay *Ronsard Poète de l'Amour*, III, 193-4.

Marie de Bourgueil.[37] Like the elegy on the death of Chateignier, there is no direct address apart from the various apostrophes. Also like the early death-elegy the style is rich in imagery, although the tone is generally less formal. Since it involves the death of the beloved, the themes, too, are somewhat different in their concentration on the beauty of the deceased and the love of the poet.

Of the eleven new elegies in 1578, most of them, as we have seen, are devoted to Ronsard's career as court poet. The themes are hardly new, and only the last elegy that we discussed comes as anything of a surprise.

More interesting in the 1578 edition is the revisional work that Ronsard carried out on his earlier poems. The book of *Elégies*, for example, is trimmed of the seven pastoral poems that had been included in it from 1567 to 1573, a poem in quatrains[38] and four sonnets.[39] As well, three elegies are rejected from the *Œuvres* altogether, and two of them had appeared in the book of *Elégies* (numbers 63 and 65). Two new elegies appear, but in one case it is only a question of title: elegy 78 appeared with the *Elégies* as early as 1567 but not until 1578 did the word elegy appear in its title; elegy 70, a new poem, becomes the first elegy of the book.

If a number of poems have been removed from the *Elégies* (now arranged in only one book), a certain number of poems still appear there which do not bear the title elegy. The very first poem is simply "Au Roy Henry III" (the poem that follows it is entitled "Elégie I") and serves as a dedication of the *Elégies* to the king. The last poem (elegy 59) is now simply entitled "Invective". Three poems developing myths are called simply by the person that they concern ("L'Adonis", "Le Narcis", "Orphée"),[40] and five poems are called "Discours" and are numbered separately from the elegies.

These *discours* do not have much unity in themselves, They are all

---

[37] Desonay, III, chapter V. Desonay resumes all the views of the various critics who have dealt with the problem of these poems and finally concludes that, except for the "Elégie" and the "Epitaphe", they are for Princesse Marie de Clèves.

[38] XII, 205.

[39] In the 1571 edition, the *épitaphe* of Rabelais appeared at the end of the last book of *Elégies*, but in 1573 it is placed with the *Epitaphes*.

[40] See numbers 52, 82, and 87.

long poems (all over 200 lines, sometimes double that number), longer than the usual elegy, but curiously the first two Genèvre elegies that Ronsard wrote (and he originally gave the name "Discours" to one of them) and which are very long, appear here as elegies and only the third one, published in 1571 (elegy 66), becomes a *discours* (number IV). The fact that all three poems are not called *discours* is all the more curious since the lengthy narrative elegy 55 is called "Discours II" in 1578. All we can say, then, is that Ronsard had a certain hesitation in 1578 about the fitness of these very lengthy narrative love-poems as elegies.

The other three *discours* are long poems of flattery: elegy 39 is dedicated to Queen Elizabeth of England, elegy 67 ("La Promesse") is dedicated to Catherine de Médicis, and another poem that never was and never will be entitled elegy, is dedicated to the bishop of Toulon.[41]

Not all the changes concerning our elegies occur in the book devoted only to them. Apart from the four elegies that we have just looked at which became *discours* in 1578, five others must be mentioned. Two early elegies (23 and 24) that had appeared in the section *Discours des Miseres de ce temps* since 1567 are now logically called *discours*. Two other early poems, which resemble each other, become *discours*: elegies 20 and 22, both poems which, it will be remembered, are autobiographical and explain how Ronsard became a poet. Finally, there is the very flattering poem to Du Lac (elegy 60) which ends with a request that he settle the poet's lawsuit.

Only three other poems are affected in the 1578 edition. Elegy 46 is rejected altogether; the fate of elegy 15 is finally settled (it becomes a *chanson*); and elegy 8 returns as an elegy after having lost its generic title in the editions from 1560 to 1573.

The importance of the 1578 edition rests in its attempt to put a little more order in the poet's works. The result of this is the loss of a number of earlier elegies and the increase in the number of *discours*, a title that grows steadily in importance especially after 1567. As yet, the purpose behind all the changes is not always clear, but the particularly long elegies, whether they be about love or praise of

---

[41] "La Vertu Amoureuse". See X, 337.

the mighty, have a tendency to go, and we have a slight inclination to remove the purely flattering poems or those closely connected with life, his own or the problems of the age.

5. 1579-1584

In the 1584 edition, six new elegies appear, and a poem which first appeared in 1564 now has the word elegy in its title. Only one of the poems is really new as a type of elegy.

Three of the new elegies are devoted to love. The section of poems for Hélène is increased by an elegy (number 79), the only one written for her. In it, the poet says that his love of seven years is now at an end: Reason delivers him from love's fetters, and he now spends his time alone in nature or with his books. The two other love-elegies (numbers 83 and 84) are *basium* poems, both modelled on Secundus. The poems add a sensual note not often found in the elegies of Ronsard.

A fourth poem (number 82) deals with love but in the development of the myth of Orpheus, and so it belongs more properly to the other mythological elegy (number 52) published as an elegy first in 1567. The Orpheus poem was written as early as 1564 and was included with the *Elégies* in all the collective editions from 1567 to 1578. It is still with the *Elégies* in 1584, but for the first time the word elegy appears in its title: "L'Orphée, en forme d'Elegie".

The edition of 1584 provides us with another preface-elegy (number 80). Written for the book on hunting by Charles IX, the poem is first published in 1584 at the end of *La Franciade*. Charles was already dead when Ronsard wrote the poem, and so the poem, although it apostrophizes Charles, addresses Villeroy (Nicolas de Neufville), who was responsible for the inclusion of the poem in this edition.[42] The poem is, of course, essentially one of praise of Charles's unfinished book and so not very different in type from elegy 81, which is another plea to Henri III to give the poet some writing to do.

---

[42] See Catalogue for full title of the poem.

The final elegy which appears for the first time in 1584 is the famous poem against the destruction of the forest of Gâtine (elegy 85). No other elegy is quite like this one, except perhaps for the "Invective" poem (elegy 59) in which Ronsard also gives vent to his feelings in strong terms.[43] Elegy 85, however, is obviously less personal in the direction of its attack. It consists of a series of apostrophes, mainly to inanimate objects, and mixed in almost equal amounts are the curses on the destroyers of the forest, the poet's memories of his happy youth in the forest and the development of the philosophical theme of the constant change in the form of matter.

In 1578 we saw that Ronsard rearranged his works considerably and renamed a number of his elegies. In 1584 this revision work went much further.

The book of *Elégies*, for example, takes on quite a new appearance. Twenty-one poems are removed from the poems given to us in 1578 and eight are added, six of them new poems to the 1584 edition and two from other parts of the *Œuvres*. In the case of the poems that remain, quite a few have title changes.

It is relatively simple to sum up the type of poem which Ronsard eliminates from the book of *Elégies* in 1584.[44] All but four of these poems are poems of praise of French and English royalty or of important nobles at court. Of the remaining four, elegy 55 was already given the title "Discours" in 1578, and elegy 44 was eliminated from the *Œuvres* altogether in 1584. Both of these poems deal with love but not in the typical elegiac fashion. Elegy 44 is Anne's poem to Diane about friendship; elegy 55 is the long narrative in which the writer explains his mother's objections to marriage between him and the lady who is to receive the letter. The other two poems are in a way poems of praise but not too obviously so. Elegy 7 is the

---

[43] It is perhaps worthy of note that the two poems follow one another in 1584.
[44] Of the twenty-one poems eliminated, two never bear the title elegy at any time: the "Au Roy" which begins the book ("Si l'homme de porter deux sceptres en la main", XVII, 17) and the "Discours III" ("C'estoit au poinct du jour quand les plumes du Somme", X, 337). Two other poems which appeared with the elegies but were entitled "Discours" in 1578 are also eliminated: see Appendix numbers 39 and 55. The others eliminated are numbered as follows in our list: 7, 9, 25, 34, 37, 40, 41, 42, 43, 44, 45, 49, 51, 54, 56, 70, 78.

blason on the glass given to him by Brinon; elegy 19, written for
Troussily, discusses poetic inspiration and the poet's own fears
concerning the effects of age on it.

Essentially, what Ronsard has done in 1584 is to eliminate the
bulk of the poems of praise from his book of *Elégies*. That does not
mean, however, that this type of poem is totally absent in 1584.
One of the new poems to appear in this edition (elegy 81) is a direct
request to Henri III that he give the poet commands. "La Promesse"
(elegy 67) not only remains in the book of *Elégies* but is called an
elegy again. Elegies 21 and 27, both what we have called previously
the *discours* type despite their intention to praise, also remain. Ronsard did not carry out his eliminations to their logical conclusion,
but for the first time it is noticeable in the book of *Elégies* that he
has one type of subject principally in mind: almost all the poems
deal in some way with love. We have already pointed out four exceptions; only three more poems can be added to them. Elegy 48 is one
of the autobiographical poems dealing with his early years; elegy
59 is the invective against his foppish critic; elegy 85 is the invective
against those who would destroy the Gâtine forest. All the others
concern love-themes.

These love-elegies are not, however, all of the same kind. If Ronsard seems closer to a conception of the elegy as a love-poem, it is
not a conception which is as well-defined as it was among the Latin
poets or in the work of Marot and many of his successors. Eleven
elegies are of the personal-address type to the lady, all of them dating
back to the 1560's.[45] As well, we have the three Genèvre elegies,
which, as we have already pointed out, are a little different from
these other elegies in their narrative character, and this difference
seems to have been felt by Ronsard since the two most narrative of
the three are called in this edition "Discours en forme d'Elegie".

The remaining elegies show greater variety. Elegy 14 still remains
with the elegies and is the only one that has no address at all; elegies
5, 61, and 77 discourse on love to various acquaintances of the poet;
the new elegies 83 and 84 are *basia*.

Only three poems remain to be mentioned:[46] elegies 52, 82, and

---

[45] Elegies 29, 30, 31, 32, 33, 35, 36, 53, 58, 62, 64.
[46] There is as well a "Discours" which we shall discuss with the 1587 edition.
Its theme is love, but it is a most unusual poem.

84, poems which develop at length the Adonis, Narcissus, and Orpheus myths. The first two are given titles here which include the
word elegy; it seems to be pure oversight that the Adonis poem
does not also appear as "L'Adonis en forme d'Elégie". In any case,
as far as classification of the poems is concerned, they can be regarded as a sort of *hymne*, as a *discours* (in their moralizing tendency)
or as a love-poem, since all three myths are concerned with love. It
is perhaps this aspect of them which accounts for their presence in
the book of *Elégies*.[47]

The book of *Elégies* in 1584 is quite a different collection from
what we found in 1578. Love is now the major theme if not the only
one. What happened to the other elegies in 1584 and what happened
to the poems eliminated from the book of *Elégies?* Elegy 44 was
eliminated altogether; elegies 8, 37, and 56 became *discours* (the
last two are written to Mary Stuart; the first is one of the dedication poems); elegies 47, 54, 73, and 76 lose the title elegy without
gaining a generic title in its place (number 47 to Jamyn about love;
number 76 partly about poetic inspiration but similar to numbers
54 and 73 in its theme of praise). The most important single change
in 1584 is the creation of a new section, the *Bocage Royal*, intended
to receive, if not all of them, a good number of the poems which
Ronsard wrote for the great and powerful. In putting the poems into
this section, Ronsard removed in every case but one the title elegy,[48]
and thus we have eleven elegies of the book of *Elégies* of 1578 which
lose their title elegy at the same time that they are put into the *Bocage
Royal*. Six of them (numbers 7, 34, 40, 43, 51, and 78) become *discours*,
number 70 regains its original title "Estrennes", and four have only
dedicatory titles (numbers 19, 41, 43, and 49).

The 1584 edition also recovers a number of elegies. All these
examples are to be found in the book of *Elégies* itself except for
elegy 2, which, after having been an elegy and an *épîtaphe*, now is
called an "Elegie en forme d'Epitaphe". Ronsard shows consider-

---

[47] This would explain as well their never having been called *hymnes*. The *hymne*
is too lofty a poem to deal with love even if the Truth is hidden in a mythological
garb.
[48] Elegy 45 is removed from the section of *Elégies* of the 1578 edition but is
called *élégie* in the *Bocage Royal* of 1584.

able affection for the "en forme de" phrase in his 1584 titles. We have pointed out already the two Genèvre elegies which have become "discours en forme d'élégie"; two of his mythological poems (numbers 52 and 82) are also "en forme d'élégie"; elegy 59, called "Invective" in 1578, is now "Elegie, en forme d'invective". Finally, elegies 66 and 67 have become elegies again after having been *discours* in 1578 and elegies before that.

In 1584, then, we can say in conclusion that Ronsard has a tendency to eliminate his courtier elegies and to favour subjects dealing with some aspect of love. This process of classification is not, however, carried to its logical limits.

6. 1585-1587

The value of the 1587 edition of Ronsard's *Œuvres* as representing his final wishes no doubt can never be determined. It must always be admitted that we are on uncertain ground if we assume that everything found in it reveals the wishes of the poet: if we accept the new poems as being authentic, we cannot be absolutely sure that their titles and especially their position among the other poems were determined by Ronsard. Nor can we be sure that the various title changes which the previously published poems underwent in 1587 conform to the wishes of the poet.[49] Nevertheless, we cannot overlook what happened to the elegies in this edition or ignore the nine new ones which appear in it.

Of these nine new elegies, only two are published here for the first time: the other seven are poems which simply assume the title elegy for the first time in 1587. Elegy 87 (which appeared as early as 1563) was always placed in the book of *Elégies* from 1567 on, and as we have already suggested, it seems to have been an oversight that it was not actually called an elegy earlier since in its treatment of the

---

[49] Isidore Silver, however, tends to accept the 1587 as being the authentic expression of Ronsard's final wishes. As early as 1950 he has argued in favour of this edition and at present he is editing it. See the introduction to his edition, *Les Œuvres de Pierre de Ronsard, Texte de 1587, Premier Volume* (Published for Washington University Press by the University of Chicago Press, 1966).

Adonis myth it resembles, as a type, the elegies about Narcissus (number 52) and Orpheus (number 82). Elegy 92 appeared in the book of *Elégies* in 1584 but was called "Discours". It is a long (282 lines) and strange poem which curses the marriage of the beloved to another man. The poet's curse is strengthened by the spells cast on the bed-chamber of the newly-weds by two old witches, whose words are given in ABAB quatrains. The poem ends with recipes to help the poet forget his love. Although by its length and its mixture of couplets and quatrains this poem does not resemble classical or neo-Latin elegies, it does, by its imitation of Secundus and Ovid,[50] create something of the atmosphere of the more bitter classical elegies, and the reference (ll. 61 *sqq.*) to the old hag who prompted the lady to marry reminds us of the familiar *lena* figure of classical elegies.[51]

The other five poems which become elegies for the first time in 1587 were all originally odes. That they should appear as elegies in 1587 is very curious, although three of them are written in alexandrine couplets rather than lyric forms. These three belong to common types among Ronsard's other elegies: elegy 90 is a poem of praise and gratitude to Martial de Lomenie; elegy 91 speaks of mankind and its tendency to add to its misery by foolish desires and fears; elegy 93 deals with his poetry and the idea that life is short and full of pain. However, what prompted Ronsard – or his editors – to put these poems among the elegies in 1587 was perhaps the desire to give examples of elegies which conformed to the proper length. According to Ronsard himself in one of the two short poems which introduced the book of *Elégies* in 1587:

> Soit courte l'Elegie en trente vers comprise,
> Ou en quarante au plus. Le fin Lecteur mesprise
> Ces discours, ces narrez aussi grands que la Mer.[52]

Elegies of this length have always been very rare among the many poems of this title written by Ronsard, and their fortune was not too

[50] See Paul Laumonier, *Ronsard poète lyrique* (Paris: Hachette, 1932), 264-5.
[51] Concerning the *lena* figure, see Jacques Bailbé, "Le thème de la vieille femme", *Bibliothèque d'humanisme et renaissance*, XXVI (1964), 98-119.
[52] XVIII, 246.

certain. Elegies 16, 46, 63, and 65 were all rejected; elegies 15 and 47
lost their elegy title. In 1584 we found two new elegies (83 and 84) of
32 and 34 lines, and, as has been suggested above, Ronsard perhaps
felt that he should add further examples of short elegies in 1587 by
renaming these three short odes in couplets (they have 28, 32, and
34 lines).

But what would be the justification for the renaming of the other
two odes? It is true that they are on the short side even if they do
exceed 40 lines in length: elegy 88 has 48 lines and elegy 89 has 60.
However, these two odes are written in lyric forms – elegy 88 in
sextains and elegy 89 in quatrains. And if elegy 89 in its development of a moral theme and its references to poetry is typical of a
number of other elegies, elegy 88 is not at all typical. The poem addresses Nicolas Denisot and asks his aid in gathering poppies which
are then presented to Sleep on an altar that they build. After this is
done, the two men return from the fields, full of hope that the poet's
mistress will find sleep in her illness.[53]

Although we have tried to suggest a concern for shortness in the
elegy as prompting the title changes in the five odes, it has to be admitted that this concern with length did not appear to prevent the
poet from putting among his elegies two new poems which have 72
and 88 lines. Otherwise they present no peculiarities. They are both
in alexandrine couplets; number 86 discourses to Desportes on life,
its brevity, happiness, and the certainty only of the present; and
number 94 is a poem of fulsome praise of the Italian poet Bartolo-
meo Del-Bene.

These nine new poems do not, as a group, show any definite tendency. The other differences concerning the elegy in this edition are
hardly more significant. If we limit ourselves first to a consideration
of the book of *Elégies* itself, we find a greater uniformity in the
titles. Now all but one of the poems in the book are given the title
elegy and are numbered from one to thirty-five: the exception is the
"Epithalame de Monseigneur de Joyeuse" which opens the book, as
it did in 1584. This means that we no longer have poems called "Dis-

---

[53] Classical elegies sometimes deal with the illness of the beloved, but the theme
is not developed in this way.

cours en forme d'élégie", "Elégie en forme d'invective" or poems
with descriptive titles like "Adonis". As in the latter case, such descriptive titles are occasionally added ("Elégie IIII. A Genèvre",
"Elegie V. Adonis"), but on the whole we simply find a series of
numbered poems.

As well as the nine new poems discussed above, two elegies (numbers 45 and 75) from other parts of the *Œuvres* are now put in the
book of *Elégies*: one is a poem of flattery, the other a love-poem.
On the other hand, five of the elegies found in this section in 1584
are missing. Four of these are rejected altogether from the *Œuvres*
(elegies 5, 36, 30, and 64); the other, elegy 82 (about the Orpheus
myth), loses its elegy title and is put in the *Bocage Royal*, a curious
change which makes us doubt the presence of Ronsard's guiding
hand.

Apart from all these changes, there are only two further poems
called elegy in 1584 which undergo any transformation in 1587.
Elegy 16 is rejected; elegy 72 loses its generic title and becomes simply "Ronsard parle a Eurymedon".

7. CONCLUSION

Ronsard prepared for his 1587 edition two short poems of introduction to his book of *Elégies* and a few lines of prose.[54] The poems have
already been referred to in our Introduction because, in them,
Ronsard gives a definition of what an elegy should be; the prose
offers an explanation why his own poems do not always follow
this definition. We might remind ourselves that at the end of his
career he defined the elegy essentially as a love-poem, although he
was aware of its supposed origin as a death-lament and its tendency
to treat any subject:

> ...maintenant on compose
> Divers sujets en elle, et reçoit toute chose.
> Amour pour y regner en a chassé la Mort.

One might feel that Ronsard was thinking of the neo-Latin elegy

[54] XVIII, 245-7.

in these lines were it not for the reference to death-elegies. Instead, his history of the genre applied most precisely to his own works.

In the second little prefatory poem, Ronsard tells us how an elegy should be written. The point most emphasized, curiously enough, is the brevity of the poem: ideally it should be about thirty lines and certainly not longer than forty. The subject should be "simple et un", decorated perhaps by "quelque fiction rare", and should come to a rapid conclusion, somewhat in the style of an epigram. This description obviously has little to do with Ronsard's own poems, especially the major point concerning length. Ronsard explains this contradiction in the few lines of prose: he would have been brief had he not written "la meilleure partie" of his elegies on command. It is true that many of the elegies were written on command, but they were not all written for others. Three of his most personal elegies, the poems to Genèvre, are among the lengthiest that he wrote. Indeed, only nine poems before 1584 do not exceed the maximum of forty lines,[55] and of these nine poems only two (elegies 83 and 84, published for the first time in 1584) still appear as elegies in 1587. Five have disappeared altogether; one has become a *chanson*; another has no generic title. Were it not for the renaming of a few odes in 1587, then, there would be only the *basium* poems to represent what he considers an elegy properly to be.

These introductory remarks of Ronsard, if they represent his real convictions at all, refer to a new stage in his thinking, one that had no opportunity to prove itself. Up to this point, however, the evolution of his thoughts on the elegy is fairly clear in outline although never tidy in detail. Ronsard's elegy is first a poem as indefinite as the *épître* in choice of subject and freer than the old *épître* in its manner of expression: the precise character of the poem as a letter is not emphasized. The style tends to be more elegant and learned than in the usual letters: the elegies constitute a highly sophisticated and varied sort of correspondence. After 1560, love begins to show itself prominently as a theme for the first time, and a much clearer type of courtly elegy is composed in aid of the politics of Catherine. The love-poems are curiously similar to Marot's elegies;

[55] Elegies 15, 16, 46, 47, 63, 65, 68, 83, 84.

the courtly poems by their length and development go beyond the normal boundaries of the *épître*.

After 1570, and until his death, Ronsard writes fewer elegies but shows his interest in the form by frequently changing the titles of his earlier poems and rearranging them in the various sections of his *Œuvres*. The guiding principle behind the new titles and the new arrangements seems to be a constantly more definite desire to make the elegy a love-poem, a desire which nevertheless does not prevent his writing an elegy about a forest or some other subject not concerned with love. Again, in speaking of Ronsard's "conception" of the elegy, we are restricted to speaking only of tendencies.

At the same time that Ronsard is eliminating many of his former elegies in favour of a clearer pattern among the remaining ones, we find that the number of *discours* and *poèmes* is increasing. From the great variety of elegies written during his early years, Ronsard is gradually creating new types of poem and trying to give a special character to each. The *discours* takes on many of the more serious *élégies d'idée*, the *poème* many of the elegies which concern ideas but lack the moralizing quality and high seriousness of the *discours*. For the *élégie de cour*, Ronsard conveniently creates his *Bocage Royal*.[56] The elegie is freed, then, of much of its diversity, and the emphasis on love in the short introductory poems in the 1587 edition is accurate at least in its pointing to this tendency.

The history of all these forms – *élégie, discours, poème* – is really the history of the *épître* after 1550. After first using the elegy to take the place of all types of *épître*, Ronsard then moves towards limiting it to the *épître-amoureuse* type, and this rejection of other types leads to further new titles. One should not presume too quickly that Ronsard ends up where Marot began, however, because these disguised *épîtres* go well beyond what the *épître* was before Ronsard and go well towards the creation of new genres.

---

[56] The only generic title (apart from one elegy) which appears in the *Bocage Royal* is *discours*. A number of these poems concern ideas and fit the summary definition that we have given the *discours*. The others which are more definitely *élégies de cour* appear to have merited the title because of their tone and erudition. The elegy included in the *Bocage Royal* is number 45, a poem of flattery but unusually light in tone.

IV

STYLE CHARLES IX

Religious troubles were, of course, not new to France when Charles IX became king, but it is during his reign that events began to take a particularly unpleasant turn. With the religious wars and power struggles at the court, the mood of the 1560's is unusually tense and serious, and this mood is reflected in the elegies of the period: more than has been noticeable before, the elegy tends towards sobriety, reflection, and concern with the events of the times. In a way, this last characteristic could be linked with the *élégie de circonstance*, which we have found from the very beginning of the century, but there is surely an important distinction to be made between a poem which deals with a *fait divers* and one which involves the nation as a whole. The latter type could be called *littérature engagée*, if the term did not already have such imposing connotations.

1. DISCOURSE, DEATH, AND DESTRUCTION

At the beginning of this period, it is the seriousness of tone rather than the historical significance of the poem that we notice. Not one of Jacques Grévin's seven elegies can be called frivolous.[1] The only one of his elegies at all concerned with love is the first one in the 1560 edition. Coming at the beginning of the second section, *Les Ieux Olimpiques*, the elegy affirms the poet's devotion to his lady. As a preface to the section, however, it does a great deal more. Grévin goes on to explain that while Greece can proudly claim to be the

[1] See Catalogue 45 and 47.

inventor of the ode, the epigram, and the elegy and Italy can boast the sonnet, France will henceforth be able to take pride in a new genre, the "olimpien", inspired by his lady. More than a love-poem, then, this elegy resembles the literary-preface type that we found in the works of Ronsard.

The idea of originality can be found in another elegy, the second of the two published in 1562 and dedicated to de Poix, a doctor. Like the poem to Olympe, this elegy is not easily categorized, for it has a strong element of flattery, it is autobiographical, and it develops certain general themes which suggest a *discours*. The poem begins with a description of man: every individual has the same physical make-up, is born the same way and, in essentials, lives the same way. It is in his will, in his mind, that man differs from his neighbour. Unfortunately the validity of another person's desires or originality is not always recognized:

> Ie me deulx seulement de uoir ces enuieux
> Reprendre mon labeur sans pouuoir faire mieux.
> I'entrepren (disent-ils) un œuure fort à faire,
> I'entrepren de parler, moy qui deuroy taire,
> Et sans auroi encor' le poil sur mon menton,
> Ie cherche les secrets du diuin Apollon. (ll. 15-20)

Apollo is proof that the study of medicine and the writing of poetry are not irreconcilable (ll. 21-8). Poetry is relaxation for Grévin (ll. 26-40), and, after a period of commerce with the Muses, "ragaillardi ie rentre en la carriere" (l. 41). He remembers, however, that de Poix has a higher conception of poetry: it is not simply a pastime:

> Là me resouuenant que la poesie est faicte
> Pour priser la science, & que tousiours un poete
> Doit enrichir ses uers, louangeant le scauoir,
> I'ay essayé De-poix, de me mettre en deuoir (ll. 49-52)

At this particular time, however, he did not succeed, and he managed only to laugh and cry over "l'enuie & la misere / Dont les hommes sont pleins" (ll. 54-5). These two types of poetry, that of knowledge and that of lament, will share the remaining elegies of our poet.

In praise of truth and knowledge, Grévin first offers us a curiosity called "sur la naissance de Typosine, Deese tutelaire de l'Imprimerie. Elegie II" (1560). The new goddess created by the poet fascinated him so much that he devoted a sonnet and an ode to her in 1562. As poems, none is remarkable, perhaps least of all the elegy, but the pride that Grévin has in the recent invention of printing is a useful reminder that many sixteenth-century writers sought new glory and did not simply prostrate themselves before the ancients. Grévin, decidedly a *moderne*, admits the difficulty of discovering great new truths, but he exults over the possibilities of the printing press in combatting ignorance.[2] The elegy which follows this one reveals some of the poet's ideas concerning ignorance: it is the study of the non-physical world and the belief in astrology. The sublunary world is the proper domain to study, and knowledge of it is greatly increased by a study of the classical writers.

In the remaining three elegies, Grévin deals directly or indirectly with the misery of human existence. The method is indirect and incidental in the fourth elegy of the 1560 book of elegies. The poem concerns the death of a young girl, Anne Boucher, and is really an epitaph (at line 22, the poem addresses the "passant"). Were it not for the elegy to "Philippes Musnier, euesque de Philadelphe" (the first poem in the book of elegies), the 1562 "Elegie sur la Misere des hommes" and the two books called *Gelodacrye*, the reader would see in this short death-elegy nothing more than a few commonplaces on the misery of life and the advantages of an early death. But the misfortunes of human existence deeply troubled this poet, who made his own life more difficult by joining the Reformers, and in the short epitaph he speaks more simply and more movingly of his feelings than he does in the other two elegies (his longest):

"Que nous sert plus long temps demourer en ce monde
"Ou le malheur redouble, & la misere abonde?
"Que nous sert plus long temps dans ce corps ocieux
"Tourmenter nostre esprit d'un soing ambitieux,
"D'un desir obstiné, qui d'autant ne r'enforce,
"Qu'il se sent alleché d'une nouuelle amorce,
"Qui tousiours nous seconde & talonne nos pas,

[2] See Hans Baron, "The 'Querelle' of the ancients and the moderns as a problem for Renaissance scholarship", *Journal of the History of Ideas*, 20 (1959), 3-22.

'Voire en nous maistrisant iusqu'au iour du trespas? (ll. 1-8)

If Grévin appears to stress the hazards of life such as they depend
on the individual, his other two elegies develop the theme more
widely in terms of human society and what it has become. The very
lengthy poem (274 lines) to the bishop of Philadelphia develops the
myth of the Golden Age, and, in the description of lawyers, judges,
merchants and the like, we have a criticism of what they have
become in the sixteenth century. The happy state of man during the
Golden Age upsets Pluto, whose realm is not increasing in numbers.
The solution to his problem is to send on earth "Cupidité", "Or-
gueil", and "Faulse religion", the three causes of all the disorder
and misery of life according to Grévin. While the poem is to be taken
seriously as representing Grévin's personal thoughts, the manner
that he has chosen to express them is very literary but nevertheless
often powerful. Less forceful but interesting for its anecdotic detail
is the 1562 "Elegie sur la misere des hommes". The poet gets off to
a rather tiresome start by speaking of the Muses and his inclination
to laugh and cry. Then, to prove to man how wretched his life is,
a description of his various ages is given. The infant is helpless and
miserable; the child must endure the hardships of education:

> Si tu es au college, helas! combien de fois
>   Ne mange-tu le lard apres les pois:
> Combien de fois, helas! te mets-tu dans la couche
>   Quand plus la faim que le sommeil te touche.
> Encor s'il aduient que tu ayes sommeil,
>   Combien de fois auras-tu le reueil,
> Auant qu'un nouueau iour rentre dans sa courtine,
>   Par l'esguillon d'une espesse uermine? (ll. 69-76)

And man's life continues in this way. It is after the description of
the ages of man, however, that the poem takes its most bitter turn
as the writer describes the sight of a "caphart", gluttonous and
sensual but a preacher of abstinence. Grévin's laughter is more
pained than his tears.

High seriousness characterizes Grévin's elegies: although there
is a slight nod in the direction of love and death, his elegies are all
much more generally involved with ideas or lament over the condi-

tion of all human existence. The poems are, then, like the *discours* type of elegy that we have so far found to be most exploited by Ronsard. Other poets during the 1560's will also be interested in this type of poem – for example, two poets whose names are closely linked with Ronsard's because of the Pléiade.

Both Jodelle and Baïf might have composed as uninteresting a piece of flattery as Habert (Catalogue 44) because the first purpose of their elegies is to flatter and grace the books of friends: Jodelle writes for Baïf; Baïf writes for Scévole de Sainte-Marthe.[3] This primary concern is worked out in such a way, however, that the resulting poems are every bit as ambiguous as many of Ronsard's elegies were.

Jodelle is inspired by Baïf's learned book on meteors to develop, along with his praise of Baïf's erudition, ideas about the importance of knowledge. All the "terreurs" and "abus" which Jodelle sees in France are caused by ignorance:

> Par la diserte leçon des Vieux (qui mesme de leur rang
>> Ont fait par ce labeur estre le docte **BAIF**)
> S'ouure la cause de tout, tant bien que la crainte, que l'erreur
>> Et la superstition fausse, se donte par eux. (ll. 11-4)

Rather tortured syntax makes the poem increasingly difficult to follow as Jodelle explains the mechanism by which man's spirit becomes freed from the weight of his body and is able to soar aloft and perceive the true nature of the universe (ll. 15-28). But there is another miracle: this same result may be gained through the art of poetry. By the study of Baïf's poem, one can reach the same understanding of the world:

> Tous les cieux vrayment figurez peut clorre de ses vers,
>> Clorre la Terre encor, l'Onde, le Vuide, le Feu. (ll. 35-36)

Baïf's elegy is identical to Jodelle's in intent and method – and prosodic form: both are in *vers mesurés* imitating the classical elegiac distich. Jodelle's poem did not have any obvious classical antecedent in its subject-matter, however. As well as Ronsard, Baïf

---

[3] See Catalogue 49 and 58.

might have had in mind the elegies of Solon: like Solon, Baïf is concerned with the problems of peace and justice. Much more directly than Jodelle, Baïf is obviously writing with the religious disturbances of the 1560's in mind. What is particularly interesting for us to see in this poem and in many others of the period is that the religious aspect of the troubles is almost totally neglected in favour of an interpretation of the events as being a purely civil problem. The address to Sainte-Marthe at the end of the poem clearly demonstrates Baïf's understanding of the matter as one of sedition:

> Puis comme l'ordre legal maintient toute chose de bon sens,
> 　　Met aux fers le mechant, orne e preserue le bon,
> . . . .
> Redrece tout ce qui va de trauers, e rabaisse tout orgueil,
> 　　Pacifiant les fais d'horrible sedicion,
> Pacifiant le debat quereleux, e la haine, e la rancueur,
> 　　Par la rigueur d'equité nourrice dousse de paix. (ll. 56-64)

Earlier in the poem he interprets the disorder as prompted by ambition, cruelty, and ignorance rather than a struggle of religious faiths:

> Mais aucuns citoiens sont enemis de la paix,
> . . . .
> Plains de fole ambition, conduis de mechante volonté,
> 　　Enuenimez é felons, d'outrecuidance piquez.
> . . . .
> Ains qui a tort a trauers taschent s'engresser e remplir,
> 　　Sans chois tout le sacré tout le public rauissans. (ll. 12-20)

The poem, then, paints a picture in its sixty-four lines of a France torn by civil conflict, resulting in harm to all because of egoism (ll. 41-4). Baïf warns of the other dangers which usually await a troubled country:

> Voici venir la cruelle furie du barbare etranger.
> 　　A ce voleur nous auons traitres ouuert le chemin.
> A Dieu des François e l'honeur, e la franche liberté:
> 　　L'antique foi n'est plus, l'Empire vieil se dechet. (ll. 47-50)

With this elegy by Baïf we bridge the gap between the *discours-*

type elegies and the group which deals quite specifically with the historical moment. It is interesting to note in connection with these poems that the title elegy had by this time become familiar enough that casual versifiers were inclined to make use of it along with the more familiar "Plainte", "Complainte", or "Déploration". These poets often remain anonymous; they generally show their lack of concern for the literary habits of the day by their indifference to the alternation of masculine and feminine rhymes and by their prosaic style, only slightly adorned by uncomplicated allusions to antiquity.

A good example of this type of elegy is the only one that we have found from the Reformist side, signed simply with the initials D. R.[4] We are warned in a short introduction that this elegiac prosopopoeia of France will be imperfect in style:

...à cause que la France est introduite, comme si desolee, & en telle perplexité, qu'elle ne peut bien discourir...

France can, however, speak at length: the elegy contains 834 lines of harsh criticism of Catherine de Médicis and the cardinal de Guise. It is interesting to remind ourselves that on the title page we are promised a demonstration of the abuses of both religious groups:

Item monstrant que tous en general, tant d'vne, que d'autre Religion, sont vne des causes d'icelles guerres, aduenues despuis l'Edict de Ianuier.

Instead, the poem simply lays the blame for the seven years of bloodshed that followed the 1562 édit de janvier on the shoulders of Catherine, who has, according to the poem, entrusted herself to the cardinal de Guise. The reality of these seven years, 1562-1569, is, of course, quite different. Catherine was as concerned about the power of the guisards, who were closely involved with Spain, as she was about the connections between the Reformers and England.[5] The author is equally unfair to Catherine concerning the édit de janvier, which allowed the Reformers to worship publicly. The édit was very much the result of her work. Instead, the author gives Charles IX

---

[4] See Catalogue 57.
[5] See Jean Héritier, *Catherine de Médicis* (Paris: Fayard, 1959), 273-394.

the credit and blames Catherine for the long list of violations of the *édit* which followed. The author's reason for doing this might have been pure ignorance. It might also have been a question of convenience, for he claims, on the part of the Reformers, complete fidelity to the King. If the situation in France has been so unsettled, it is because the Guise party is trying to overthrow the legitimate monarchy, and the Reformers are trying to save it.

Reformers were obviously not necessarily any fairer in their appraisal of events than the Catholics. If it must be admitted that our writer has understood the ambitions of the Guise family, he has not understood the rôle that Catherine was playing. Is this the result of her unfortunate talks at Bayonne in 1565?[6] In any case, the writer insists on Catherine's complicity with "ce maudit Cardinal" (l. 34) and suggests the breaking of the Salic Law as the Original Sin which has brought about the years of war and carnage:

> Pour donc auoir souffert la Loy Salique enfraindre
> Par trop tard ie me puis de vous iustement plaindre
> Quels maux ay-ie enduré, par vous desia trois fois,
> Et si endureray, ainsi que i'apperçois? (ll. 59-62)

The poem simply repeats over and over again these few basic ideas: the Salic Law, the ambitions of the cardinal to rule, and the breaking of the *édit de janvier*. The themes are simple, and they are treated simply. Only occasionally does our poet adorn his matter with references to Roman history (see folio B vi recto). And although the poem is written in alexandrine couplets, the non-alternation of masculine and feminine rhymes gives us a hint that the roughness of style mentioned in the preface is not simply for greater realism in the apostrophe of France to her people, but that the work is that of a versifier rather than that of a poet, the work of someone not too aware of the literary practices of his day. Indeed, the presence of the word "Item" from time to time in the poem carries us back a very long way.

In the same year of 1569, we have from a professional and a Catholic poet another elegy of lamentation over the troubled times.

---

[6] Héritier, 326-331.

Claude de Pontoux[7] states his point of view clearly in the opening
passage of the poem:

> Nous n'aurons iusque icy, dont il en soit memoire
> Par chronique ancienne, ou par aucune histoire,
> Ouy, connu, ny veu, temps plus pernicieux
> Que cestuy qui produict tant de seditieux,
> Par lesquelz auiourd'huy si malheureux nous sommes
> Les hommes auiourd'huy sont loups garoups aux hommes. (ll. 5-10)

The word "seditieux" is particularly interesting: as in Baïf's
poem and, in fact, in all these elegies, dogma appears to be of no
interest whatsoever. Indeed, Pontoux doubts that religion has any
real part in the troubles of the country:

> Qui cause ces malheurs? c'est dame Ambition,
> Ayant pour sa fourriere vne Relligion (ll. 55-6)

The only way out is to crush "les ambitieux / Les traistres, les mu-
tins & les seditieux" (ll. 141-2).

A harsh lesson for troubled times. Pontoux shows as much concern for them in another poem published in 1569 which is ostensibly
occasioned by a royal death, the Queen of Spain, Elisabeth de
France, daughter of Catherine and Henri II.[8] Elisabeth died in
October of 1568; a reference to harsh winter (l. 73) suggests that the
poem was written a few months later when the third civil war was
being fought. This explains the first twenty-six lines of the poem,
which ask the "Nobles guerrier(s) Françoys" to lay down their arms
and to restore peace in France. This opening evocation of France
in the throes of war is not forgotten during the rest of this long poem
(296 lines), and the references to the misery of life give greater
weight than is usual to the commonplaces concerning the peace of
death and the good fortune of the departed:

> Pleine de cruauté [i.e. France], pleine de desarroy,
>   Opiniastre & rebelle à son Roy
> Nous viuons en la guerre, en paix elle repose, (ll. 143-5)

In a mood of escapism, the poet creates a vision of the peace of

[7] See Catalogue 53.
[8] See Catalogue 54.

Heaven to form a contrast with earthly life (ll. 149-266) and concludes:

> Ah! que ne suis ie mort, pour iouir à iamais
>   En ce sainct lieu de tant heureuse paix.
> Ie ne verrois icy regner tant de miseres.
>   Tant de forfaictz meurtres, rages, choleres,
> Ie ne verois icy le piteux desarroy
>   Qu'en France on faict pour tourmenter le Roy. (ll. 267-272)

Elizabeth seems hardly central in this deploration; the poem is mainly another version of Pontoux's *Elegie des troubles et miseres*.

This linking of individual death with the religious, or civil disturbances is characteristic of the elegies written during Charles's reign: obviously the poets held to the Great Man view of history. The death of these influential individuals could inspire either great sense of loss and despair or, on one particular occasion, great joy. In the latter vein we have the two poems about the death of Gaspard de Coligny, a *Chant d'Allegresse*[9] and an anonymous *Elegie Satyrique*.[10] The writer of the *Elegie satyrique* was in no way a tender-hearted person. The poem exudes his hatred not only for Coligny but for all the Reformers, and it is not only the murder of Coligny which gives him reason to rejoice but also the massacre of *la Saint-Barthélemy* (ll. 44-46). Nor is he content with so many deaths: he begins his poem by calling on the Furies to punish Coligny and picks up the theme again at line 59 with the additional request that all heretics be tormented:

> Furies donc laschez voz dragons, voz couleuures,
> Couleuures, crocodilles, sifflonissent leurs leuures,
> Voz serpens, vos lezardes, voz aspicqz sans merci.
> Bourreller de Colligny, ces complices aussi
> Sans mercy Caluinistes obstinez, zuingliens
> Zuingliens, Bezeistes, & tous Lutheriens
> Terriens Epicures, attheistes sanglantz,
> Sanglantz tous vous assistent, pour pasture avez dentz, (ll. 59-66)

---

[9] *Chant d'Allegresse sur la Mort de Gaspar de Colligny, iadis Admiral de France* (Paris: Nicolas Chesneau, 1572), in-4.
[10] See Catalogue 61.

After recalling again the glory of *la Saint-Barthélemy* (ll. 75-6), the poem ends in praise of the king.

When the death was on the Catholic side, however, Catholic poets expressed an appropriately different feeling. Another anonymous poet in 1563 reveals that for him the death of the duc de Guise is a tragic loss for France.[11] He begins his poem by calling on France and Paris to deplore this loss which threatens the whole structure of the country (ll. 1-8). The defunct was the protector of the Church which the Reformers are determined to destroy. Beginning at line 30, the poem develops the theme of the destructive ambitions of the Huguenots, mixed from time to time with lament and praise for the duc of Guise. Almost all of the second half of the poem is in the form of a prayer, the last part of which asks for a new Scipio, a new Hannibal to save France.

After this poem, short (68 lines, decasyllabic couplets) and unpretentious, we have to wait a few years before any new elegies of this type are found. Guise was killed just after the first civil war; in 1567, at the beginning of the second war (the battle of Saint-Denis) the Catholic side lost another great general, Anne de Montmorency. In 1568 two poems appear about his death, and again there is considerable attention given to the events of the time, although perhaps a little less than in the poem about the duc de Guise. These two poems, by Sorel and D'Amboise, are more ambitious than the preceding one: they are both slightly more than two hundred lines in length and are considerably more literary in their allusions and their form (alexandrine couplets, alternation of masculine and feminine rhymes).

Sorel[12] presents us first with a problem: did he write only one elegy or two poems of that title. Part of the title of the book promises "plusieurs Elegies"; inside its covers we find two poems bearing the title. The strange thing, however, is that the first of these poems ("Elegie à Monseigneur du Mortier") is a sonnet. Immediately following it is the long poem, simply called "Elegie" but equally addressed to Du Mortier. Is the sonnet conceived of as an elegy or is it simply a sort of preface to the long poem? It is a question that

---

[11] See Catalogue 48.
[12] See Catalogue 51.

cannot be answered with certainty, but the second possibility seems the more likely of the two.

The theme of the sonnet is one that will be developed at length in the elegy. While it talks of the Golden Age, it manages to refer to the inclement weather that Jupiter has sent to France. This, Sorel will describe as an omen that should have warned France of the second war, for at the end of the summer of 1567 the wind and cold played havoc over the country (ll. 105 *sqq*.). The elegy as a whole is concerned with omens, because Sorel seems to believe that Heaven always warns man of impending trouble (ll. 1-4). He traces such omens back to Catherine's dream about Henri and her warning to him, unfortunately not heeded (ll. 5-83). The death of two kings so close together was another omen and led to outbreak of sedition (ll. 84-104). Finally, the weather was a warning for the last war:

> Oncques furent les vents si mutins & enflez
> Armez, herrissonez, dedaigneux, boursoufflez,
> Qu'ils furent contre nous, vn peu auant l'Automne. (ll. 111-3)

The poet describes at length this omen and almost forgets his subject – which is ostensibly the death of Montmorency but which turns into a panegyric of Du Mortier and expresses the hope that he will take the place of the defunct (ll. 179-202).

Rather curiously, the poem by D'Amboise[13] also deals with omens but at less length in favour of more greatly developed praise of Montmorency and more explicit references to the loss suffered by France (ll. 30-1). But everything is the will of God, and every living thing must die (ll. 50 *sqq*.):

> De là, vient le desir de sçauoir les presages,
> Auant-coureurs des maux, & des humains orages, (ll. 73-4)

Line 89 begins another panegyric of Montmorency in which he is compared with classical heroes and his great battles are reviewed. The career of the defunct offered ample material for such a theme, and it is not until line 190 that the subject of deploration returns.

More poems can be cited in this category of death-elegies which

---

[13] See Catalogue 50.

bear witness to the historical moment. There is a sort of collective lamentation for those who died in the battle of Hervaux;[14] there is a rather confused work by Jean de La Jessée about the death of Henri de Foix;[15] and by Belleforest we have a deploration for Gilles Bourdin.[16] On the other hand there are very few death-elegies which leave out of consideration the upheavals of the country. One exception is Guillaume Aubert's lament for Joachim du Bellay,[17] a thoroughly unoriginal but floridly written poem, of interest, perhaps, only in its emphasis on Du Bellay the man as well as the poet. Another exception is the extraordinary poem by Pontoux on the death of a pig.[18]

Published in 1569 like the two other elegies by Pontoux, this one has a totally different source of inspiration and indeed follows directly from the poet's interest in and translation of Ortensio Landi's deplorations of a variety of animals. The idea appears to have been most congenial to Pontoux for he devotes more lines to his lament over Grognet than he did for the Queen of Spain! It is, perhaps, the length of the poem which detracts from its charm, for Pontoux was not a good enough poet to be able to deplore the death of his pet successfully in mock-heroic style for 402 lines. It is not until line 67 that the reader, or the person to whom the poem is addressed (a friend, Gaulard), is told why the poet is so upset. For sixty-six lines he repeats his grief in the most exaggerated terms:

> HA GAVLARD, c'est faict de ma vie,
> Elle est de-ia demi rauie.
> Mon amy Gaulard, ie me meurs,
> Ie voy les filandieres Sœurs, (ll. 1-4)

The humour of this introduction is not simply in its contrast with the actual cause of the grief but in many of the details given to prove the depth of the poet's despair:

> Et s'on me parle de viande,
> Tant soit elle exquise & friande,

---

14 See Catalogue 55.
15 See Catalogue 64.
16 See Catalogue 60.
17 See Catalogue 46.
18 See Catalogue 52.

> Ou tendre comme venaison,
> On me parle d'vne poison,
> Ie hay plus le manger & boire,
> Qu'un venin de vipere noire,
> Que l'arsenic ou reagal: (ll. 33-9)

Once the writer informs us of the cause of his lament, an extremely long description and panegyric of the pig begins. Needless to say, there never was a pig to compare with the defunct (ll. 75-92). Physically it was beautiful, and in describing its charms, Pontoux gives us what amounts to a *blason* of the pig (ll. 105-200). If this description idealizes Grongnet, the description of his preferences in food brings us back to reality (ll. 210-248), as does the passage regarding his various habits:

> Grongnet auoit telle nature
> Qu'il faisoit par tout son ordure: (ll. 249-250)

Pontoux's indifference is admirable (ll. 251-268). At line 269, we are given a character portrait and a description of the friendship which existed between the writer and his pet. Pontoux has only one bad experience to recall: Grongnet bit him on one occasion, but he was quickly forgiven (ll. 361-374). The poem ends with the poet's desire to bury his pig "Dedans ce grand parc des couchons" (l. 395), beside an elm-tree on which he will carve an epitaph:

> Cy gist Grongnet que l'on veit estre
> Le plaisant mignon de son maistre. (ll. 401-2)

Pontoux has provided us with something extremely rare. If all elegies are not sad, they are almost never amusing. In its long series of octosyllabic couplets, this poem provides several moments of *esprit gaulois*, a refreshing change from the normal elegiac themes and moods and especially during the reign of Charles IX.

2. THE LOVE-POETS

So far during these years, we have not found the elegy to be 'joyeuse' or 'récréative', in the sense of dealing with the supposedly in-

consequential theme of love. It is true that along with an elegy on
"le vray bien" Etienne du Tronchet in 1569 gives us a *terza-rima*
elegy about the beauty of his lady,[19] but during the 1560's we have
the impression that, apart from Ronsard's sudden interest in the
personal love-elegy, poets were not inclined to lament their lady's
cruelty. Actually, however, there were three poets especially who
devoted considerable energy in this direction, but their poems were
destined to appear in print sometime after their composition. These
three poets teach us something important about the love-elegy
during these years, something which again tends to set Charles's
reign apart in our history of the genre.

By the number of his poems, the most important love-elegist of
this period is Claude Turrin, whose *Œuvres poétiques* were published posthumously in 1572 by François d'Amboise and Maurice
Privey.[20] The exact date of Turrin's death is not known, but it is
likely that he died a year or two before the publication of his works
and that the poems which he left behind him were written between
1561 and 1570.[21] In the *Œuvres poétiques*, we find two books of
elegies, the first book containing thirteen poems all dealing with
love, the second book containing five poems on a variety of subjects.[22]

The first elegy gives a résumé of the most common themes that
we shall find throughout the thirteen poems of the first book.
Addressing his lady, the poet makes clear that, while his appearance
is sufficient indication of his wretched state, he wants to tell her
what torments he is suffering. This he does while he sings her
praises:

[19] See Catalogue 56.
[20] See Catalogue 62.
[21] Turrin's first printed work dates from 1561: *Les Charites, prises de Theocrite*
(Toulouse), in-4. This work appears to be lost, but Marcel Raymond in *L'Influence de Ronsard sur la Poésie Française*, 2 vols. (Paris: Champion, 1927), II,
5, note 2, suggests, after Du Verdier and Goujet, that the work contained what
appears as the second eglogue in 1572: "Eclogue 2. Margot, ou le despité, à
l'imitation du troisième Idyllie de Theocrit", folio 84 recto. The title of the
volume would indicate, however, the second elegy of the second book: "Les
Charites Prises de Theocrite. A feu monsieur de Longs-court, Abbé de Cit. etc.
Elegie 2.", folio 30 verso.
[22] The title-page is inexact since it speaks only of "élégies amoureuses".

Ie reçoy grand plaisir & mon mal se contente,
Quand, louant voz beautez, mes angoisses ie chante. (ll. 9-10)

These two themes are dealt with in the first forty lines of the poem. We are then given a few precise details: he fled her (l. 43 *sqq.*) but was as tormented as before, and he did not return until she became ill (ll. 55 *sqq.*). Now that he has returned, he is full of despair again, and we are given another description of his appearance to prove it (ll. 71-84). This misery causes him to think constantly of death:

Ie n'eu onque plaisir qu'à repenser comment,
Ie pourroy par la mort acheuer mon torment. (ll. 75-6)

Indeed, he is so unhappy that he is certain that he will soon die, and he promises his lady that he will haunt her (ll. 109 *sqq.*).

At the end of this poem (ll. 151-4), the poet brushes aside the lady's claim that she loves him. The next two poems show us, however, that they had moments of relative calm and that the fears of the poet were perhaps exaggerated. The second elegy is full of woe, but after describing again the effects of love on him and after telling his lady the story[23] of the youth who committed suicide outside the door of his beloved, the poet ends by saying:

Helas! si ie me meurs, ce ne sera par vous.
Maistresse vous auez le visage bien doux
Vous faites cas de moy, & mon peu de merite,
Ne vous rendit iamais encontre moy depite,
Ie ne doy pas mourir pour estre mal traité.
Ie n'ay veu dans voz yeux vn brin de cruauté. (ll. 159-164)

In the third elegy however, he claims to be already dying, and he even composes his epitaph. This poem gives us the first real clue as to the difficulty which exists between the two: the lady is very wealthy and the poet is poor. He accuses her of refusing her favours for this reason (ll. 65 *sqq.*), and he will repeat his accusation when she chooses another man as her husband.

---

[23] From Theocritus XXIII. There are significant changes, however, especially regarding the sex of the cruel one and the death of the latter. Otherwise Turrin gives quite a close translation of the Greek poem.

In elegies IV and V, the poet is absent again from his mistress, physically absent, but as tormented as ever by thoughts of her (elegy IV) and by fantasies (a simple, happy life on the *Iles Fortunées*). In elegy VI, he has returned to his mistress, who seems, momentarily, to love him. He is back to his gloomy state in the following two elegies, and we are prepared, therefore, for the ninth elegy in which he expresses his desire to leave the lady in whom he can no longer have any faith. The reason for this violent mood is that their plan to live a simple life of shepherd and shepherdess seems to have gone amiss:

> Ie ne croy plus ce que vous me disiez,
> Quand priuement au soir vous deuisiez,
> Auecque moy: vous ne voudriez pas estre
> Simple bergere, affin de mener paistre
> Vostre troupeau, & que l'equalité,
> Ne fust contraire à vostre honnesteté.
> Vous n'aimez plus: vostre amour est flaitrie, (ll. 9-15)

Refusing to believe that her "parens" have anything to do with her attitude, he chastises her for not having warned him before he became so enslaved in his love (ll. 109 *sqq*.). In elegy X and XI, we learn that there is a rival and that the lady intends to marry him. Elegy X is essentially a description of his lonely sorrow; elegy XI claims his intention to remain faithful in spite of his lady's action. He is less idealistic in the last two poems: elegy XII expresses delight that "lon vous abuse" (l. 48), that the lady's beauty is already beginning to fade somewhat (ll. 61-4), and elegy XIII is a prayer to the gods for deliverance.

The second book of elegies is quite different. The five poems that make up this second part belong essentially to the *discours*-type of elegy or to other categories that we suggested for the elegies of Ronsard. The first poem, for example, is a poem of flattery, dedicated to "Tres-excellente Princesse Madame Marguerite Duchesse de Sauoye", and was written in the hope that she would help the poor – that is, indigent – poet. This concern for his poverty comes out in two other elegies of this book. In the second poem, "A feu monsieur de Longs-court", entitled "Les Charites Prises de Theocrite"[24] the poet complains bitterly about the lack of interest in poetry among the great:

> Qui est-ce toutefois...
> ...mon Prelat qui reçoit
> Noz graces de bon œil? mais mon Prelat qui est-ce
> Qui de mille presens richement les caresse?
> Ie les voi plus souuent tout-confittes d'emoi,
> Les piés nus tramblotans... (ll. 9-14)

The sad truth is that the poet's contemporaries are interested only in money and do not believe that the poet is the sacred interpreter of the gods and has the power of conferring immortality on the mortal (ll. 25-51). The plaint occurs again in the fourth elegy (to "François Sayve Dijonnois") in which the poet gives a lengthy account (310 lines) of all his miseries – his slavery in love and his disillusionment as a poet. At line 149 he tells us of the "grand seigneur" (l. 150) who promised to finance him, of the immortalizing poetry that he wrote for the seigneur's antecedents, and of the latter's breach of promise:

> C'il qui feignoit me porter dedans l'œil
> Apres auoir euanté le cercueil,
> De ces ayeus, & d'vne æsle plus forte
> Guinde aux cieus leur memoire ia morte,
> Ne me connoit, & ne veut auiourd'huy,
> Que pour vn rien ie me targue de luy,
> C'il qui debuoit me servir de Mæcene,
> Me secourir, & me mettre hors de peine,
> Le seul appuy, & le dous honneur mien,
> Ne me veut plus reconnoistre pour sien. (ll. 202-212)

The poet ends his poem by cursing the Muses and advising the young to take "autre chemin" (l. 303).

The other two elegies deal with love but are not love-poems of the type found in the first book of elegies. Elegy III, addressed to Ronsard, describes love as a sort of "daimon" impossible to exorcize; the last elegy ("A Chrestienne de Baissey Damoiselle de Saillant") is principally an account of Venus's love for Anchises and

---

[24] See Theocritus XVI. Again Turrin follows his model closely although there is a greater adaptation of the material to the conditions of the poet's own life and times.

the vengeance of Mars. This tale, which accounts for 212 of the
poem's 290 lines, leads to the rapid conclusion (eight lines) which
prays for vengeance on his beloved and her fiancé:[25]

> Fais qu'à tous deux ces nopces soient fatales,
> Fais eclairer les torches infernales,
> Affin qu'ils soient d'eux mesmes sacagez,
> Et que leurs fils deuiennent enragez. (ll. 287-290)

These two elegies, then, deal with Turrin's love, but their principal
interest is in the development of ideas or stories of a general nature.
They remain essentially poems about love, like the ones that
Ronsard wrote before 1560.

The whole question of Ronsard's influence on Turrin's elegies

---

[25] With regard to this poem, it should be mentioned that critics have assumed
that it was Chrestienne de Baissey herself who was the beloved of Turrin and the
subject of all his love-poems. (See Emile Picot, *Les Français italianisants au XVIe
siècle*, 2 vols. [Paris: Champion, 1907] II, 59; Charles Oulmont, "Un Chantre
de l'Amour au XVI siècle [Claude Turrin]", *La Nouvelle Revue*, 1913, 435;
Marcel Raymond, II, 4). This view seems to be based on the notice by La Mon-
naye in *Les Bibliothèques Françoises de La Croix Du Maine et de Du Verdier*
edited by Rigoley de Juvigny, 6 vols. (Paris: Michel Lambert, 1772), I, 154.
Such a view hardly seems possible. There are four poems which address this lady
directly: the two sonnets which introduce the liminary poems (folio v recto),
the elegy and an ode (folio 88 verso). It is true that in the elegy (line 26) and in
the second of the sonnets there are references to the poet's love for this lady, but
it is not a love that inspires the same sentiments that we found in the first book
of elegies. The elegy tells us that this lady is incapable of love because her whole
devotion is turned to writing poetry (ll. 23-50), a detail which forms the subject
of the ode and the first sonnet as well. Indeed, in the sonnet, the poet expresses
the hope that the lady will not fall in love because, if her poetry would then be
like Sappho's, she would also suffer like Sappho, and he has no desire to see
the lady undergo the pangs of love. The elegy gives us the further detail that
while the lady is insensitive to the arrows of Cupid, she is kindly disposed to
those who do suffer the torments of love, and it is for that reason that Turrin
addresses his poem to her, just as lovers "vont au temple d'Erice, / Et pour affin
que Venus soit propice" (ll. 59-60). Altogether then, it is difficult to see Chrestienne as the lady in the first book of elegies, a lady who seems to have given
herself to love, to have been fickle and to have had little interest in poetry. The
last lines of the elegy to Chrestienne refer to this other lady and to her marriage.
How can these lines be reconciled with what the poet says of Chrestienne in the
first part of the poem? The only solution is to see two women in the (poetic) life
of Turrin: the first inspired a passionate love and a bitter disappointment in the
poet and is the lady in the first book of elegies. Chrestienne, a great lady of
Dijon, a poetess, is respectfully loved by Turrin, who does not really expect her
favours.

has been raised by Marcel Raymond,[26] but, while he favoured the attitude of a direct influence of Ronsard's *Recueil de nouvelles poésies,* lack of precise evidence made him cautious in his conclusions. It seems unlikely that Ronsard had much if any influence on the first book of elegies of Turrin. It is not until the *Recueil de nouvelles poésies* of 1564 that Ronsard wrote love-elegies of the personal type, and Turrin certainly need not have depended on Ronsard for examples: as we have seen from our résumé, the themes of Turrin's poems are extremely common ones in the elegies before 1560. Also, while Ronsard's poems are very much in the *épître* style of Marot, Turrin's use of address is much less precise, more similar to that found in the classical elegists. The arrangement of Turrin's elegies into two books, the first dealing with his love for one woman and tracing the development of the story, is again more reminiscent of the classical elegists than of Ronsard. In the *Recueil...* of 1564, in the *Elegies, Mascarades...* of 1565 and in the *Œuvres* of 1567, Ronsard shows no desire to create a harmonious unity in the grouping of his elegies.

There is also the all-important question of style. Although, as Raymond points out, both writers use a Petrarchan style,[27] it is not of the same quality. Ronsard scarcely goes beyond the sort of developments that Marot gave to Petrarchan themes; Turrin, however, shows a constant desire to decorate lengthily and to complicate his small number of themes – his happy sorrow, his death, the eyes of his mistress:

> Maitresse helas! si vostre œil ne m'eclaire,
> Si ie ne voy dedans mon hemisphere
> Vostre soleil, si ie n'ay mouuement
> De ce beau tout que lon fait en aimant,
> Ie ne suis rien, si vostre œil ne m'enflamme,
> Maitresse il faut que ie viue sans ame. (Book I, elegy VI, ll. 85-90)

Turrin has frequent recourse to mythology as well, which Ronsard used sparingly in the love-elegies of this period, and to other long developments of a classical or Petrarchan nature. There is the story of the lover who commits suicide from Theocritus in the

---

[26] Raymond, *L'Influence de Ronsard ...*, II, 5-6.
[27] Raymond, II, 6.

second elegy; a description of the *Iles Fortunées* in the fifth elegy; a nocturnal appearance of Cupid who enters the poet's body in the eighth elegy. On other occasions, Turrin simply adapts lines from the classics to his own purposes.[28] The first book of elegies, then, does not so much resemble Ronsard's love-elegies, surprisingly free of classical or direct Italian models, as they give us a clear foretaste of the elaborate neo-Petrarchan style, which will dominate in poetry after 1570. If Ronsard's influence is found anywhere in Turrin's elegies, it is in the second book, and here the influence is only indirect. As we pointed out earlier, the five elegies of this book fall into categories which were common in the elegies of Ronsard both before and after 1560 (themes of flattery, autobiography, the phenomenon of love). In a general way, it is the *élégie-discours* that we are reminded of in these poems, popular with Ronsard and Grévin.

If Turrin's elegies give us a foretaste of the neo-Petrarchan style, Jean de la Taille's six elegies, published in 1573[29] but dating back from the 1560's,[30] take us back in time rather than forward. Four of the six poems are very definitely *épîtres amoureuses*[31] and are written in a relatively simple style even while they deal with Petrarchan themes such as we found in Turrin's poems. The first and last elegies, for instance, are not very different in subject-matter from what we found so frequently in Turrin. In the first elegy La Taille also wants his mistress to know the torments which he suffers and the effects of his love:

> Bref ie ne puis durer en ta presence
> Ny moins encor supporter ton absence,
> Et sans pouuoir ny dormir ny veiller,
> Au lict ne fais qu'en pleurs me distiller. (ll. 37-42)

His love and his suffering are caused, as we might expect, by the

---

[28] See for instance the passage beginning line 37 in the second elegy of the first book, a translation of the famous poem by Sappho ("Celuy, Belle maitresse, egal aux dieux me semble, / Qui assis pres de vous vis à vis vous contemple", 37-8).

[29] See Catalogue 63.

[30] Three elegies refer to the civil wars: II, IV, and V.

[31] In the first line of the first elegy we read: "L'extreme amour me contraint de t'escrire." In the other cases the epistolary nature of the elegies is indicated by details of absence or separation.

beauty of the lady (ll. 17-20), and also because she seems to have decided on a marriage to someone else (ll. 85 *sqq.*). The poem ends with a plea for pity, which will be to kill him (ll. 157-162). The poet is equally desperate in the sixth elegy. He has left his mistress because of her harshness towards him, and again the poem's purpose is to keep her informed about his misery, which is more acute than when he left her. He repeats several times the lines

> Las, il faut bien que ie sois peu aymable
> Ou qu'en amours ie soys bien miserable

as he gives an account of his situation. Again there is reference to the lady's marrying another man (ll. 21-32); again he thinks of death (ll. 71-6). Instead of killing himself, however, he wanders about lamenting (ll. 166 *sqq.*), and by the end of the poem it appears that he will not have to plunge his sword into his body for he is dying in any case (ll. 223 *sqq.*). He says his good-bye, gives some advice to his lady and composes his epitaph.

What distinguishes La Taille from Turrin is not, then, a difference in matter but a difference in style. Whereas Turrin adorned his themes with learned references, La Taille is normally satisfied with a bald statement of feeling or fact. If images appear, they are generally drawn from nature, as in Du Bellay and Marot:

> Comme vne fleur perd son beau teint vermeil,
> Comme la neige, o[u] la cire au soleil,
> Ou au feu fond, comme d'un sort magique
> Vn beau poulain languit, & meurt etique,
> Ainsi ie fonds, ie seiche, & meurs pour toy, (I, ll. 47-51)

Instead of complicated mythological allusions, La Taille occasionally refers to great heroes, such as those in *Amadis de Gaule* or *Orlando Furioso* (see elegies III and IV).

Greater reference to the times also helps to create a different atmosphere in these poems. In elegy II, the poet writes to a relative[32]

---

[32] According to René de Maulde, who edited La Taille's work during the last century (*Œuvres de Jean de la Taille Seigneur de Bondaroy*, 4 volumes (Paris: Léon Willem, 1878-1882), the person addressed is probably Geneviève Berthomier who was married to Jean de La Taille, seigneur d'Hanorville et de Faronville. See vol. II, xcviii, footnote 1.

to console her about the absence of her husband who is fighting
with the catholics. He assures her that if he were to meet her husband on the battle-field, and on the opposing side, he would not
forget their blood ties. Elegy III does not have any reference to the
wars of the 1560's, but its answer, elegy IV, mentions that the poet
is about to leave to fight:

> Ioinct que m'amour vous seroit inutile
> (Contraint d'aller à la guerre ciuile)
> Où combattant (& vous ayant mon cueur)
> Comment sans cueur pourroy-ie estre vainqueur? (ll. 61-4)

These two poems are strange. Elegy III is a letter sent to the poet
by a woman who has decided to reveal her love and to express her
grief over the poet's preference for another lady, whom she considers to be unworthy of him. She refers to his lack of pity, and this
is confirmed by his answer in elegy IV. He admits that his corre-
spondent has her merits:

> Non que soyez indigne, ou mal-habille,
> Ains plutost belle, & honneste, & gentille, (ll. 17-8)

But Love always arranges things badly, and they are both fated
to love the unattainable.

Elegy V again reminds us of the wars, for the poet is at camp,
away from all his ladies. This poem is a death-elegy, and, as is usual
with this type of elegy, there is the use of apostrophe rather than
address. The subject here is quite original: instead of the lover's
dying because of the separation from his lady, it is the latter who
has not been able to live without him!

> Puis que i'ay sçeu, que n'ayant peu attendre,
> Mon long retour, ny peu viure, & souffire
> Ma longue absence, elle a voulu mourir: (ll. 6-8)

When he calls on "Soupirs" to lament with him (ll. 25 *sqq.*), we
find a *précieux* quality coming into La Taille's normally simple
style:

> Que mes soupirs & mes larmes deuinnent
> Vents, & ruisseaux, que ioints ensemble ils viennent
> Faire vne mer, où soit plus dangereux
> De nauiguer qu'en l'Ocean si creux. (ll. 33-6)

The lament continues with the poet's wish to be in the tomb with his lady! It is not, however, necrophilia. Indeed the poet is led to love of God:

> Mais si au Ciel ton ame est iointe à DIEV,
> Ie veux n'aymer que luy, & dire Adieu
> A Cupidon, iusqu'à tant qu'vn iour i'aye,
> Ainsi que toy, la iouissance vraye
> De l'immortelle & parfaitte beauté,
> Dont i'ay en toy quelque rayon noté. (ll. 127-132)

Like Turrin, La Taille has presented us with a book of elegies which has an overall unity. All six poems are in decasyllabic couplets; five of them are *épîtres*; five of them deal with love (for the death-elegy is a love-poem as well). The difference between Turrin and La Taille is not, as we have pointed out, one of conception so much as one of style. Whereas Turrin, as a result of his humanistic culture and his direct contact with Italy, was interested in the adornment of his themes, the less cultivated La Taille concentrated almost always on the simple statement. His poems take us back in time, back to the simple and naïve Petrarchan style of the poets before 1550, back to the *épître amoureuse*.

Jean Passerat, our third important love-poet of the 1560's might well seem greatly out of place here since his first elegies were not printed until 1597.[33] These twelve poems, forming a book of elegies,[34] are largely concerned, however, with Passerat's love for Catarina Delbene, from 1560 until her departure from France in 1568.[35] The poems add a new dimension to the love-elegies of these years in that they illustrate a distinctly classical influence not obvious in either Turrin or La Taille.

Many of the themes, for example, are clearly inspired by those favoured by classical elegists. This does not mean that Passerat has used the classical poems as source material in detail: he takes the over-all theme and composes independently from that starting-

---

[33] See Catalogue 131. Our page references are to the edition of Prosper Blanchemain, *Les Poésies Françaises de Jean Passerat*, 2 vols. (Paris: Lemerre, 1880).

[34] I, 38-58.

[35] See Edgar von Mojsisovics, *Jean Passerat, sein Leben und seine Persönlichkeit* (Halle: Niemeyer, 1907), 6-7.

point. For instance, the second elegy is a plea to the gods to cure his
lady of illness, a theme treated by Ovid, Tibullus, Propertius, and the
French Ovid, Jean Doublet. Passerat's poem is obligated to the
tradition established by all these poets and not to any one of them
in particular: he writes an original work in the classical style.
Elegies IV and V are even more obviously classical: it is the elegiac
commonplace of the door that separates lover and lady. Passerat
elaborates on this idea by composing both an address to the door
and the door's answer.[36] When the lover begins his speech to the
door (IV), he has already spent the whole night before it in the hope
that he might gain admittance to his lady. The misery of his fruitless
waiting reminds him of his past vigils when he persisted through
all types of weather and at all hours of the day (ll. 1-24). These
memories make him angry, and so he begins to curse the door by
wishing all sorts of unpleasantness for it (ll. 25-40). The harshness
of his language seems unwise, however, and so he begs forgiveness –
and also pity: even if the door were only opened half-way, he would
be happy (l. 50). He thinks for a moment that his plea has had
results, but it is only the wind, and not the bolt, which is making a
noise (ll. 60-2). This disappointment causes him to conclude with
the vigorous line, "Adieu l'espoir, & au diable la porte!" (l. 64).
The door's answer is even more entertaining (V). After telling the
lover to be sensible and to go away (ll. 1-8), the door then proceeds
to quote the various things which the lover says to it, from sweet
praises (ll. 9-15) to harsh accusations (ll. 16-32). The door is concerned by the latter, but it goes on to tell his accuser that it is as
feather-brained as a bird and more entertaining to the passers-by
than a parrot (ll. 33-51). Finally the door says that it is sick of the
physical abuse that it receives and explains the only way that the
lover will gain admittance:

> Conte & reconte vne Iliade entiere
> De tes malheurs, de ta peine & misere:
> Vante toy d'estre vn tres loyal seruant:
> Ce sont propos en vain iettez au vent:
> Qui veut entrer, qu'argent il nous apporte,
> Sans ceste clef on n'ouure point la porte. (ll. 71-6)

[36] Catullus provides us with a poem which is a *dialogue* between the lover and
the door. See number 67 of his works.

It is obviously the classical elegy and not Mlle Delbene that inspired this poem.

These themes are clearly drawn from antiquity. Others are less
clearly so but in the context seem likely to have been. The bitter
complaint to Cupid in VI is, for instance, both classical and commonplace in other traditions; the opening lines of VIII which appeal
to the lady to devote her youth to love also have a rich background
of reference. In Passerat's book of elegies, however, the atmosphere
is mainly classical. That atmosphere is heightened by the presence
of two poems which do not concern his lady at all but rather the
death of two pet birds, a linnet (VIII) and a sparrow (IX). Again it
is to be noticed that the dead sparrows lamented by Catullus and
Statius did not precisely influence the poems of Passerat: he again
prefers to work independently from a given idea. Passerat, apparently an animal lover,[37] combines an attractive irony (mock-heroic
style) and considerable realistic detail in his deplorations (references
are not lacking in VII to the civil disturbances of the 1560's).

In the love-elegies Passerat manages the same quite happy combination of realism with mythological adornment, another characteristic of the classical elegy highly recommended by Du Bellay. In X
we have the poet's sorrow at remaining in troubled France as his
lady leaves him to go to Savoy and also his apprehension about the
dangers of her trip:

> Les chemins ne sont seurs: helas! où va Madame
> Temeraire qu'elle est! Ie crain mille malheurs,
> Qui peuuent aduenir parmy tant de voleurs.
> Ie crain ces rocs aigus, & montagnes cornues,
> Dont le sommet venteux se cache dans les nues. (ll. 20-4)

His fears become much more fanciful as he goes on: he thinks
that Aquilon will fall in love with his lady (ll. 25-8). The last part of
the poem becomes studded with classical allusions as he refers to
the great powers of the poet-musicians of mythology, whose powers
he would like to have:

> Tantost pour l'arrester à mon amour parfaite
> De l'enfant d'Apollon la lyre ie souhaite:

---

[37] See Mojsisovics, *Jean Passerat...*, 52 *sqq.*

Tantost ie veux choisir, pour ma douleur charmer,
La lyre que porta le Dauphin par la mer
Au bord Tenarien, flaté de sa musique. (ll. 43-7)

Since he does not have the powers of Orpheus, Amphion, Arion,
and Linus, he finally calls upon his tears to stop his lamentation:
"Trop peu sent de douleur qui sa douleur peut dire" (l. 64). A less
happy example of Passerat's devotion to mythology is the first
elegy, which may be summarized briefly as follows: the poet begins
by wishing that he could escape love by flying with the wings of
Dædalus, by turning into a fish like Glaucus or by being swallowed
up by the earth like Amphiarus, the husband of Eriphyle (ll. 1-14).
However, Zeus, Neptune, and Pluto were no less the slaves of "cest
Archer" (ll. 15-28). And why fight love when even Hercules was
powerless (ll. 31-2)? Just as Mars delights in the misery of war, so
the god of love takes pleasure in a lover's tears (ll. 37-40). Thus,
every idea of the poem is illustrated by an allusion to a classical god
or hero.

Passerat's elegies are largely classical in theme, then, and in an
important element in style. Classical too in length (the average
length is about fifty lines). If not precisely classical, at least Passerat
is anti-*épître amoureuse* in his extreme hesitation in using a realistic
and consistent address in his poems: only VIII speaks throughout to
his lady.

Apart from the book of twelve elegies, Passerat wrote eighteen
more original elegies, fifteen of which probably belong to this same
period. These fifteen poems, scattered haphazardly throughout the
poet's verse,[38] are less classical than the book of elegies but quite
close to the characteristics that we have found for the elegies of the
Charles IX period. Seven of the fifteen elegies are concerned with
love but only three are in any way at all in the love-plaint category:
two deal with separations, but Passerat writes them for others
(Blanchemain I, 113 and 130), and one subtitled "D'Amour Coque-
mar" (I, 104) becomes finally more of a *discours* on love's night-
mares than the horror of a personal experience. Other amatory
discours are to be found (I, 107 and 120), and finally, two coldly

[38] See Catalogue 143 and 145.

witty developments: a series of puns on the word *dextre* (I, 106) and a comparison between the poet and a ring (I, 72). The latter is a far from original idea which has a way of popping up every now and then in elegies: Ronsard has given us an example (elegy 46) and Desportes will soon give us another.

Death is another theme that we find among the remaining elegies of Passerat, but they are about people rather than pet birds. The grief expressed rarely seems particularly personal although there is, as is typical, a certain pretence of involvement. In the elegy on the death of Adrian Turnèbe (II, 107), Passerat apostrophizes Ronsard and Marot as he talks of his grief, and in this case the grief is no doubt genuine. The lament broadens early in the poem to include all the ills of France in the throes of civil war (ll. 33 *sqq.*). References of this type are much more in place in the elegy on the death of le comte de Brissac (II, 117), who died in battle in 1569, but Passerat does not dwell on the point and almost prefers to mention Achilles and the Trojan wars. Classical references also abound in the poem on the death of Madamoiselle de Mausparaute, sister of Henri de Mesmes (seigneur de Roissy) (II, 111), but the poet suggests that, rather than lament like the gods and goddesses, they should follow the advice of the dead woman: "Pendant qu'il est permis, viués heureus, (dit-elle)" (l. 33). In an elegy on the death of another woman, Madamoiselle de l'Espine (II, 118), we are given a mainly harsh criticism of the incompetent doctors who tried to cure her: throughout his elegies Passerat takes many swipes at the medical profession.

Four miscellaneous elegies make up the twenty-seven Passerat composed early in his career – two prayers, a poem of praise and a gift-elegy. Clearly Passerat is principally a love-poet in his elegies but only in his book of elegies does he favour the personal type of love-poem. Otherwise he is rather in the tradition of the 1560's by favouring a more intellectual and general approach to themes of love. He is also a man of the 1560's by his quite numerous references to the troubled times in all his elegies.

A few more love-elegies published in the early 1570's might well have been written during the preceding decade but they would not alter the picture of the elegy that has emerged from the poems that we have discussed. The 1560's clearly constitute a rather special moment in the history of our genre. The first unusual characteristic is the preference given to the death-elegy over the love-elegy, a preference which is indicated by the number of poets drawn to each of the two types of elegy rather than by the number of poems composed. There are further oddities concerning the appearance of these two types of elegy. The love-elegy shows no dominating tradition. Each of the poets studied seems to have been drawn to a different source. Before and, as we shall see, after this period, there is always one style which overshadows all other modes of loving and expressing that love. In the death-elegy we have already sufficiently emphasized the tendency to broaden out the lament to include the exceptional historical conditions of the day.[39]

These death-elegies thus link themselves to the Ronsardian *discours*-elegy, and this too is a prominent type of elegy for the first time in our history of the genre – Grévin, Passerat, Turrin, three important contributors to the *discours*-elegy apart from those poems involved with the wars and death. The whole period thus becomes largely characterized by a seriousness of purpose and manner which is unusual in the progress of the elegy throughout the century.

As we noted with Ronsard, the title elegy was a convenient coverup for poems which would have been called *épître* by his more old-fashioned contemporaries. We also noted how gradually the nature of these disguised *épîtres* changed to the point of new genre creations. The same sort of processes can be seen at work among the poets of the 1560's, but especially it should be emphasized how strikingly casual our poets are about the sort of sustained personal address which is so essential to the *épître*. About half of our elegies during Charles's reign use apostrophes or a vague and intermittent

---

[39] This *engagé* quality of the elegy is also noticeable in some translations that we find during this period. In 1569, we find an *Elegie Sur La Defense de la Ville de Poyctiers, assiegée par les Rebelles*, and to our surprise the original Latin poem is not in elegiacs but in hexameters. Not dealing with the wars but with other abuses is the *Elegie au Iesuite Qui List Gratis En L'Vniversité A Paris* (1565), and again the original Latin poem is not in elegiacs. In his *Premieres Œuvres* of 1569, Scévole de Sainte-Marthe finds very much to the point the translation of an elegy by Solon on justice and the public good.

address which bears little resemblance to the old *épître*. It is no doubt this relative independence from the *épître* which accounts for a fairly large number of exceptions to the usual alexandrine or decasyllabic couplets. Baïf and Jodelle both imitated the classical distich as closely as is possible in French by composing their elegies in *vers mesurés*; Grévin, Turrin and Pontoux imitated more conventionally by forming couplets of an alexandrine and a decasyllabic line. There are also a few poems in quatrains (Turrin, Passerat) and in sextains (Belleforest).

A final point to be made is the seemingly greater popularity of the title elegy. A fairly large number of poets – both sophisticated and naïve – use it, and especially to be noticed is the relatively frequent number of *books* of elegies. Between Marot and Ronsard's edition of 1567 there are few poets who arranged their elegies into books but in the space of a few years we have Grévin, Turrin, La Taille, and Passerat.[40] La Taille and Grévin decided on this arrangement even though the number of their elegies is hardly very great. What appears to be happening is that the elegy is coming to be considered an important genre worthy of having its own place among the works of the poet instead of being scattered throughout the *chansons* and sonnets.

---

[40] The unity of Passerat's book of elegies suggests that they were intended as a book when written and not simply at the time of publication.

V

STYLE HENRI III

1. PHILIPPE DESPORTES

What we shall term the style of the reign of Henri III actually began slightly before his accession to the throne: it might be said to date from the *Premières Œuvres* of Philippe Desportes, published for the first time in 1573. This volume was dedicated to Henri, and its contents were to influence greatly the poetry of his reign. Specifically in the case of the elegies, however, critics tend to believe that Desportes was an unoriginal follower of Ronsard. We shall attempt to reveal enough that is new in Desportes' elegies to justify our contention that they represent the beginning of a new period in our history.

Twenty-one of the thirty elegies which Desportes has left us appeared in 1573.[1] Since the earliest of them appear to go back as far only as the end of 1569 or the beginning of 1570,[2] we are not surprised that these twenty-one poems bear a certain similarity to one another. They are, in fact, so similar that Lavaud has admitted that "la lecture de ses élégies est monotone et même quelque peu fastidieuse".[3] Almost every new poem reminds the reader of the one that he has just read, so limited is the poet's repertoire of ideas.

The only subject that we find throughout these elegies is love, love that is a torment, love that the poet was fated to experience (I, i, 54-6). Miserable as he is, the poet delights in his fate because it is

---

[1] See Catalogue 68. We are using the critical edition of the elegies prepared by Victor E. Graham (Genève: Droz, 1961).
[2] See Jacques Lavaud, *Un poète de cour au temps des derniers Valois* (Paris: Droz, 1936), 138. I, vii refers to the battles of Jarnac and Moncontour.
[3] Lavaud, 202.

proof of his humanity (I, vi, 1-10). Indeed, there is even the possibility of a certain glory in such a terrible love:

> ...je croy qu'en mourant pour une beauté telle,
> On s'acquiert, comme en guerre une gloire immortelle. (I, viii, 101-2)

These considerations explain much of the poet's determination to remain faithful no matter how cruel his mistress might be (I, xvi, 73-86). In addition, he can hardly imagine love that is not painful – he wants to suffer:

> Je dy que ma douleur qui de vous prend naissance,
> De mon loyal service est digne recompanse:
> Et que le mal d'Amour, qui me guide au trespas,
> Vaut mieux que tous les biens qu'on reçoit icy bas.
> Aussi durant mon mal ce qui plus me travaille
> C'est helas! que j'ay peur que le tourment me faille:
> Car je gouste en souffrant tant de contentement
> Que je ne crains rien tant que d'estre sans tourment. (I, i, 61-8)

Silent and unobserved suffering is not what he means, however. As we have found throughout the love-elegies of the century, many of Desportes' lines are taken up with a description of his pains and anxieties. A more modern touch is that he sometimes stages his complaint in nature (see I, iv and xiv).

It is, as we would expect, the lady's beauty which causes such torment. At times we almost believe that only her eyes exist, since the poet talks so frequently and so passionately about them. It is with the eyes of the lady that Fate managed to enslave the poet to love:

> Dès que je vey vos yeux j'oubliay toute affaire,
> Mesme je m'oubliay: car je ne peu distraire
> Mes yeux de vos regars, mes yeux me trahissoyent:
> Car volontairement vers vous ils s'adressoyent
> Et voyant flamboyer vostre lumiere sainte,
> Estonnez et ravis, ils vacilloyent de crainte,
> S'en retiroyent un peu, puis ils vous regardoyent
> Pendant que tous mes sens de frayeur se rendoyent,
> Et que cent mille esprits pleins de subtile flame
> Troubloyent mon sang esmeu, ma raison et mon ame. (I, ii, 105-114)

The lady's eyes do not constitute her only attraction, however:

her other physical charms (and only her physical charms are ever mentioned) come to the aid of the eyes in keeping the poet a slave. Indeed, if she were to lose her beauty, she would no doubt lose her faithful servant (see I, xvii, 57-80).

These well-worn themes provide Desportes with what he considers to be sufficient subject-matter for his elegies. There is almost nothing in the way of events or actions. One situation, however, that does arise frequently is an absence of some sort. In I, xvii, the writer has had to depart; in I, xviii, he asks his lady to return. He speaks of the sorrow of an absence (he was at camp) in I, x and the dangers of it in I, vii: his lady has believed gossip (another common theme) about him while they have been separated. In I, ii, he reveals sadly that absence cannot efface his love: he has tried to no avail.

The above résumé of themes suffices to indicate the character of the first group of elegies, and we should remember that 1573 saw the publication of just over two-thirds of Desportes' elegies.[4] The few themes that we have discussed are repeated by the poet with untiring frequency. Only two poems depart somewhat from the sort of formula that the poet used. Elegy I, ix develops the Golden-Age theme, and explains modern decadence and misery in love as the punishments of *Amour*; I, xix tells the story of Philandre, who, abandoned by his lady, attempts to commit suicide and gives a diatribe against the fickleness of all women.

The second book of elegies, published ten years after the first book, provides us with only five poems.[5] Lavaud does not linger over them at length in his study of Desportes, because he feels that

> Malgré leur tenue, malgré leur incontestable valeur littéraire, elles n'apportaient guère d'accents nouveaux.[6]

This is not altogether true: if there is not a dramatic difference between the two books of elegies, there is some change nevertheless that is immediately felt by the reader. The reasons for the difference are not difficult to find.

---

[4] See Catalogue 71, 78, and 105 for the remaining elegies.
[5] See Catalogue 105.
[6] Lavaud, 285.

First of all, there is a difference in sources. The precise sources that have been found for the elegies of 1573 are mainly Ronsard and Ariosto,[7] especially the latter. In the second book of elegies, three of the five poems have classical sources. Lavaud shows the important borrowing from Tibullus I, ii in Desportes II, i; the second elegy is based on Catullus 8 and 76; the third elegy has Ovid *Amores* III, xiv as its source. The change in sources brings a change in theme. In the first book of elegies, we find the poet's insisting on his fidelity which nothing will diminish. In three of the five poems in book II, the poet wants to be free. In the first elegy, he accuses the lady of being too cold and too nervous. Since he prefers women to be passionate and unconcerned about dangers, he gives a warning that he might be tempted to look elsewhere. In II, ii, he makes a plea to the gods to cure him of his love. In II, iv, a poem which resembles in most respects the elegies of the first book, the writer ends his poem by the unexpected affirmation that he will pardon his beloved if she will simply teach him how to stop loving her as she has stopped loving him. In I, x, the poet is also abandoned for another, but there he insists that he will remain faithful nevertheless. It is II, iii which is the most surprising. Based on Ovid, as we have pointed out, the poet expresses his chagrin, not about his beloved's infidelities, but about her indiscretion. She can do what she pleases just as long as he is not forced to know about it. Only the last elegy of the second book resembles particularly the earlier elegies but even here the large number of precise details of what seems to be a true story distinguishes it from its predecessors.[8] Indeed the poem belongs most properly to the narrative-elegy, and, as we pointed out in connection with the first book of elegies, what makes the 1573 poems so monotonous is their almost complete lack of events: they are love-plaints in the narrowest sense of the term.

There is something new in the second book of elegies, and La-

---

[7] All the research on this matter is resumed and added to in the notes of Victor E. Graham's edition of the elegies.

[8] Even though Lavaud is probably correct in stating that the elegies are important as examples of Desportes' writing as court poet, 137, precise details are extremely infrequent. Only about three elegies of the first book refer to a place or time that can be identified: we have mentioned I, vii, which refers to the war of 1569; I, x and xiv both make references to camp and the wars.

vaud's insensitivity to it is in keeping with his statement that Desportes had "une certaine répugnance" for imitating the classical poets.[9]
We, on the other hand, must not fall into the error of overestimating
the classical influence or the originality of the second book. Only a
few poems are involved, and the classical sources are somewhat
adapted to suit the usual 'purity' of Desportes' poems.[10]

It is, then, much easier to define Desportes' conception of the elegy
than it was Ronsard's. Desportes deals with only one subject, and
always in such a similar way that especially the first book of nineteen elegies has an air of great unity. The nineteen elegies which compose the book do not in fact all belong to the same experience or
even the same person. Some of them deal with loves of Henri III.
In I, vii, ix, and xvii, we are involved with the love of a prince; in I,
vi, xvi, and xviii, the writer speaks of his temerity in loving a lady of
such exalted station. Other contradictions can be found. In I, iii, viii,
and x, the poet speaks of his past happiness with the lady, of their
once reciprocal love; in I, xii and xiii, the lady has never looked upon
him with favour. The person involved in I, i, ii, and xvii has had
previous love-affairs; in I, xii, he falls in love for the first time. The
unity of the book is an illusion, then, created by the singleness of
subject, form (all Desportes' elegies are in alexandrine couplets),
themes, and style. As in most love-elegies in the sixteenth century,
direct address to the lady is usual, and in some cases the epistolary
nature of the poem is evident (especially I, v, xiv, and xv). There are
exceptions, however. Elegy II, v and two of the elegies in the *Amours
d'Hippolyte* have no address; I, xix and II, ii have apostrophes. The
Desportes elegy is, then, a poem in alexandrine couplets, containing
a love complaint usually addressed to the beloved.

Does this conception of the elegy stem from Ronsard? Both
Lavaud and Raymond think so.[11] Such a view is surely an exaggeration. In the editions of Ronsard that Desportes would know when
he published his *Premières Œuures* in 1573, he would find many
different types of elegy placed together without any order or unity

[9] Lavaud, 189.
[10] Compare Desportes II, iii and its source, Ovid, *Amores*, III, xiv.
[11] Lavaud, 202; Marcel Raymond, *L'Influence de Ronsard sur la Poésie Française*, 2 vols. (Paris: Champion, 1927), II, 87.

at all. Less than a quarter of Ronsard's elegies at this time dealt
with love (only about a dozen elegies are at all like Desportes').
Stylistically, we found that the love-elegies of Ronsard closely res-
embled those of an earlier period. For the most part simple and naïve
in tone and expression, they followed very closely the *épître amoureuse* tradition.

Desportes, too, is essentially in this tradition, but he did not need
Ronsard as an example to follow, and stylistically there are certain
differences which, we feel, result in the old *épître-amoureuse-élégie*
taking on a new appearance. In at least one way, Desportes, like
Ronsard, shows a certain concern for simplicity: there is an almost
total absence of mythology. This is, of course, a difference between
the elegies of Desportes and the classical elegy. To make up for the
absence of mythology – because Desportes certainly needed something to clothe his few ideas – our poet indulges in long similes, epic
similes, frequently imitated directly from Ariosto. In his love-elegies
of the 1560's, Ronsard occasionally used the same sort of simile,
and sometimes both poets used the same source,[12] but Desportes'
tendency towards this sort of development goes far beyond Ronsard's, becomes an important element of his style and will be seen
in many other poets after him. Sometimes the image is very long,
as at the beginning of I, xvii. Here the lover compares himself to a
"pèlerin" who loses his way at night, when he tries to journey by the
stars, but finds his way when the sun appears. Even some of the less
developed similes (e.g. I, viii, 107 *sqq.*, and I, ii, 117 *sqq.*) are of the
epic type.

As well as decorating his ideas with similes, Desportes' other
great resource is lengthy development and analysis of emotional
states. This characteristic has led Lavaud into crediting Desportes
with the creation of a sort of psychological elegy. The example that
he cites is I, iii,[13] and it is a good example. What Desportes does,
however, is elaborate at length on the elements contained in Petrar-

---

[12] The miser-image in Ronsard's elegy 35 comes from Ariosto's *Orlando Furioso*,
XLV, 34. Desportes uses this image in I, xv, but his source is Ariosto rather
than Ronsard since he goes on to imitate the images which Ariosto has following
that of the miser nervous about leaving his gold.
[13] Lavaud, 203-5.

chan love-poetry. In the sonnet, or even the *chanson*, there is little room for such analysis: in the elegy mentioned above Desportes makes explicit what would be suggested in a few lines of a shorter form. The delight in such minute analysis (perhaps description is a better word) no doubt accounts for the increasing interest in the elegy that we find during the years following Desportes and the vogue of *stances* as well. In these two forms, the poet could allow himself as many lines as he wished to set forth his torments, jealousy, his hopes, or lack of them, and his undying fidelity.

Further decoration of his slim matter is found in the use of metaphor, but here Desportes is less original since his inspiration comes from the followers of Petrarch, the quattrocentists. While the elegies are less *précieux* than the sonnets to Diane and to Hippolyte, we still find the typical exaggeration in such passages as the following description of the lady's forehead:

> Qu'il vienne voir ce front large table d'yvoire,
> Plaine, claire et polie, où l'Amour à sa gloire
> Tient appendus devant les noms et les escus
> De tant de Chevaliers heureusement vaincus:
> Le mien s'y reconnoist le plus haut de la bande, (I, vii, 57-61)

The eyes of the lady also benefit from numerous eleborate developments. In the same poem, they become a sort of universe:

> Yeux, où l'enfant Amour tient son celeste empire,
> Yeux, où le beau Soleil tous les soirs se retire,
> Yeux, les lampes du jour, aux rayons gracieux,
> Qui font honte à la Lune et aux astres des cieux,
> Qui font en mesme point vivre et mourir ensemble, (*ibid.*, 41-5)

Sophisticated and *précieux* expression, lengthy description of feelings, elaborate similes: these are the main stylistic traits of Desportes' elegies.

As far as Desportes' conception of the elegy is concerned, we can see that he did nothing that was really new: he composed the most common type of elegy that we have found in the sixteenth century, and he followed it with a single-mindedness that Ronsard never displayed. He is, then, in the French tradition such as it had developed, with the added dimension of the neo-Petrarchan style that was becoming popular at the beginning of the 1570's, largely through the influence of the salon of the maréchale de Retz.[14] Indeed, Lavaud explains the general absence of classical sources in favour of Petrarchism as a result of this famous salon and the court:

> C'étaient les charmes de plus hautes dames que Desportes avait à vanter et il ne pouvait guère le faire dans le style familier des Latins... C'est pourquoi le pétrarquisme devait tant trouver de faveur dans ce milieu...[15]

This explanation is interesting, but we have seen that French writers have always preferred, from Marot to Desportes, the Petrarchan idea of love to the Latin. While Desportes' precise milieu no doubt had some influence on him, again he simply follows the tendencies of the whole century.

Finally what justifies our putting Desportes at the head of a new chapter is the exclusiveness of subject-matter in his elegies and their style. While not all the elegies that we find after 1573 were inspired by Desportes, his example was very important in setting the general pattern that we shall find, and it is a pattern that is represented before him not so much by Ronsard but rather by a poet like Turrin.[16] During the reign of Henri III love comes to dominate the elegy again, and in the neo-Petrarchan and heavily ornamented style that Ronsard hesitated to adopt. No greater indication of Desportes' influence at this stage of the elegy can be shown than the obvious impact that his elegies had on a poet like Amadis Jamyn.

2. AMADIS JAMYN

Jamyn gives us thirty-four elegies in his *Œuvres* of 1575,[17] and only

[14] Lavaud, 72-106; Raymond, *L'influence de Ronsard...* II, 65-8.
[15] Lavaud, 190.
[16] Concerning the difficult question of the Ronsard-Desportes relationship, see Mary Morrison, "Ronsard and Desportes", *Bibliothèque d'humanisme et renaissance*, XXVIII (1966), 294-322 and Claude Faisant, "Les relations de Ronsard et de Desportes", *BHR*, XXVIII (1966), 323-353.
[17] See Catalogue 72. All our quotations will be from this edition unless otherwise noted.

one poem does not have love as its basic theme. Since Ronsard – let us repeat – does not show a definite preference for the love-elegy until 1584, one feels that already Jamyn is looking more to the fashionable Desportes than to his master Ronsard.[18]

It is not a study of the themes of Jamyn's love-plaints that can elucidate the problem of influence. We find the well-worn ideas that are common to all our poets. Again the love depicted is in the Petrarchan rather than the classical tradition. As usual, the lady's eyes are responsible for the poet's misery; as usual a good deal of space is devoted to the celebration of the lady's beauty. Tormented by her image whether he is separated from her or not, he swears fidelity while lamenting his chronic frustration and unhappiness. Into these formulas Jamyn injects a few details equally familiar to us: the lady's scepticism concerning her suitor's sincerity; his social inferiority to the lady; the theme of separations, which nevertheless receives a somewhat original treatment in one elegy:

> Ie croy que vous m'aimez d'affection non feinte,
> Et pour cela ie crains de refroider vn peu,
> Vous voyant fort souuent, la puissance de feu
> Feu qui doux & gentil allume nos pensees
> L'agreable fureur également poussees,
> "Le mépris est enfant de la satiété, (folio 275 verso, ll. 12-17)

Jamyn's themes point to his being a man of his century rather than a pupil of any one master. His style is more revealing. Although his elegies are shorter (usually around seventy lines) than those by either Ronsard or Desportes, he delights in the art of decorating his themes with long similes, mythological allusions and complicated metaphors. Jamyn is decidedly much richer in style than Ronsard was in his love-elegies of the 1560's, and he also outdistances Desportes in the embroidery of an old idea. Nevertheless, it is Desportes who comes to mind as one reads through Jamyn's elegies. We have concentrated on Desportes' great affection for the epic type of simile,

---

18 The problem of these influences has been dealt with by Raymond, II, 113 *sqq.*, and by Theodosia Graur, *Un Disciple de Ronsard, Amadis Jamyn (1540-1593), Sa Vie, Son Œuvre, Son Temps* (Paris: Champion, 1929), 73-5. The conclusions are not identical.

used to a very limited extent by Ronsard in his elegies. Jamyn shows
a particular affection for expressing his feelings by means of the
concrete scenes which these similes evoke. In the elegy "En te lais-
sant ie ne t'ay point laissée" (folio 90 verso), he recounts in sixteen
lines (ll. 7-22) the agony and death of a man bitten by a mad dog in
order to conclude quite simply:

> Aussi ie croy que l'Amour enragé
> Tout venimeux m'a de mesme outragé: (ll. 23-24)

In the same poem he borrows from Vergil (*Æneid* IV, ll. 68 *sqq.*)
the image of the wounded hind, which he develops in nine lines
(ll. 44-52), and this too explains his inescapable torment. Many
examples of this type of simile could be given, but perhaps one further elegy will serve to show to what degree Jamyn indulged in this
particular type of elaboration of his ideas. In the elegy in the *Meslanges* "Auec le beau Soleil le iour monte vers nous",[19] the poet in
the space of fifty-six lines manages to develop four long similes, as
well as a number of shorter ones. First, to describe the lady's beauty
and inaccessibility, Jamyn thinks of a diamond ring:

> Tousiours on donne prix au Diamant bien clair,
> Qui d'vn lustre poli nous darde maint éclair,
> Et qu'vn habile Orfeure vsant de main sçauante
> En chaton de fin or aux yeux nous represente,
> Pour en ceremonie à quelque iour pompeux
> Luire dessus le chef d'vn Prince genereux.
> 　Autant que telle pierre à la force indomtee,
> Par vnique valeur, est au monde vantee,
> D'autant sur les beautez ton prix a merité,
> Mais ie voudrois pour moy qu'il ne fust indomté. (ll. 5-14)

Part of his trouble, he feels, is that the lady does not really know
the torments that he suffers, but he is incapable of making her feel
them because the poet is like the painter who can give an image of
snow but cannot reproduce the coldness of it. The poet can talk about
his being "plein de souffre & de flame", but he cannot make the lady
actually experience what he does (ll. 26-32). At line 41, the image of

---

[19]　1577 edition, Catalogue 79, folio 273 recto.

the sympathetic vibration of a lute when another is struck is created to express the close rapport between the souls of lovers (ll. 41-6). And immediately following the lutes, the poem concludes (ll. 47-56) with the simile of the mandrake: when growing beside vines, the mandrake causes the subsequent wine to have beneficial, soporific effects. He pleads with his lady to change "le fort vin qui m'enyure la vie" (l. 52) so that his misery will be less painful.

Thus, by use of lengthy images expressing common themes of Petrarchan love-poetry Jamyn exaggerates a tendency that we saw in Desportes. What we do not find in Desportes, however, nor in the love-elegies that Ronsard wrote in the 1560's, is an equal delight in mythological allusions. In this one respect, Jamyn's elegies are somewhat reminiscent of the classical elegy. In an elegy which expresses the concern of the lover over the lofty station of the lady,[20] we are told that even Venus abandoned Mars for a lowly shepherd (ll. 65-6) and that many gods changed their form:

> L'vn se faisoit Serpent qui merqueté se glisse,
> Et l'autre qui d'Amour ne pouuoit s'estranger
> Daignoit bien se vestir de la peau d'vn Berger,
> Et pourtant d'oliuier la champestre houlette
> A sa fluste apprenoit les plaintes d'amourette
> Pour adoucir son mal: Le grand pere du vin
> En la grappe vineuse échangea son diuin
> Pour tromper Erigone: Et le bruyant Neptune
> Pour tromper pres sa Dame vne heureuse fortune
> Prit forme d'vn Cheual crineux & hamnissant (ll. 72-81)

One of the richest poems in mythological allusions, however, is the one addressed to "vne Gouuernante"[21] who is interfering in the love of the poet. Unlike the worship of Ceres, men and women should not be separated when they worship Venus, and both day and night are suitable for adoration of the goddess. Since the old woman, a sort of *lena* figure, does not understand this, she is likened to the dragon who

> Gardoit tousiours aux niepces d'Atlante
> L'or des pommiers de leur forest luisante:
> Tu es semblable à celuy que Iason

---

[20] Folio 176 recto.
[21] Folio 92 recto.

Fit endormir pour auoir la toison:

....

    Tu vas gardant aussi d'vn mesme soing

Ce qui resemble à la forme d'vn coing,

Qui est semblable à la pomme hesperide,

Et au present que conquit l'Esonide: (ll. 37-54)

The poem continues with references to Argus and Io, Juno and Jupiter, Pluto and Proserpine and concludes with the wish that the old woman be transformed into a dog, like Hecuba, if she continues to frustrate his love.

Our discussion so far of the style of Jamyn has no doubt given the impression that his elegies are extremely artificial. While this is generally true, our poet can, on occasion, create a certain realism by his painting of scenes and activities that do not find an origin in classical or Italian sources. In two poems[22] he talks with affection of the Loire and of his hunting. In another poem[23] he describes the dancing of the popular "volte" at a ball. While Jamyn's elegies tend to be more florid than Desportes', at the same time he can be on occasion more realistic than the latter poet.

It is nevertheless from Desportes that Jamyn received his lessons. The exclusiveness of love as his theme and the generally neo-Petrarchan style are rather unmistakable marks of Desportes' habits. To this Jamyn simply adds a slight originality in his use of mythology and much greater concentration of matter, which even causes a measure of obscurity.

Ronsard is perhaps not completely absent from Jamyn's verse, however. About a dozen of the thirty-four elegies of 1575 are not clearly in the love-plaint style although love is still the basic subject. First of all there is a *discours* type of elegy. The beloved is still the person addressed, and the purpose of the poem is still to convince the lady that she should accept the poet's love, but the whole body of the poem is a general argument. In the elegy "Au temps iadis la belle Cythere" (folio 102 verso), the poet develops the rather striking idea that love is first of all spiritual and should become "corporelle" (folio 110 recto). Two poems (folios 105 recto and 212 recto) argue

[22] Folios 112 recto and 114 recto.

[23] Folio 122 recto.

against honour; another elegy discourses on the lady's praiseworthy honour and fidelity (folio 27 verso). It is in this last elegy also that we have a confirmation of our classification of these poems as *discours*:

> Ce bref discours qu'ici ie te propose
> Tend à ta gloire & non à autre chose, (folio 228 verso, ll. 23-4)

As well as treating general ideas, Jamyn sometimes gives his poem over to a long, colourful narrative. This is especially the case in a long elegy which recounts the writer's falling in love with the beautiful Callirée beside a fountain. The scene is a completely imaginary one, which the poet creates as richly as he can:

> Vne source y estoit d'eau viuement coulante
> Iusqu'au fond sans limon comme argent sautelante:
> D'odorantes couleurs ses bords estoyent garnis,
> Là sentoit bon la fleur du beau sang d'Adonis:
> Là rougissoit la fleur du sang d'Aiax éclose:
> Là commandoit le Lys, là boutonnoit la Rose,
> Là son pourpre odorant la Violette auoit,
> Et celle qui tourne au soleil s'y trouuoit. (folio 126 verso, ll. 27-34)

This description is indicative of the whole interest of the poem. In this charmed setting, the poet is wounded by Venus's arrows, by a love just as extraordinary in its effects as the landscape in which it takes place:

> Pour esteindre le feu qui m'alloit deuorant
> Tout plat ie m'accoudé sur le bord murmurant,
> Et du creux de la main puisé l'onde azuree
> Pensant que ma chaleur en seroit moderee,
> Pour le moins si du tout elle ne s'esteignoit.
> Helas! mais comme en l'eau ma bouche se baignoit
> Elle aualoit encor dauantage de flame,
> Qui, soufreuse, asprissoit la fieure de mon ame:
> (folio 128 recto, ll. 3-10)

Two more elegies show the same tendency as this one in their descriptive and narrative interest. In "Ie rechantois la guerre & les alarmes" (folio 132 verso), the poet manages to fill his love-poem with the story of Helen and Troy; in "Las! que mon lict semble dur à mes os" (folio 134 verso) he creates his own story. *Amour* visits him at night, but transforms himself into the image of the lady:

> Il prit ainsi les traits de ton visage
> Tout l'ornement de ton diuin corsage,
> Et toute nuict à moy se presenta.
> Loin de mes yeux le dormir s'absenta (folio 135 verso, ll. 3-6)

Similarly decorative are two elegies which create a personal symbolism concerning objects (a ring, on folio 101 verso[24] and on the colours of his lady's "jartieres", given to him as a gift).

This group of elegies, somewhat different from Jamyn's usual love-plaints, do remind us of similar elegies by Ronsard. Curiously enough, however, instead of finding justification in an example like Ronsard, Jamyn shows a certain hesitation about these poems as elegies. Already in the 1577 edition of his works,[25] six of the elegies of 1575 lose their generic title for a descriptive one; in 1579[26] there are twelve such poems. If we still recognize them as elegies it is only because they are listed as such in the index. The poems involved are precisely the ones that we have discussed in the second group: "D'vn Anneau", "De la transformation des Amans", "Contre l'Honneur", "Pour les Iartieres", and so on. What confirms Jamyn's hesitation concerning these elegies is the fact that one of the early poems becomes a *discours* in the 1579 edition.[27]

However, complete clarity does not reign in the situation. In the same edition that an early elegy becomes a *discours*, a new elegy appears which is far more of the *discours* type than the rejected poem. The poem, "A Monsieur de Mandes",[28] listed with the elegies in the index, has nothing at all to do with love. Instead it is a mixture of praise and of ideas on public duty and the importance of rhetoric. Still listed with the elegies in 1579 is a poem in the first

---

[24] For the basic idea Jamyn could have had as a model either Ronsard's elegy 46 or Desportes' *Les Amours de Diane, Premier Livre*, L1 (p. 99 in the edition of Victor E. Graham [Genève: Droz, 1959]).

[25] See Catalogue 79.

[26] See Catalogue 88.

[27] The elegy "Tes yeux au cœur m'ont versé tant d'amour".

[28] Folio 305 verso (1579 edition).

book of the *Œuvres* which is nothing more than a piece of flattery of Catherine de Médicis. Perhaps its subtitle (1575) explains Jamyn's calling it an elegy: "A la Royne mere du Roy, Regente, faicte apres la mort du Roy Charles IX".[29] The poem does not, however, do any more than refer to the death of Charles; its subject is the greatness of Catherine. Another poem which remains an elegy in 1579 is a poem of flattery of two sisters.[30]

There is, then, some slight confusion in the idea that Jamyn had of the elegy. We are astonished, for example, to see in 1577 that he renames a 1575 elegy as an *épître*[31] at the same time that he adds a new elegy[32] which is less a love-plaint than the new *épître*. In 1583 he adds another example to his poems of flattery[33] and in 1584, as well as giving another group of love-plaints, he publishes two satirical elegies.[34] Whatever confusion of types we find, however, there is an overwhelmingly clear tendency to write of love: out of forty-seven poems scarcely half a dozen treat other subjects. In the love-plaints, the style shows him to be in Desportes' camp; in the other elegies the inspiration is perhaps Ronsardian. Altogether, Jamyn is more a poet of Henri III's reign than he is faithful to the 1560's.

3. THE LOVE-POETS[35]

Jamyn's case will be the typical one of these years: when the poets speak of love, and they prefer to, they are 'modern', and that means they resemble Desportes more than they do Ronsard. This tendency is, of course, most clearly noticeable in the works of those poets who wrote several elegies. It is the case of a poet like Pierre Boton,[36] but

[29] Folio 14 verso.
[30] Folio 264 verso.
[31] Folio 274 verso.
[32] Folio 273 recto (1577 edition).
[33] See Catalogue 98.
[34] See Catalogue 109.
[35] For works containing love-elegies, see Catalogue: 65, 66, 67, 69, 70, 73, 74, 75, 80, 82, 84, 85, 87, 89, 90, 93, 99, 100, 101, 102, 103, 107, 108, 110, 111, 118, 119, 133, 144, 149.
[36] See Catalogue 67.

he is such a curious and eccentric poet that he is perhaps better left in his earned obscurity.

It is more to the point to look at the works of Pierre de Brach[37] because his familiarity with the pre-1570 Ronsard is evident on a number of occasions. It is not, however, so evident in the elegies which express his *mal d'amour*: in these poems he writes in the most modish neo-Petrarchan style. Again it is the style which is revealing and not basic themes, and in his style one notices especially his affection for the long, epic simile. Indeed, the length sometimes goes far beyond anything that even Jamyn attempted, as in this unusual comparison:

> Ainsi voit on dans la sale d'escrime
> Un fier-a-bras, qui faisant peu d'estime
> Des plus adroits, en tirant promettra
> De donner touche, à l'endroit qu'il voudra.
>   Mais toutefois lors que quelqu'vn se treuue,
> Qui d'vn cœur masle & d'vne forçe neufue,
> Coup dessus coup l'enfonce viuement.
> De son escrime il perd le iugement,
> Et en son jeu il n'a loisir d'attendre
> Pour assaillir, pressé de se deffendre :
> Si que souuant les apprentis lui font
> Porter la touche, & la vergogne au front :
> Ainsi que j'ai dessus ma face peinte,
> Auec la honte, vne amoureuse attainte,
> Qui me perça d'outre en outre mon cœur,
> Me laissant vaincre, ayant esté vainqueur.[38]

Not always are the similes so highly developed, however, nor are they always so unexpected. In another poem, we are given the usual comparisons between the eyes of the lady and the sun, clouds, and absence.[39] It is, however, the epic simile which reigns supreme as a stylistic device. Only very occasionally does the poet decorate his themes with mythology, and, when he does, it is of a very familiar nature. In one poem he speaks of his fear that Aimée will tempt the gods:

---

[37] See Catalogue 74. Page references are to the original edition.
[38] Folio 42 verso, ll. 23-38.
[39] folio 27 verso, ll. 117-128.

Le chaut pipeur du cigne blanchissant,
Et l'or pluyeux qui tomba iaunissant
Dedans la tour, & la forme empruntée
De ce taureau, par qui fut emportée
Dessus son col comme un leger fardeau
Sa proye aimée a nage dedans l'eau.
Cela me fait soubz vn mauuais augure,
Craindre aduenir sur toi mesme aduanture,[40]

The eleven love-elegies of Jean de Boyssières[41] are equally in the
poetic style of the 1570's; he too has affection for the long simile.[42]
What adds a touch of originality to this forgotten poet is his writing
a sort of verse-novel (in his *Premières Œuvres*) about his love for
Sylvie. The genres are varied, but each poem provides simply a link
in the chronologically told chain of circumstances which leads him
to desire death. In this sad but conventional story, the elegies are
the *épîtres* that he sends to his cruel lady (and the *discours* are, for
Boyssières, spoken communications).

For fear of simplifying too extremely the tendencies of the love-
poetry during these years, it is salutary to consider another particularly prolific writer of elegies, Jean de La Jessée. In 1583, he published forty-nine elegies,[43] six of which had already appeared in
1578[44] and all of which were probably written between about 1570
and 1578.[45] The poems are written for the three women that he loved,
Marguerite, Sévère, and Grasinde,[46] and in each section of the

---

[40] Folio 22 verso, ll. 55-62.
[41] See Catalogue 80 and 87.
[42] See Catalogue 80, folio 4 recto, ll. 37 *sqq.*; folio 63 recto, ll. 1-13.
[43] See Catalogue 103. Our page references will be to this edition.
[44] See Catalogue 82.
[45] In any case, Grasinde was the third and last love of La Jessée and at least a
part of the poems to her appeared in 1578. It is, therefore, probable that the
poems to Marguerite and Sévère were completed before 1578, although it is
possible that La Jessée added poems to his earlier affairs. The fact that these
three loves had (as well) a purely literary side is revealed by the presence of two
of the 1578 elegies to Grasinde among the elegies to Sévère in 1584. (Elegies IV
and V in 1578 are numbered IV and XIII in the 1584 elegies to Sévère).
[46] Marguerite was identified as Jeanne d'Albret by Cénac Moncaut in "Jean
de La Jessée", *Revue d'Aquitaine*, VI (1862), 370. Raymond, II, 164-5, corrects
this supposition and argues convincingly in favour of Marguerite de Valois.
Neither Sévère nor Grasinde has been identified.

poet's *Amours*, the elegies occupy a book in themselves. It is interesting to note that in the several hundred pages which recount the difficulties of the poet in his love affairs, the elegies, with two exceptions,[47] are the only poems which are not in strophic forms. We have, then, in the three books of elegies a common form, decasyllabic or alexandrine couplets, and a form which is not used for poems of any other title among the other poems of the *Amours*.[48]

Similar to the unity of form is the single subject of love throughout these forty-nine poems. And since our poet had little success with his three ladies, all forty-nine poems resemble one another in their themes; it is only in a few cases that their arrangement in the various books matters very much. As we might expect as well, the unhappy love-affairs of our poet resemble in their general lines those of the poets that we have already studied.

More interesting is, again, the question of style. This is a subject which the poet himself raises in a number of his elegies, and, according to his statements, we should expect him to be somewhat different from his contemporaries. In all three books, he claims to be against the excesses of his fellow poets:

> Ie suis esmerueillé d'vn tas de Petrarquistes
> (O combien peu, Raison, à ce Dieu tu resistes!)
> Qui se dueillent en France, ardantz, & langoureus,
> Tant en leur rime ilz font les transis Amoureus!

and further:

> Qu'on m'oste le Bandel, qu'on m'oste le Petrarque,
> L'Arioste, & Bocaçe, et tous ces Escriuains
> Qui traitent ce subiect, leurs œuures me sont vains:[49]

Love is not communicated in a style that is florid and learned:

> Pour chanter grauement ma veine i'enfleray
> Et dans l'eau d'Helicon trois fois me plongeray.

---

[47] The exceptions are two "Fantaisies" in *La Grasinde Livre Premier* (pp. 1298 and 1304). The lines in these two poems are, however, shorter than in the elegies (seven and eight syllables).
[48] Variety of title is not lacking either. As well as the usual *sonnets, chansons, complaintes* and *stances*, La Jessée gives to his poems such titles as *Gayeté, Fantaisie, Regret, Eprise* and *Mignardise*.
[49] *Marguerite*, elegy VIII, ll. 109-112 and ll. 130-132.

Bref seule vous seriez la Venus que i'implore,
La Pallas que ie sers, la Iunon que i'adore,
N'estoit que ie voy bien que ces motz empoulez,
Poëtiques, obscurs, et de nouueau moulez,
Sont scabreux pour l'Amour: car il fuit ce langage.

and so he will be simple:

C'est pourquoy desormais enclin à vous complaire
Ie serray plus aisé, coulant & populaire,
Pour vous rendre admirable & sans rien emprunter
Parmy la France iray voz honneurs raconter:[50]

In actual fact, however, La Jessée's style is not nearly so simple as he would lead us to believe. If the books to Sévère and Grasinde are more "populaire" than the one to Marguerite,[51] all three are essentially the same and only on occasion less modern than the poetry that we have just been considering. Typical of his contemporaries is the lengthy development of the Petrarchan themes, the excessive descriptions of the lady's beauty, whose eyes are especially powerful:

Voyla comment depuis ma Gorgone m'enroche,
Voyla comment ie meurs si tost que i'en aproche:
Voyla comment chetif! ie suis si desastré
Par ses regardz qui m'ont cruëllement outré,
Regardz qui font languir mon ame maladiue,
Mon ame qui languit trop plus morte, que viue:
Car est-il en ce monde vn plus facheus trespas,
Que d'ainsi trespasser, & ne trespasser pas?[52]

When he is banished from his lady's presence, his poem abounds in images of darkness and light (*Marguerite*, elegy VII). Like his contemporaries, he shows a certain affection for the epic simile:

Ie suis pareil à l'homme attaint d'hydropisie,
Duquel et la chaleur, & la soif s'est saisie:
Il veut boire tousiours, le boire est son desir,
Et seulement a boire il prend tout son plaisir:
Ainsi ie n'entreprendz, ne refuse, & n'excogite,

[50] *Sévère*, elegy VI, 1246, ll. 13-19 and ll. 23-26.
[51] La Jessée refers to this change himself: see *Sévère*, elegy XIII, ll. 55-60.
[52] *Marguerite* II, ll. 29-36.

> Sinon ce qui me nuit, me tourmente, & m'agite:[53]

La Jessée was at times, however, a little old-fashioned, rather than simple as he promised. Very curiously La Jessée reminds us even of the *rhétoriqueurs* when he describes his passing sentence in *Amour*'s courtroom, peopled by *Bel-aceuil*, *Soupçon*, *Faus-raport*, *Vangence*, *Danger*, *Fureur*, and a host of other abstractions.[54] More unexpected than this allegory is a reminiscence of the style of 1500:

> Si d'vn chant enchanteur i'ay sceu plaindre les plaintes
> D'vn Amant non aymé, ses feintises non-feintes,
> Ses souspirs souspirantz, ses sanglotz sanglottez,
> Ses dolentes doleurs, & regretz regrettez:[55]

The *rhétoriqueur* side of La Jessée remains unobstrusive, however. What strikes us more is the frequent use of mythology, which had not ceased to exist in the poetry of Henri III's reign but which was not abundant. Similar to the early Pléiade, La Jessée likes to decorate his themes with mythological allusions, and their range is considerable. Much more erudition is required of the reader to follow the examples that La Jessée gives of divinities who loved mortals than in a similar passage by Jamyn.[56]

Is this affection for mythology the result of our poet's great affection for Ronsard and for the work of the Pléiade,[57] or is it a desire to write elegies inspired by the classics? In one of his elegies, La Jessée promises to compose for his lady poems in the classical style. After referring to the Roman elegists, he says:

> La Romaine Eraton, & la Muse Françoyse,
> Me feront celebrer vostre beauté courtoyse:

[53] *Marguerite* I, ll. 57-62.
[54] *Sévère* I, 1215-1217.
[55] *Marguerite* I, ll. 1-4.
[56] Compare La Jessée, *Marguerite* XX, ll. 33-56 and Jamyn *Œuures*, 1575, folios 176 recto and 181 recto.
[57] Throughout the *Œuvres* of 1584, Ronsard's name is frequently mentioned, and in the last elegy to Grasinde he proclaims that his verses will render the lady as famous as Cassandre, Olive and Francine (ll. 85-93). In his three books of elegies (*Marguerite* V, *Sévère* VI, and *Grasinde* I), La Jessée also recounts in minute detail the birth of his love for each lady, the conversations which they had and so on. Elegies of this type are rare, but they resemble Ronsard's elegies to Genèvre. See Raymond, II, 167-8 for a general discussion of Ronsard's influence.

I'ay leurs outilz en main, (Mes communs passetemptz)
Pour vous parangonner à celles de leur tempz:
Car de vous esgaller aux filles de nostr'-age,
Madame, ie crandroy vous faire trop d'outrage,
Pour ne paroistre assez: le graue Antiquité
A tousiours enuers nous plus grande autorité![58]

As well as the mythology, what strikes us is the arrangement of
the love-elegies in books which have a certain unity and the occasional sensuality of the classical poets rather than of his contemporaries (as in his description of a dream in which he found himself in
bed with his beloved).[59]

However, we have been able to see that, especially since the 1560's
French poets have been inclined to arrange their couplet poems in
books of elegies which are not very different from La Jessée's: con-
sistency of form and subject-matter, the title elegy for what was once
an *épître*. We have also had occasion to point out since the 1560's
the tendency for the *épître* origin of the elegy to become increasingly
vague, despite a Boyssières. With La Jessée this tendency is even
clearer. If a number of the elegies are *épîtres* (absence of the beloved),
our poet is much less concerned about the characteristic of address
than many of his contemporaries were. Sometimes he gives a general
address, as in the case of the fifth elegy in the book to Sévère in which
all "Amantz" are asked to listen to his plaint; sometimes, unlike an
épître, the apostrophes are as lengthy and as important as the address
to the beloved, as in the first elegy to Marguerite; and in eleven
poems,[60] there is no personal address and only short, occasional
apostrophes.

Some variation from poet to poet is to be found, therefore, although the main lines are remarkably clear. The 'variations' of
these years are most inclined to turn up in poets who experimented
little with the elegy. Marie de Romieu, Béroalde de Verville, Jean
Bertaut, and Flaminio Birague,[61] among others, produced narrative
elegies. Birague, for instance, tells us at length how Cupid died after

[58] *Marguerite* V, ll. 601-8.
[59] *Sévère* X.
[60] *Marguerite* II, VI, VIII, IX, X, XI, XII, XIII and XV; *Sévère* I and X.
[61] See Catalogue 89, 99, 142 and 110.

seeing the portrait of the poet's lady and recounts for us with considerable local colour the love-plaints of the "Pescheur amoureux" and the "Pasteur amoureux".[62] Pontus de Tyard[63] writes a bizarre love-poem involving two women, which has received a perhaps overly subtle philosophical interpretation from a modern critic.[64] Le Loyer provides us with a curious pastoral elegy[65] in which the beautiful women of Anjou become nymphs frolicking in the Loir. He also composes an elegy in which he justifies his writing of love: his verses soothe his torments; he is helpless to write of any other subject; love is, in any case, a subject favoured by the Muses. This sort of discourse of self-justification is to be found as well in Filber Bretin[66] and in Scévole de Sainte-Marthe.[67] Sainte-Marthe is more notable, however, for his non-conformist casualness about using the almost constant alexandrine or decasyllabic couplet form in the elegy. One of his variants is a couplet made up of alternating alexandrine and six-syllable lines; Nicolas Rapin[68] writes in precise elegiacs of *vers mesurés*. Sainte-Marthe also writes elegies in quatrains (as does Robert Garnier)[69] and in sextains. A final curiosity might be mentioned: the Tabourot-Du Pont delightful satire of all our serious love-elegies,[70] noteworthy for its humourous and improper rhyme which continues throughout the whole poem.

There is an independent, original side to our love-elegies, then, and sometimes these are the poems which are most interesting to read. A good example is Jean de Sponde's one elegy,[71] which has a first section in couplets and a second part in stanzas with a two-line refrain! On the other hand, it is ultimately never a question of originality that accounts for the distinction of some poems among all the dross. Among the most conventional poems in form and mat-

[62] See Catalogue 110, folio 55 recto, 56 recto and 57 verso.
[63] See Catalogue 65.
[64] See Albert-Marie Schmidt, "Pontus de Tyard ou l'amour famélique", *Table Ronde*, 97 (janv. 1956), 84-8.
[65] See Catalogue 75.
[66] See Catalogue 73.
[67] See Catalogue 84
[68] See Catalogue 149.
[69] See Catalogue 66.
[70] See Catalogue 100.
[71] See Catalogue 133.

ter there are still a few which stand out as exceptional statements of the familiar. No better example of this type of elegy can be given than the two poems by Jodelle:[72] typical in many ways of the *épître amoureuse* tradition, they have a profundity of thought and emotion not frequently met with in the love-poetry of the sixteenth century.

4. THE DEPLORATIVE ELEGY[73]

Once again love outweighs death as a theme in the history of the elegy. A fair number of deplorative elegies are composed, however, particularly after 1580, and as usual they offer more variety than the love-poems. Sixteenth-century writers never settled on any common form when they dealt with death. All collections of death-poems offer a huge variety of generic titles and very frequently the same title is used for many different types of poems. A glance through the book of epitaphs by Ronsard alone illustrates this, and his vagueness is typical of the century. It is not surprising, then, that elegies deploring the death of an important person or of a friend should also give rise to a certain amount of variety.

There is great experimentation in form, first of all. Five poems make some attempt at reproducing the elegiac distich. Marie de Romieu, Guy Lefèvre de la Boderie, and Jérôme d'Avost[74] employ the now familiar couplet formed with an alexandrine and decasyllabic line. Nicolas Rapin imitates the classical distich more seriously by composing in *vers mesurés*.[75] With Robert Garnier there is a certain ambiguity. In his "Elegie sur le Trespas de feu monsieur de Ronsard",[76] the alexandrines alternate with lines of six syllables. We could interpret this as an experiment in the elegiac distich, but the rime-scheme ABAB suggests that the poet simply intended to write his poem in quatrains.

---

[72] See Catalogue 70.
[73] For works containing deplorative elegies, see Catalogue 74, 89, 90, 91, 95, 96, 97, 112, 113, 114, 115, 116, 117, 121, 142.
[74] See Catalogue 89, 91 and 97.
[75] See Catalogue 95.
[76] See Catalogue 112.

The poem that we referred to by La Boderie has another peculiarity in addition to its use of distichs: it is a dialogue between *l'Esprit* of the defunct and *le Passant* in which an argument is engaged concerning the merits of life and death. This is not our only example of a dialogue elegy: we have found an anonymous poem called "Elegie En laquelle entreparlent Le Passant et la Muse" inspired by the death of Mary Stuart.[77]

Both these poems with their *passant* remind us somewhat of the epitaph; three other poems have a closer connection with it. Marie de Romieu calls her one death-elegy "Epitaphe ou Elegie Funebre de Feu Messire Jan Chastelier", but the poem itself is more a typical deploration than a literary evocation of a tombstone epitaph. Jérôme d'Avost adds an epitaph of six lines to his lament on the death of François de Belleforest. It is Jean Bertaut who comes closest to writing an epitaph-elegy,[78] but the term epitaph must be understood, of course, in its widest sense. Bertaut, like most of the poets of the sixteenth century, did not intend to write a real epitaph that could be placed on a stone: his poem of 104 lines makes that clear. He nevertheless begins his poem by an address to the *Passant* and speaks of the life of the defunct in a way reminiscent of an epitaph.

The death-elegies of the 1580's also provide us with a certain amount of variety concerning the type of address involved. Unlike the love-elegy, we have noted throughout the death-elegies of the sixteenth century the tendency towards apostrophe rather than address. It is this tendency which makes Pierre de Brach's very personal poems sent to friends after the death of his wife seem so unusual.[79] To his friend Malvin[80] Brach writes a familiar *épître* retracing in detail the illness of Aimée, her last words, his promise never to remarry and his emotion when she finally passes away. In the elegy "A Monsieur de Raymond Conseiller en la Cour",[81] Brach reproaches his friend for not being faithful to his dead wife. For Brach, death does not dissolve marriage vows, and it is because

[77] See Catalogue 117.
[78] See Catalogue 142.
[79] See Catalogue 74.
[80] Dezeimeris edition, I, 214. Brach's wife died in 1587.
[81] I, 250.

of Raymond's lack of fidelity before his wife's death that he has become so easy a prey to temptations after it. Finally, in an elegy to "Monsieur de Massiot Conseiller en la Cour",[82] memories of his married life are evoked as our poet reviews his past, and he states that he has no desire to become a magistrate, a position to which he had been elected by a Bordeaux grateful for the poet's services. The poem is written in a very casual vein: even more than the two preceding elegies, it is a familiar letter dealing capriciously with various thoughts of a man who appears to be weary of life (ll. 183-194).

Somewhat in the same style is a poem by Jean de Vitel written at the death of his poet-friend Jean Vivien.[83] Although much more ornate in style than Brach's poems, Vitel expresses his sincere grief and addresses his whole poem to the lady whom Vivien loved. The elegy that we have spoken of by Garnier is addressed to Philippe Desportes, but the address does not begin until line 67, and Ronsard is apostrophized rather lengthily as well. Another curious example is an elegy signed only with the initials L. M.: "Elegie à Mademoiselle Camille de Morel, Sur la Mort de Monsieur de Morel son pere".[84] As well as an address to the daughter, there are apostrophes to the defunct; as well as the usual praise of the latter, the poem very strangely is quite as much a poem of flattery of the daughter. In this way, it resembles Rapin's elegy on the death of De Thou[85] in which the son-in-law of the dead man is spoken of in glowing terms beginning at line 33.

The poem by Rapin does not, however, address the still-living son-in-law, and, like the bulk of the poems of the 1580's as well as the death-elegies of earlier decades, it contains apostrophes. The effect of apostrophes rather than a personal address is generally that of a more formal and literary style. This is clearly shown in Isaac Habert's elegy on the death of the "bergere" who suckled him when he was an infant.[86] In a case like this we might have expected

---

[82] I, 255.
[83] See Catalogue 121.
[84] See Catalogue 96.
[85] See Catalogue 95.
[86] See Catalogue 90.

a much more personal sort of poem, not too ornamented by erudite references. Despite the humble origin of the dead woman, however, Habert writes a complaint in the classic style with a first section which expresses his grief, with apostrophes to cruel Atropos and to the gods of nature, and a second section which expresses the *consolatio*:

> "Mais puis que l'on ne peut forcer l'arrest fatal
> "Du seuere destin, & que l'Orgue infernal
> "Pour appaiser Pluton ouure la gueule sombre
> "Pleine d'horreur, d'effroy, de peur, de triste encombre,
> "Sans cesse receuant les ames que Charon
> "Conduit dans son bateau sur les flots d'Acheron
> "Pour faire compagnie aux Ombres & aux Manes
> "Des ayeux trespassez, qui des eaux Letheannes
> "Ont beu à celle fin de perdre souuenir
> "De ce monde où iamais ils ne peuuent venir,
> "Et puis que tous les corps composez sont muables,
> "Subiets aux accidens, & tousiours variables,
> "Il ne faut s'estonner s'ils vont au monument :
> "Car tous ceux auront fin qui ont commencement. (ll. 35-48)

The poem ends with a final address to the gods of nature to prepare the tomb of the dead woman.

Although all the death-elegies do not follow this pattern, Habert's poem is typical of the style generally found. Much more than the love-elegies, those concerning death are filled with classical allusions. It is indeed rare to find any allusion to the Christian God and the Christian idea of Heaven: our dead seem to people the Elysian Fields, and, when it is Ronsard who joins their numbers, it is he who becomes the god of all he surveys.[87] This does not mean that the poems are completely divorced from reality: a sketchy outline of the dead-man's life is sometimes given, and, when he met his death in as dramatic a way as Edouard du Monin, references to it are found. The poet's nephew, François Granchier, says:

---

[87] There is a lengthy description of Ronsard in the Elysian Fields in the poem by D. I. E. M., Catalogue 113. This poem has been reprinted in *Le Tombeau de Hugues Vaganay Humaniste Lyonnais Recueilli de Plusieurs Excellens Personnages. Ensemble Vne Elegie Pour le Tombeau de Pierre de Ronsard Prince des Poetes François* (Lyon : Imprimerie de Lyon, 1937), 95-105.

La muse des François a ia frippé la porte
Du monde terrien, non pas de volonté,
Mais vn meurtrier sanglant à l'encontre irrité,
Fasché de son honneur, aussi de sa science,
D'vn poignard la banni du monde & de la France.[88]

A somewhat lengthier account is given in an anonymous poem[89] but it is interesting to see that, even in the case of Du Monin, references to his unusual death were not considered necessary. In the three elegies found in a collection devoted to his death and that of one of his friends,[90] not one of the poems refers to the murder by stabbing.

The death-elegies are on the whole, then, very literary poems with only unremarkable references to reality. It is this point that strikes us particularly after having seen, in the preceding chapter, a number of death-laments that were so much concerned with the whole situation of France. France was by no means stable in the 1580's either, but our death-elegies give only a slight hint of the continuing civil disturbances. Marie de Romieu makes a few passing references to the troubles of the times, and so do two poems on the death of Ronsard:[91] R. Cailler quickly refers to Henri III's successes in establishing order, and Garnier speaks of "la povre France en son corps outragée / Par le sanglant effort / De ses enfants" (ll. 163-5). However, Garnier goes on to show greater concern for the little appreciation of poetry among his contemporaries...

5. THE OCCASIONAL ELEGY

Although our rather numerous death-elegies show little interest in the problems of the times, a number of other poems deal with the subject almost exclusively. Both elegies by Guillaume du Buys, for example, are on the theme of civil wars, but in a much more fanciful way than we found in the 1560's. In the first of these poems,[92] the

[88] See Catalogue 114. Ll. 24-8.
[89] See Catalogue 115
[90] See Catalogue 116.
[91] See Catalogue 112.
[92] See Catalogue 92.

fifty-four lines at the beginning (almost a third of the total length) develop the image of the struggles of a pilot of a boat in stormy waters. After this over-developed image, the poet manages to refer more specifically to the troubles of his country. When he explains them as God's punishment for the excesses of his contemporaries, the reader is not certain whether such a non-partisan attitude is a blessing or lamentable simplicity. Du Buys's second elegy is scarcely more interesting. This time, with many extraneous details, the poem begins by describing the poet in his garden, where a starling comes to tell him all about the state of France. It is the bird, too, that prays to God for an end to the civil troubles (ll. 154 *sqq.*). A mere twelve lines remain of the poem after the bird finishes its speech.

In four other elegies on a similar theme we are in a very different atmosphere. Nicolas Debaste takes himself seriously as a defender of the catholic church and composes two elegies which are more *discours* than lamentations on the bloodshed and destruction of the wars.[93] Again the poems are different from those that we found in the 1560's, because, with Debaste, we are presented the situation on religious grounds, whereas the earlier poems dealt with the problems politically. The titles of these lengthy poems indicate the angle from which the writer speaks of the problems: "Elegie, par laquelle le Poëte demonstre comme l'Eglise Apostolique & Romaine à tousiours remporté victoire de ses ennemis. A Monsieur Charpentier Docteur en Theologie, & Theologal de l'Eglise de Chartres" and "Elegie, par laquelle le Poëte prouue contre les Ministres, comme saint Pierre a esté premierement Pape seant à Rome. A Monsieur Loret, Chanoine de Chartres, & Prieur de Gallardon". These poems are not simply learned discourses, but it is in a third elegy that Debaste gives fullest vent to his feelings: "Elegie, par laquelle le Poëte deplore le massacre, duquel les Huguenots ont vsé en la personne des Ecclesiastiques, & comme aussi ils ont bruslé beaucoup de Temples. A Monsieur Bonneaux, Chanoine de Chartres".[94] Here he calls upon all the youth of France – and the older men who are still living – to come forward to crush the Calvinists since they have become peaceful and the moment is opportune (ll. 277 *sqq.*)! Just

[93] See Catalogue 111. The poems are found on folios 62 verso and 68 recto.
[94] Folio 74 recto.

before this rather cruel passage, however, Debaste asks the priests of his church to reform themselves: lack of fidelity to the church among the population is, apparently, largely the fault of the clergy, even for so ardent an apologist of the church as Debaste (ll. 211 *sqq.*).

Also concerned with the times, but with a different aspect of them, is an elegy by Claude de Trellon.[95] Like Jamyn, Trellon writes a diatribe against court life, not out of hate but pity since he has withdrawn to his "Hermitage" (the title which he gives to a section of his poems). His distaste for the court is the result of many factors, but prominent among them are the usual criticisms of the ambitions of courtiers which lead to hypocrisy, flattery, and artificiality (ll. 13-52). Another poem dealing with the purely social decadence of the times is the anonymous diatribe against the immodest and 'un-Christian' clothing and make-up of the stylish young ladies of the 1570's.[96]

The elegies dealing with the times are therefore few in number, distinct from the deplorative elegy and quite different in style and intent from their counterpart in the 1560's. It is only Brach who in an epistolary elegy to his friend Malvin[97] writes in some realistic detail about the wars, but even here the intimate nature of the poem is different from the earlier style.

All these poems are easily assimilated with the *discours*-type of elegy, which still appears from time to time during these years. The title *discours* itself, however, has become so popular by the 1580's that the elegy is not overly rich in examples of this type. When they do appear they tend to be more familiar in style than the *discours*. Isaac Habert,[98] for instance, answering a friend's letter, discusses at some length the physical and psychological differences among humans and the havoc which the four humours can do to the body. All of this is a prelude to a discussion of his own illness, but at line 41 he begins to generalize again concerning the effect of time on the body. The poem ends with praise of his friend's poetry. Habert's elegy is a mixture of elements, then, and this should not surprise us because,

[95] See Catalogue 119.
[96] See Catalogue 77.
[97] See Catalogue 74. The poem is on folio 131 verso.
[98] See Catalogue 90.

more than anything else, it is simply a familiar letter. This is true of the two other elegies which show some *discours* tendencies. Rapin writes to his friend Parent about friendship, the evil of promiscuity and his admiration for Horace and the Pléiade;[99] Le Poulchre writes to his friend Brissonnet about his law suits, the improvement in education since antiquity, the limitations of Cupid's powers and how one can have success with women.[100]

There is, then, a casual and personal quality about these poems, and every now and then we meet with very autobiographical poems. Agrippa d'Aubigné's elegy is one of the more interesting examples,[101] but even as literary an exercise as Vitel's elegy about a plague which forced him to seek a healthier climate is none the less a real experience in his life.[102] Birague and Debaste[103] offer further examples but the bulkiest and perhaps most interesting of the autobiographical elegies is Guy Le Fèvre de La Boderie's "Elegie A La Boderie lieu de naissance de l'Autheur".[104] In 352 lines the poet recounts his youth in Normandy (in the valley of the Lambron River) and how he became a poet. When he comes to the part of his life which he spent working on the polyglot Bible for Philip II, he is filled with bitterness against the Spanish (ll. 81 *sqq*.). The evocation of all the wrongs that have been done to him leads him to an expression of his faith in God, and it is on this note that the poet ends the résumé of his life.

La Boderie's poem begins with an apostrophe to his birthplace in which he praises the countryside, the valley, and the river. It is momentarily, therefore, an encomiastic elegy, another type which continues to appear during these years. Du Monin praises the city of Amiens and the Bourbons.[105] Naturally it is praise of humans that we normally find. When Boyssières does not speak of love in his elegies, he writes fulsome praise of various people whom he seeks

[99] See Catalogue 94.
[100] See Catalogue 118.
[101] See Catalogue 76.
[102] See Catalogue 121.
[103] See Catalogue 110 en 111.
[104] See Catalogue 91.
[105] See Catalogue 104.

as patrons.[106] Debaste, Vitel, d'Avost, La Boderie all contribute examples of this type of elegy.

A final type of occasional elegy which might be mentioned is the Ronsardian "A son livre". Brach and Debaste have both given us examples,[107] and in both cases Ronsard's presence is precisely felt.

The first thing that is striking in the period that we have just discussed is the great number of elegies that were written. Not every poet during the reign of Henri III felt it necessary to try his hand at elegies, but more than forty poets produced about three hundred of them. It is true that, especially during the 1570's, a few poets wrote large numbers of elegies: Desportes composed thirty, Jamyn forty-seven, Brach eighteen and Boyssières seventeen. Nevertheless, it is not easy to find a collection of poetry during these years which does not offer at least one poem bearing the title elegy.

In subject-matter, the elegy becomes more involved with love than in the years immediately preceding Henri's reign. Indeed, the genre now seems rather escapist when one remembers how large a number of elegies during Charles IX's reign became earnestly involved in the events of the day. Poets now are more interested in writing at length and with great frequency about love, and the only thing that makes these poems of much interest to us is the fact that, like Desportes and unlike the typical Ronsard love-elegy of the 1560's, the elegy is becoming ever more distant from the *épître amoureuse*. Poets no longer take much interest in keeping up the pretence of writing letters to their beloved but allow themselves the freedom of longer, literary developments, forget about their address and indulge in frequent and often lengthy apostrophes. The love-elegy and the *épître* are no longer necessarily the same.

This is true, as well, of many of the elegies which deal with subjects other than love. The origin of these poems also is ultimately, no doubt, the *épître*, but, since the subjects that we found in them (flattery, requests, autobiography and so on) were found in abundance among the elegies of Ronsard, it is likely that Ronsard, already one step away from the *épître*, provided our poets with a model which easily led to still further separation from it.

[106] See Catalogue 80, 81, and 87.
[107] See Catalogue 74 and 111.

Finally, the death-elegy remains a comparatively rare type. Just as love inspired the use of many different verse forms, no one type of poem became associated with the deploration of the dead. Granchier in his book on the passing of Du Monin writes, besides sonnets and epitaphs, a "Colloque funèbre", an "Elégie" and an "Odelette"; Vitel expresses his grief in poems called "Eclogue", "Larmes et Regrets", "Complainte", a dialogue poem and one "Elégie". Further, the death-elegies themselves do not follow at this period, and have not followed in earlier periods, any particular pattern (as the love-elegies do); we are never sure what to expect of them. Also, it can only seem strange that the elegy title should be used so seldom for deplorations. It occurs certainly less often than *épitaphe* and perhaps even less often at this time than *stances* or *complainte*.

The elegy, a popular type of poem during the reign of Henri III, is again essentially a love-poem, but, no matter what its subject-matter, the *épître* character of the elegy is on the wane. This is perhaps not noticeable among the death-elegies, since they have never been particularly associated with the letter, but in all the other types of elegy it is a development which is striking and important.

VI

THE LAST DECADE

All the way through the sixteenth century writers complain that poetry has become too common an activity, that the unskilled and untalented boldly inflict their mediocre verses on the reading public. One of our elegies, written in 1600, again laments this situation:

> Je n'aime plus les vers, et toute ma colère
> Est de voir tant d'esprits, qui se meslent d'en faire,
> Nous brouiller des papiers que pour livres en vend[1]

During this last decade of the sixteenth century, however, although poetry remains as vigorous as ever, the number of elegies tends to fall off after the almost excessive production of them during the reign of Henri III. By extending ourselves beyond 1600 slightly to include a number of elegies that were perhaps composed in the last years of the sixteenth century and which are by poets, in any case, whose literary career belongs to the sixteenth century, we have not managed to find as many as a hundred elegies. There is a falling-off in number, then, but at the same time an exaggeration of the preference of the preceding years for the elegy to be a love-poem: only twenty of our elegies will deal with other subjects.

1. THE LOVE-ELEGY

Apart from remarking on the popularity of the love-elegy there is little else that need be said: the poets at the end of the century do not try to renew the patterns that we already know so well. Trellon

---

[1] See Catalogue 141. Ll. 1-3.

adds two further groups of elegies to his first collection of 1587[2] but there is nothing particularly novel in them. The 1597 poems have a certain local colour, however, since they reflect the poet's stay in Marseilles.[3] Also prolific in the writing of love-elegies is Siméon Guillaume de La Roque, but in the 1595 group of twelve[4] it is only the last elegy which is at all original. In this poem he changes his address from Caristée to his friend Malherbe, and instead of telling his friend about his difficulties with Caristée, he develops the theme that love is an art that should be learned:

> Amour est vn mestier que chacun doit apprendre,
> C'est vn discours encor' qu'il faut sçauoir entendre,
> C'est vne large mer ou lon se perd souuent
> Si lon n'est bon Pilote & si lon n'a bon vent: (ll. 13-16)

Part of this training in love involves the destruction of the foolish idea that love is durable:

> Aussi est ce vn erreur que de voir vne flamme
> S'amortir dans le cœur d'vn homme ou d'vne femme,
> De forcer la nature en l'osant r'allumer
> Et comme au parauant se vouloir faire aimer: (ll. 37-40)

Something of the same cool-headed detachment is expressed in a practical situation in 1597[5] when the poet, in a section of his volume called *Diverses Poesies*, is again having difficulties with a lady. In the fourth elegy, he analyses to what extent her beauty has faded during the last year:

> Le temps a du depuis que i'en suis eslongné
> Vn peu terny [cest] œil que m'auoit desdaigné,
> Son taint n'est plus si vif, sa bouche si vermeille,
> Sa voix ne sonne plus si douce à mon oreille

[2] See Catalogue 127 and 132.

[3] Trellon, after his imprisonment in 1594, went to Italy and returned to France by way of Marseilles. See Pierre de Lacretelle, "Note sur Claude de Trellon", *Bibliothèque du Bibliophile et du Bibliothécaire*, 1906, 29-38, 133-138. In the third elegy, Trellon mentions specifically being in Marseilles (l. 37), and the description that he gives of his surroundings in the seventh elegy (ll. 7-24) suggests the port city again.

[4] See Catalogue 128. La Roque is also responsible for Catalogue 123, 134, and 147.

[5] See Catalogue 134.

> Ce corps n'a plus la grace, & les traits de Cypris,
> Aussi n'en suis-ie plus si viuement espris. (ll. 71-6)

This theme is more forcefully treated in a poem found among seven new elegies which La Roque published in 1609.[6] In the eleventh elegy of that edition he attempts to retain the lady's favour, rather oddly, by telling her that she is neither young nor beautiful enough for the young Adonis with whom she has fallen in love. His interest in the perfecting of one's knowledge of love, as he recommended in his poem to Malherbe, appears again in 1609 when he writes an elegy[7] involving useful tips on seducing women. A final elegy by La Roque which offers a somewhat original theme is number XXI in 1609. Here the poet delights in what he presumes will be the unhappy marriage of a "mignon" (l. 3) who laughed at the poet's past difficulties in love. The poet, who claims to be free of love's tyranny (ll. 5-6), looks forward to the torments that the impudent young man will have to suffer.

There are slight touches of the unconventional, then, in the elegies of this period. Out of six poems, Claude Expilly provides two which are a little off the beaten-track.[8] In his first elegy we learn that the poet's love was bizarrely inspired by hearing the lament of a woman at her beloved's grave: the poet does not see the mourner, but her words of sorrow are sufficient to make him fall completely in love. The last poem in his book of elegies is a curious speech by *Amour* concerning his powers and also their limitations, since he appears to be helpless in ending the misery of three young lovers whom he has caused to fall in love with three "nymphes" (l. 51).

Marc Papillon de Lasphrise is surprisingly chaste in his elegies:[9] how curious that a poet given to eroticism should avoid it when writing in a genre where it is sanctioned by the classical tradition. He does beg for Noémie's favours before she marries an elderly man (second elegy), but the sonnets remain a good deal more overtly sensual than his elegies. Michel Guy de Tours' tendency to weep

---

[6] See Catalogue 147.
[7] The poem is actually "Elegie XX" but is numbered erroneously "Elegie XVII". See La Roque, 448.
[8] See Catalogue 130.
[9] See Catalogue 135.

seems only to dampen his sensual ardour.[10] Only his "Songe en Forme d'Elegie A Madame Renee La B. Sœur de son Ente" (folio 22 verso) is noteworthy. Here curiously, it appears that it is the woman who is more anxious than the lover to enter into holy matrimony, and she refuses to see him until he promises that he will marry her. Before the promise is given, we have a lament and a curse against women, followed by an apology when Ente finally opens the door. It is interesting that this elegy, which strikes us as being original and, up to a point, different from so many others, is in fact a translation of the fifth elegy in Book I of Ovid's *Amores*.[11] Guy de Tours is responsible for the dream framework and little else. The point is, of course, that French elegies inspired by classical poems still distinguish themselves by the end of the century.

Finally we might mention the nine elegies of Etienne Pasquier.[12] Published for the first time in 1610, they perhaps belong to a much earlier period, but the preface by André du Chesne and Pasquier's own introduction leave the dating an insoluble problem. The *Ieux poëtiques* are divided into five sections which trace the loves of man through the various stages of his life, from youth to the final part charmingly called "Vieillesse Rechignée". Pasquier explains that his purpose was to create "...un theatre des affections humaines, que i'ay voulu representer soubs ma personne".[13] While he goes on to say that the work is fictional, it is perhaps implied that the poet had at least passed through these stages of life.

Five of the nine elegies are found in the first section, called "Loyauté". It is indeed the most elegiac part of the book since it deals with the young and innocent man who is "esperduëment idolastre en un seul object".[14] The loyalty has lasted at least six years (see the second elegy, l. 15), ample opportunity for some of the most typical themes of the sixteenth-century love-elegy to find

[10] See Catalogue 136.
[11] See James Hutton, "Michel Guy de Tours: Some Sources and Literary Methods", *Modern Language Notes*, LVIII (1943), 431-441: see 441, note 16.
[12] See Catalogue 148.
[13] For our text of the *Jeux Poëtiques*, we are using *Les Œuvres d'Estienne Pasquier...*, 2 vols. (Amsterdam: la compagnie des libraires associés, 1723), in-fol. See II, columns 827-8 for Pasquier's preface.
[14] II, column 827.

their appropriate place. Despair and hope during a long-suffering fidelity, which is finally disappointed and turned to a desire for vengeance. The still apparent style during these years to ornament themes with long images is particularly in evidence in the third elegy where a boat trip is seen to have many parallels with the poet's love. So long and elaborate is Pasquier's delving into the similarity that his poem almost becomes an allegory.

Two elegies appear in "Liberté", the second section of Pasquier's work, but they are to be distinguished from the preceding poems – if at all – only by a slightly more violent tone. The one elegy in the third part, "Ambition", is a real curiosity, however. The man, now married, provides instruction to his wife on her duties and behaviour. Shades of *L'Ecole des Femmes*! With Pasquier's last elegy, found in the part devoted to old age, we are back to the familiar themes, the lesson being, apparently, that oldsters behave like youngsters when newly wounded by Cupid.

Our last group of love-elegies in the sixteenth-century is not very new, then, insofar as the subjects are concerned: very few have themes untypical of the love-elegy of the preceding years of the century. They are interesting, however, in their confirming a tendency that we emphasized in the preceding chapter: the love-elegy can scarcely be called an *épître amoureuse*. That does not mean, of course, that there are no examples of the elegy as a letter. In the second book addressed to Félice, Trellon tells us that he is writing to his lady and is waiting for a letter in reply to another one that his valet has delivered for him.[15] Examples as clear as this one are, however, extremely rare. All the elegies in Trellon's second book to Félice should be letters since the poet is separated from his lady, and so, when he addresses her, presumably it is in the form of a letter. However, the poems rarely appear as letters. The fourth elegy,[16] for instance, gives much more attention to apostrophes than to addressing the lady: she is, in fact, spoken to directly only in the last four lines of the poem. The first elegy of Guy de Tours[17] is similar. It too is a letter to his lady written during an absence, but

[15] See Catalogue 132, folio 164 recto.
[16] Folio 162 recto.
[17] See Catalogue 136, folio 8 recto.

in its long description of how he passes his time and his recounting in direct discourse the words that he addressed to the lady's *château* and park, we easily lose sight of the fact that the poem as a whole is a letter. In other poems, where the address is quite clear, the reader is nevertheless not absolutely certain that the poem is intended as a letter. In Pasquier's advice to his wife,[18] are we to presume that this was a letter or perhaps spoken advice? The written poem as a verbal communication certainly does occur, as we have seen in the past and as we still find in the last years of the century. Papillon's second elegy[19] to Théophile, for example, contains lines like these:

> Meditez mes discours, escoutez ma parolle,
> Ne croyez que ie sois des conteurs de friuolle. (ll. 35-6)

A dialogue poem by Trellon,[20] a conversation between a "chevalier" and his "dame", is obviously a further example of the "spoken" rather than the "written' poem. Also to be included in this category would be, probably, the sort of poem which has a general address or which involves a series of apostrophes. Pasquier addresses one of his elegies, not to a single lady, but to all women,[21] and again the poem takes on the character of a spoken communication. In an elegy by La Roque,[22] the poet addresses his lady in the first line of the poem, but the last paragraph begins:

> Dames, oyez ces mots que rien ne vous empesche
> De cognoistre l'erreur d'vne longue recherche (ll. 113-4)

The loss of the epistolary character of the elegy is normally due to other factors, however. In some cases it is simply that the address has an unimportant rôle in the poem. In many cases it is only as the poem is coming to its conclusion that the reader becomes aware that it is intended for a precise person. In the first elegy of the first book to Félice,[23] Trellon gives us a rhetorical display of apostrophes in the first fifty lines of his poem before he finally addresses

18 Pasquier, II, col. 878.
19 See Catalogue 135, p. 81.
20 See Catalogue 132, folio 110 verso.
21 Pasquier, II, column 863.
22 See Catalogue 134, p. 45.
23 See Catalogue 127, folio 107 verso.

Félice in the last two lines only. In other cases, it is not so much the lateness of the address but the important rôle of the apostrophes which destroys the epistolary character of the elegy. Guy de Tours, in a poem[24] which addresses the beloved at the beginning, nevertheless ends by another address, or apostrophe, to the old men who try to hinder his love:

> Cessez doncques, cessez vieillars de me reprendre
> Et de plus apres moy vos paroles despendre,
> Car l'homme n'est point fol, ny n'est point animal,
> Qui cerche les vertus et déteste le mal. (ll. 51-4)

In another poem by the same poet,[25] there is definitely question of a double address (to the lady and to her disapproving father), a situation which certainly robs the poem of any pretence at being a letter.

Another curious type of elegy which escapes classification as an *épître* is that in which the lady is addressed in the second person but spoken of in the third person as well. In the first paragraph of a poem by La Roque,[26] the lady is first addressed directly but is then spoken about rather than spoken to. Guy de Tours[27] again provides us with an example and a much more impressive one. In the first twenty-four lines of the poem, the lady is spoken about in the third person; from lines 25 to 56, she is addressed directly; from lines 57 to 64, the address gives way to indirect references; and from 65 to the end of the poem, the lady is again spoken to directly, but throughout these last 160 lines of the elegy there are numerous apostrophes and developments of general ideas which suggest a *discours* rather than a personal communication.

Thus at the end of the sixteenth century, the love-elegy is the most favoured type of elegy, but it has for the most part lost its epistolary nature; in the rest of the poems the address is either absent or such that it is impossible to interpret the poem as a letter. The situation has come to the point that, in the case of certain poets the character of a personal address, epistolary or otherwise, does

---

[24] See Catalogue 136, folio 24 verso.
[25] Folio 216 verso.
[26] See Catalogue 134, p. 50.
[27] See Catalogue 136, folio 102 verso.

not seem a necessary characteristic of the love-elegy. Over half of La Roque's twenty-three love-poems have peculiarities in the address; only one elegy out of six by Expilly has the sort of address that we associated earlier with the elegy.

2. THE DEATH-ELEGY

When deploring a death the poets at the end of the century show largely the same tendencies that we have already found. First of all, no one form or title dominates the death-poems; secondly, the elegy itself is almost least-favoured of the possible titles. If one leafs through the *Tombeau* section of Trellon's *Œuvres*,[28] one finds *stances, discours, sonnets, sextains, complaintes* (stanzaic), one poem called "épitaphe" (folio 220 verso) and no elegies. Guy de Tours even writes a "Madrigal en Forme d'Epitaphe Pour Messire Frere Claude de l'Hermite, Cheualier de l'ordre de S. Iean de Hierusalem ..."[29]

We do have five death-elegies, however, and, as we might expect from our earlier chapters, they are filled with the familiar commonplaces but offer no very unified appearance. Pierre Sallière offers us our first example, a poem on the death of his employer: "Elegie Sur Le Trespas Du defunct Sieur des Cresnais, par P. Lucas Salliere, Precepteur de son fils".[30] Cresnais is praised for his bravery, and grief is allayed by the reassuring knowledge that a fine son survives the dead man. Le Chevalier is as conventional for his ideas but more literary in style;[31] Le Cauchois writes one of the most nondescript deplorations of the century.[32]

Finally, Passerat has left us two elegies, composed in 1599 for Henri IV when he lost his mistress Gabrielle d'Estrées.[33] Both

---

[28] See Catalogue 132, folios 199 verso – 227 recto.
[29] See Catalogue 136, folio 232 verso.
[30] See Catalogue 122.
[31] See Catalogue 124.
[32] See Catalogue 125.
[33] See Catalogue 145. We have used *Les Poésies Françaises de Jean Passerat, Publiées avec notice & notes par Prosper Blanchemain*, 2 vols. (Paris: Lemerre, 1880). The poems are found in Vol. II, pp. 65 and 87.

poems are supposedly the words of the king (Niré) himself. In the
first of them, he tells of his misery, caused by the death of the extra-
ordinarily beautiful Gabrielle (Fleurie). In a way strangely typical
of love-elegies, Passerat lists the qualities of each feature of her face:

> Son front, large & serein, estoit des mieus polis,
> D'où prenoient leur blancheur les belles fleurs-de-lis.
> L'ebene des sourcils se voustoit en arcades:
> Les Amours en ses yeux dressoient leurs embuscades. (ll. 27-30)

Also typical of love-elegies is the description of the lover's misery
(ll. 81 *sqq.*). The second elegy is equally ambiguous since it involves
a dream, presumably, in which Fleurie appears and explains the
reason for her death. As in an elegy by La Taille, it is the lover's
departure for war which has caused a mortal grief in the lady.

Our five deplorative elegies are not of much interest in themselves,
then, and it is more to the point to stress their rarity and to point
out their little involvement in history. There are allusions to fighting
the Ligueurs[34] and to the misery of life,[35] but references like these
are infrequent and quickly disposed of in the poems.

3. MISCELLANEOUS ELEGIES

Nor indeed are many other elegies, in the last decade of the sixteenth century, concerned with the times. Only one is exclusively
devoted to precise, historical events, an anonymous poem published
in the important year 1598: *Elegie Sur L'Heureux Succez De La
Paix.*[36] Unlike our poems in the 1560's, this one expresses joy over
the peace that has finally come to France after so many years of war
and bloodshed:

> Nous voüerons nos cœurs purgés en sacrifice,
> Nous leuerons nos ames, & du blasme le vice,
> Et du venin brouillant cent fois nostre memoyre:
> Semerons en chantant à la celeste gloire: (ll. 11-4)

[34] See Catalogue 122, ll. 42 *sqq.*
[35] See Catalogue 124, ll. 81-2.
[36] See Catalogue 137.

The elegy quickly leads to praise of the king, who has brought this peace to the country (ll. 23-36), and then a passage about Philip II of Spain indicates that the poem must have been written after the Treaty of Vervins on May 2, 1598:

> Philippes Roy second d'Espagne genereux,
> Au royaume de Naples, & la Cicile heureux,
> Ia concede vne paix à l'invincible France, (ll. 37-9)

While this is the only elegy which deals directly with the times, a slightly earlier elegy by Loys Papon[37] refers to the unfortunate state of France but not exclusively to the religious and purely political difficulties of the period. Addressed to his close friend Anne d'Urfé, the poem may be dated 1595 with considerable certainty since this was the year that d'Urfé retired from public life to spend his time in a new home in the country.[38] The poem begins with a description of general upset and abuse: in the church (ll. 1-8), in law (ll. 9-13), in civil obedience:

> Lorsqu'on voit aux tocsains les armes acroupies,
> La milice retifue au secours du pays,
> Les Roys de leurs vassaux hays ou retrahis
> Et du feu violent d'ambicieuse poincte,
> La flame du deuoir aux noblesses esteinte,
> Par mescontentement de fragiles despitz. (ll. 14-9)

On the other hand, the great indulge in luxury and have no thought for the poor (ll. 20-5). This state of affairs indicates that it is the moment to withdraw to safety (ll. 26 *sqq.*). References to the abuses continue, but the theme of withdrawal quickly dominates the poet's attention and leads to praise of d'Urfé and his decision to move to the country, far from the cares of the world (ll. 56-94). For his retreat, d'Urfé has built a house, which is praised (ll. 95-121) and which occasions further praise of its builder:

> MARQVIS c'est la maison, ou d'vn libre loyzir,
> Loing des mondanitez de ces cours hypocrites,
> Vous faictes reformer, ces hymnes si bien dictes,

---

[37] See Catalogue 126.
[38] See Sœur Mary Jerome Keeler, *Étude Sur La Poésie et Sur le Vocabulaire de Loys Papon Poète Forézien du XVIe Siècle* (Washington: Université Catholique d'Amérique, 1930), 34, note 67.

Auxquelles tout rauy, en louables discours,
Vous peignez les effectz des pudiques amours, (ll. 122-6)

The poem is only incidentally concerned, then, with large problems: its real subject is praise of a man and his house.

We might expect the series of elegies which Papillon de Lasphrise
addressed to the king to mention more seriously the events of the
day, all the more so since the poet had been in his earlier years a
soldier who took a most active part in the disturbances of France.[39]
The three poems addressed to Henri IV in 1598[40] are, however,
little more than poems of praise: there are references to war and
peace, but, as Papillon himself says, his purpose is to praise the
king.[41] In the 1599 edition of his works,[42] Papillon adds another
elegy to this section of his poetry, and the purpose of all his praise
becomes clearer: he quite frankly asks for money, but money that
is due to him for services rendered to Henri III:

Ie me suis aduisé d'autre bouche parler
Priant ta Majesté comme icy ie la prie
Que si elle ne veut graitifer ma vie
Qu'elle me baille au moins cela qu'elle me doit
Ce sont neuf cents escus SIRE qu'il me faudroit
Deus du prix de mon sang pour FRANCE en guerre dure
Ayant ma compagnie au siege de LA MVRE
D'vne Monstre arrestée & controlée aussi
Le Role dans mon Coffre est inutile icy
Voudriés vous refuser vne si iuste debte
Que vous deués si bien, bien que ne l'ayés faicte,
Mais comme heritier grand, d'vn grand troisieme HENRY (ll. 16-27)

We are, then, in the realm of the flattery-demand type of elegy
rather than in the type concerned with historical events. Papillon is
generally a very personal sort of poet, however, and even in this
type of poem he makes us feel the human situation that underlies the

---

[39] See A. Van Bever, "Un capitaine poète du XVIe siècle Marc Papillon de
Lasphrise (1555-1600?)", *L'Ermitage*, IV (1905), 231-241, 296-309: see 304.
Papillon retired from war in 1591.
[40] See Catalogue 135.
[41] See in the first elegy ll. 68-70 and in the third elegy ll. 41-50.
[42] See Catalogue 138.

typical sort of praise which many poets addressed to kings and to the great.

In two more elegies that Papillon has given us, the autobiographical element becomes pre-eminent. In 1597, there is a long elegy (318 lines) apostrophizing France for the purpose of furnishing her with arguments that can be used to defend him against criticism. In so doing the poet recounts his exploits and analyses his character. In 1599 another elegy, apostrophizing his book, deals with his whole family with considerable detail about such prosaic matters as marriages and property. These poems recall in type the autobiographical elegies of Ronsard; the idea of addressing his book probably comes as well from Ronsard.

Ronsard's elegy was a prefatory poem, and this is a type still found, if not from the pen of Papillon. There are two such poems at the end of the century, by Philippes Perault in Virbluneau's volume[43] and by Nicolas Vauquelin des Yveteaux in the 1600 edition of Desportes' works.[44] Perault's poem is a very slight piece telling the reader that Virbluneau is the perfect guide to an understanding of chaste love. The poem by Vauquelin is a more impressive work. We have already quoted its beginning: Vauquelin complains that since too many people are writing poetry it has lost the sacred character that it had at its creation in the Golden Age. Now that poetry is open to all and not simply to those favoured by the Muses, we have cycles that are reminiscent of the seasons: there is an early period of growth and final decay (ll. 77-80). According to Vauquelin, however, French poetry has gone from a primitive stage (ll. 89 *sqq.*) right into decadence:

> En cet âge dernier...
> (Apollon) Se voit dedans l'enclos d'une estroite prison,
> Et reduit sous le joug de pointes figurées,
> Souffre contre son gré ses bornes mesurées
> Par des ieunes esprits, dont le foible cerveau
> Veut produire à la cour un langage nouveau,
> Qui plaist aux ignorans, et nostre langue infecte
> De rymes et de mots pris en leur dialecte.
> ....

[43] See Catalogue 139.
[44] See Catalogue 141.

Leurs vers ont par travail plus de subtilité
Que de force requise à l'immortalité, (ll. 115-128)

Desportes is, of course, an exception: his poetry alone belongs to a period of maturity between development and decay. He is the example for poets to consider:

L'Amour n'auroit sans luy ny flamme ny cordage;
Et comme cet Amour débroüilla le nuage
De la masse confuse où tout le monde estoit,
Lors que chasque element sans ordre combatoit,
De tant d'esprits confus cet esprit nous dégage,
Et la France luy doit la reigle du langage. (ll. 145-150)

As we have seen in the elegy, it has been, in fact, the Desportes style that has most impressively served as a model for love-poets in the last quarter of the century, and clarity of language will increasingly be a reality and not simply an ideal.

Only two elegies remain to be discussed: La Roque's address to all "miserables pecheurs" to worship God, (a curious poem that contrasts the beauty of Nature, God's gift to man, and the horror, lengthily described, of Christ's body after the Crucifixion); and a *discours*-elegy by Papillon de Lasphrise. We have already referred to a few elegies which resemble *discours*: one by La Roque addressed to Malherbe, the Pasquier elegy of advice to a wife, and one of Papillon's own elegies which he called *discours* in a later edition.[45] None is so purely concerned with the development of an idea as an elegy among his *Diverses Poésies* published in 1597.[46] As is often the case with Papillon, the idea is a rather unconventional one. He finds it strange that men prefer to marry widows

...qui ont eu plusieurs sortes d'espoux,
Deux, trois, quatre, cinq, six dont quelque laide, ou belle
A eu chaque mary diuers ans auec elle,
De qui le naturel estoit luxurieux,
Ioüant... au jeu delicieux, (ll. 4-8)

How strange to prefer to marry women who have had such experience behind them rather than a woman who has had "un seul Amy

---

45 See Catalogue 135, p. 532. Renamed in Catalogue 138.
46 See Catalogue 135, p. 453.

honneste" (l. 10). For Papillon, this is nothing but "folle opinion" (l. 12):

> Penseroyent-ils qu'Hymen eust ceste vertu telle,
> Qu'ayant faict vne femme il la refist pucelle? (ll. 21-2)

These reflections lead to a diatribe against the hypocrisy of marriage and the revelation that the poet himself prefers liberty and variety, which contribute to the perfecting of one's knowledge of the pleasures of love (ll. 39-46).

Although none of these last fourteen elegies that we have discussed is obviously an *épître*, Papon's poem to Anne d'Urfé, the Papillon elegies to Henri IV and the one to his friend Montigny have a consistent, personal address. The above poem by Papillon is also addressed to a friend, Saincte Coulombe, but here a certain ambiguity arises from his apostrophes to the foolish and hypocritical people who do not share his ideas on love and marriage. Another three elegies by Papillon do not have a personal address but apostrophize his book, France, and his muse, Clio. Three more elegies are of this type: La Roque speaks to all mankind ("miserables pecheurs"); Perault is concerned with the reader of Virbluneau's book; and the anonymous poem about the peace of 1598 contains a number of apostrophes, principally to the women of Lyons. Finally, Vauquelin provides us with an example as confused as any that we have found in the sixteenth century. The first 136 lines of the elegy about Desportes have no address at all; from line 137 to 160, Desportes is spoken of in the third person, but he is addressed in lines 161-176; the last lines of the poem suddenly address the poet's lady, Anne. Altogether, then, only five elegies by Papillon and the one elegy that Papon has given us can be likened in any way to the *épître* genre.

In summing up this last period in our study of the elegy, we notice first of all that no new types of poem have been offered to us: the subjects remain typical of what we have found at least since the 1550's. Love still holds the main interest of our poets; death is of slight importance; and the elegy is considered to be a fit title for poems which have little or no lament attached to them at all – the poems of flattery and request, autobiographical elegies, liminary elegies, poems which develop ideas. These are all types which we found in the works of Ronsard and his contemporaries and most of these types were to be found before 1550. We cannot point to any new development, then, in the use of the genre.

There is a tendency, however, for the love-elegy to gain favour over all other types to a greater degree than has been usual in its history throughout the century. More than three quarters of the poems discussed in this chapter deal with love; the remaining poems show no other strong tendency. It is impossible, of course, to determine why the love-elegy should become so imposing during the last decade of the century but the example of Desportes no doubt encouraged this tendency. Desportes was still a most influential and popular poet at this time, as can be seen by a glance at a bibliography of his works. The character of his language and his style, which Vauquelin remarked on in his eulogy, was being felt more and more strongly in the writing of most poets: our elegies in the 1590's usually display little erudition in their images and developments, and the syntax and vocabulary are generally clear and uncomplicated. The example of Ronsard, however, is not to be ignored. After 1584, the reader would notice that the book devoted to elegies in Ronsard's works contained mainly love-poems, and, because of the great number of title changes, the other parts of the collected poems would not offer so very many examples of elegies treating other subjects. It is, perhaps, not too far from the truth to suggest that it was the example of both Ronsard and Desportes, the two poets whom the men of the 1590's must have studied with their greatest attention, that contributed to the emphasis on love as a subject.

As for the total number of elegies, it does not seem particularly great when it is remembered that some of them were published after 1600 and that others were perhaps composed before 1590. The reason for a certain slowing down in the writing of elegies can be attributed to the preference at the end of the century for lyric forms rather than for poems in couplets. If we look through the works of a typical enough poet like La Roque, we find that apart from his elegies, there are only a very few other poems in couplets: a few *discours* and a *hymne*. This tendency towards strophic verse explains a further decrease in the writing of elegies in the seventeenth century.

That the fate of the couplet and of the elegy should be connected is not, of course, surprising. Ever since Marot, the couplet had been the favoured form, although from time to time certain poets either tried to imitate the classical distich or chose quite arbitrarily a strophic form. At the end of the century we find no more attemps at imitating the distich, and only three poems depart from either decasyllabic or alexandrine couplets. One of these three exceptions is still in couplets, but Pasquier seemed to feel that a seven-syllable line was more appropriate for his *basium* elegy. Our other exceptions are by two very obscure poets who wrote only one elegy each: Le Cauchois very strangely gives the title elegy to a double sonnet, and Virbluneau writes his elegy in *huitains*. There are no significant experiments, then, at the end of the century: the couplet is the accepted form of the elegy.

CONCLUSION

In summing up the work of the Pléiade, Henri Chamard found himself bound to admit that the elegy was "le plus singulier, le plus déconcertant... le plus obscur"[1] of the genres still to be used after the *marotiques*. Certainly it is *déconcertant* and *obscur* in the case of Ronsard, whose elegies undergo more second thoughts and title-changes than any other genres in his writing. The elegy is also perhaps *déconcertant* if one tries to see the century in terms of the great names alone: the elegy's history is not always what one would expect from a knowledge of the examples to be found in anthologies.

Despite the difficulties of trying to put tidiness and order into the sixteenth-century's sizable production of elegies, it is possible to see certain patterns and a certain evolution in the use of the title. In its beginnings the elegy is absolutely *not* new insofar as its form, content, and style are concerned. A number of existing French genres are simply disguised by a new title, and the most important disguise is Marot's perhaps devious use of the glamorous new word for his rigidly conventional *épîtres amoureuses*. Marot does not succeed in converting everyone to his approach, however, and already in a poet like Fontaine in 1545 there is considerably greater freedom in the use of *épître* conventions. Also visible in Fontaine's writing is a mixture of styles which will be exemplified in the love-elegy of the 1550's and 1560's, giving to that period as a whole a character of indecision. Bérenger de La Tour and Jean de La Taille appear to be latter-day Marots as against Forcadel and Turrin, who seem to exploit a précieux strain in sixteenth-century poetry, one of

---

[1] Henri Chamard, *Histoire de la Pléiade*, 4 vols. (Paris: Didier, 1939-40), IV, 162.

lush elaboration of predictable commonplaces. At the same time, we find Doublet's attempt to become France's Ovid and (although his poems were published much later) Passerat's similar interest in the classical elegy during the following decade.

All this production of love-elegies in various styles (between 1550 and 1570) must be seen against the works of Ronsard and the influence of the historical moment. Until the mid 1560's Ronsard went against the current by disguising all his *épîtres* as elegies and omitting almost exclusively love-themes. Thus the elegy comes to deal with many subjects, and, although quite clearly epistolary in nature, the tone and style begin to be more serious, leading the way clearly to the *discours*. The civil disturbances of the 1560's also encourage the use of the elegy for subjects more serious than love, and the surprisingly prominent deplorative elegy of the 1560's is different from earlier – and later – examples by seeing broad historical issues in the individual death.

The 1560's are thus troubled times for the history of the elegy. Ronsard only begins to show interest in the love-elegy during these years but continues to exploit other types more enthusiastically; deplorative elegies are unusually common; poetic style is not bound by any one source or tradition. In comparison with all of this, the reign of Henri III appears as not only the richest period for the production of elegies but also the clearest in its tendencies.

Desportes ushers in the new age of love-elegies with a type of poem which is hardly blatantly original but which nevertheless combines a number of features which become the accepted principles for most of his contemporaries. His elegies are still basically *épîtres amoureuses*, but they reflect what has been happening with increasing clarity during the preceding decades: the nature of the address is not emphasized as epistolary and its presence is weakened by the use of apostrophe. The use of the epic simile mirrors stylistically the poet's emphasis on lengthy analysis or description of the lover's experience. An enormous production of love-elegies during the 1570's and 1580's follows these habits of Desportes. At the same time the fairly numerous death-elegies return to a much more literary and flattering style – their usual vein except for the 1560's – and the elegy of ideas, the *discours*-type, becomes less common than during the 1560's as the title *discours* itself becomes more common.

During the reign of Henri III the love-elegy predominates easily, and, although the total number of elegies declines at the end of the century, the proportion of love-elegies to other types is greatly increased. Thus the last quarter of the sixteenth century reveals the triumph of love as the proper subject of the elegy, and by the end of the century the connection of the elegy with the *épître* is extremely weak. The elegy is no longer the familiar in disguise but often a genuinely new type of poem in French, a remarkably loose and free form. By the use of couplets, the prosody was, of course, the freest conceivable in the sixteenth century; by removing the conventions of epistolary address and even the concept of address at all, the elegy came frequently to be used as an intimate expression or analysis of emotional states. This type of elegy had already appeared on very rare occasions in the earlier part of the century: one thinks of the beautiful poem by Pernette du Guillet, and at the same time one also thinks of an interesting general comment on the Lyons poets by Albert-Marie Schmidt:

> Avant eux, les plus grands poètes français…mêlaient sans doute des traits biographiques à leurs poèmes, mais aucun d'entre eux ne s'essayait (sauf Villon) de peindre sa *personnalité* dans son incohérence, dans sa variété durable, dans sa complexité, dans sa plénitude.
>
> Pour la première fois, au contraire, en France, les poètes lyonnais entendirent, de propos délibéré, créer non pas une *littérature subjective* mais une *littérature personnelle*. Ils firent concourir littérairement tout ce qu'ils savaient, tout ce qu'ils voyaient, tout ce qu'ils sentaient, tout ce qu'ils aimaient, tout ce qu'ils souhaitaient, à l'expression de leur personne, c'est-à-dire de leur *individualité propre* en tant qu'elle pâtit, agit, progresse et s'accomplit, en chaque point de la durée, sur tous les plans de l'être et du cosmos.[2]

It would be incorrect to apply this comment to all our elegists at the end of the century, but it is true, and it is very significant, that the elegy had become a genre which would easily permit this revelation of the writer's *personnalité* and *individualité propre*.

The evolution of the elegy throughout our century is thus not

[2] A.-M. Schmidt, "Poètes lyonnais du XVIe siècle", in *L'Information littéraire*, IV (1952), 90-94, 127-130. See 130.

without its surprises. We have suggested that the most famous poets are not necessarily always the most important in their influence or experiment. Marot has no influence until after his death; Doublet and not the Pléiade is responsible for the most notable contribution to classical imitation; it is a host of little poets who finally cause the breakdown of conventions of address and not really the Ronsards and the Desportes. The overall evolution of the elegy is perhaps unusually dependent on the many rather than the few, although we have emphasized the rôle of Desportes in clarifying a number of important trends in the later years of the century.

One could perhaps be surprised as well by the only incidental rapport between theory and practice with regard to the elegy. Sebillet describes very well only what happens in Marot's elegies; Ronsard's or Du Bellay's comments do not even apply with particular point to their own poems! On the whole the theorists are embarrassed by their knowledge of classical theory and practice and of sixteenth-century practice. Attempts at reconciliation do not turn out to be more than partially appropriate.

The real surprise in store for the student of the elegy is the lack of influence of classical theory and practice, which must have been well known to at least many of our poets. Paradoxically, when we come upon elegies which seem somewhat unusual, they often turn out to be precisely those which have some element of classical imitation – one thinks of Doublet, Passerat, the second volume of Desportes, and Guy de Tours. Also paradoxically the Pléiade poets are strangely disinclined to imitate the Latin elegists. They made a few attempts at recreating the distich (Ronsard, Baïf, Jodelle); they borrowed some images and ideas – but images and ideas which they as willingly used in other genres. Other poets showed little more enthusiasm, but if one can point to any moment of particular interest in the classical elegy it would be during the 1550's. The signs are slight, however, and one must conclude that the French elegy does not find, except sporadically, a distinctive prosodic form, the really crucial distinguishing feature of the classical and neo-Latin elegy; nor does it exploit the Latin vein of erotic love-themes, although ultimately it will be primarily a love-poem. The sixteenth-century poet could adopt almost wholesale the typical Pindaric or Horatian themes for his odes and also base his prosody on classical examples, but when it came to the elegy the pagan approach to the war of the sexes was simply not *à propos* or permissible. When one remembers how apologetic poets always were concerning their love poetry devoid of any overt eroticism of the classical type, one suspects that 'permissible' might be the appropriate word. Finally it is interesting to note that the main development in the sixteenth-century elegy, the freedom from address, is not inspired by classical practices.

The elegy, a minor genre with only infrequent examples of great poetic worth, is finally a very significant and original experiment in the sixteenth century. In a culture where rhetoric had such a fundamental rôle in defining poetry, its nature and its practices, it would be hard indeed to conceive of poetic statement as free from an expression of rapport between a speaker and a person spoken-to. In practice the poetry of the sixteenth century rarely provides us with examples where such a rapport does not exist. Thus the creation of a free poem like the elegy was an important step in the creation of truly intimate verse. No other genre provided the formal freedom of the elegy; only with the formal freedom of the couplet was the freedom from a rhetorical framework truly meaningful. In the elegy alone could a poet express himself with any amount of expansiveness and with complete choice in directing his statement. One might conclude that the elegy became the ideal romantic genre.

CATALOGUE OF *ÉLÉGIES*

(Excluding Ronsard)

It would be sanguine in the extreme to suggest that the following list of elegies is absolutely complete. It is hoped, however, that the obscurity of so many of them and the listing even of some which are no longer to be found today will inspire in the reader a certain confidence that nothing very obvious or important has been overlooked. The matter of Ronsard's elegies is so complicated that a separate listing seemed in order: a catalogue of them follows this one.

The elegies are listed here according to their date of publication if there is a sixteenth-century edition. In a few cases where a manuscript was not published until the nineteenth or twentieth centuries, the date of composition is the determining factor. More information is generally given about the rarer, earlier elegies than about the all too common later ones.

The general bibliography should be consulted for full details concerning critical works mentioned in the Catalogue: here, they are identified as briefly as possible.

The following abbreviations are used:

B. N.	–	Bibliothèque Nationale, Paris
B. M.	–	British Museum, London
Ars.	–	Arsenal, Paris
Maz.	–	Mazarine, Paris
dc.	–	decasyllabic couplet(s)
ac.	–	alexandrine couplet(s)
oct. c.	–	octosyllabic couplet(s)

nd. – no date
np. – no place of publication
ns. – new system

1505

1. d'Auton, Jean, "La Complaincte de Gennes sur la Mort de Dame Thomassine Espinolle, Genevoise, Dame Intendyo du Roy, Avecques l'Epitaphe et le Regret", in the *Cronicque de France de l'an mille cinq cens et cincq*. There are no contemporary editions; for the text and notes on the mss. see the edition of the *Chroniques de Louis XII par Jean d'Auton* prepared by R. de Maulde La Clavière, 4 vols. (Paris: Renouard, 1889-1895), II, 1 and IV, 13.

The poem is made up as follows: an introductory section of 76 lines in dc.; "Complaincte elegiacque" in stanzas (1-6 rhyme AABAABBCCDCD, 7-18 rhyme ABABBCCDD; all lines are decasyllables); "Epitaphe parlant par la bouche de la deffunte", dc.; "Regret que faict le Roy pour la mort de sa dame intendyo" consisting of a *ballade* and a *rondeau*.

1512

2. d'Auton, Jean, "Epistre elegiaque par leglise millitante transmise au roy trescrestien loys douziesme composee par frere iehan dauton abbe dangle hystoriographe diceluy seigneur", in *Poëmes en forme d'Epitres, composés par les Beaux-Esprits du tems de Louis XII. Roy de France écrits et peint(s) en Italie, pendant son Sejour, dediés à la Reine Anne de Brétagne Son Epouse*, ms. in folio (vellum, 113 folios and 11 miniatures), Library of Leningrad.

D'Auton's poem (498 lines, dc.) dates from 1512. We have been able to get a microfilm of the whole manuscript. Concerning it, see Maulde La Clavière's edition of d'Auton, I, xxxii.

1516

3. Michel de Tours, Guillaume, *La Forest de conscience contenant la chasse des princes spirituelle* (Paris: Michel le noir, 1516), in-8 (B. M. 241. g. 35). A second edition appeared in 1520, same place (B. N. Rés. Ye. 3214).

The one elegy in this volume is in oct. c., 295 (sic) lines, and is entitled "Elegie sus le propos de peche et vanite".

1518

4. Michel de Tours, Guillaume, *Le Penser de royal memoire* (Paris: pour Jehan de la Garde et Pierre Le Brodeur, 1518), in-4 (B. N. Rés. Ye. 376).

The one elegy is preceded and followed by prose and is a segment of the poet's argument. The title is "Les elegies/ thre(n)es et lamentations/ de Leglise contre les gens ecclesiasticques dissoluz et aultres" and it is in dc. (216 lines).

1526

5. Michel de Tours, Guillaume, *Les elegies threnes & complainctes sur la mort de tresilustre dame madame Claude: iadis en son viuant royne de France* (np., 1526), in-16 (B. N. Rés. Ye. 1426).

Despite the plural of the title there is only the one poem (492 lines, dc.), but it is followed by a passage of prose. It is unlikely that the prose is intended as part of the elegy since it begins: "Ainsi que de plus fort en plus fort me lamentoys et formois en längoisse de ma piteuse poictrine mes elegies complainctes et clameurs..." (folio B ii verso). We thus go from lament to 'action' in this change from verse to prose (Hope appears before the prostrate poet etc.).

1534

6. Marot, Clément, *La Suite de l'adolescence Clementine* (Paris: veuve Roffet, nd.), in-8 (B. N. Rés. Ye. 1534).

The date of this edition is either 1534 or the end of 1533 (see Mayer, *Bibliographie*, II, 16). This first edition of elegies by Marot contains twenty-one examples, the first twenty which are found in most modern editions (for example, Guiffrey) plus a poem called "La X. Elegie en forme de Ballade" ("Amour me voyant sans tristesse"), which V.-L. Saulnier numbers as IX bis in his study of the elegies: the poem has been placed among the other *ballades* since the edition of 1544. We do not accept as an intended elegy Saulnier's XX bis, the *rondeau* "Contre raison Fortune l'esvolée". Unlike the *ballade*, this poem (which comes at the end of the elegies only in the 1534 edition) was not numbered as an elegy. All twenty-one of the first elegies by Marot deal with the theme of love.

1536

7. Corrozet, Gilles, *Triste Elegie ou deploration. Lamentant le trespas de feu et treshault et puissant prince Francoys de Valloys Duc de Bretaigne et Daulphin de Viennoys: Filz aisne du Roy treschrestien Francoys premier de ce nom Roy de France. Recentement apres toutes aultres mise a lumiere* (Paris: Corrozet, 1536), in-8 (B. N. Rés. Ye. 1410).

There is some question about the authorship of this poem. We have decided to accept S. M. Bouchereaux's attribution of it to Corrozet; references to this poem are found in his articles in 1948, p. 148; 1949, pp. 149-150; 1954, p. 261. The poem is written in eleven sections followed by an epitaph, a ballad (a dialogue) and a dizain. The eleven parts contain an allegory, the *autheur* alternating regularly with four personifications. The principal stanza-form used is ABAABBCC, either dc. or oct. c.

8. Le Blond, Jean, *Le printemps de l'Humble esperant, aultrement dict Jehan Leblond, seigneur de Branville, où sont comprins plusieurs petitz œuvres semez de fleurs, fruict et verdure qu'il a composez en son jeune aage, fort recreatifz, comme on pourra*

veoir à la table (Paris: A. Langelier, 1536), in-8 (B. N. Rés. Ye. 1652).

Contains an "Epistre elegiacque de lhumble esperant a sa dame en Rythme alexandrine" and an "Epistre delegie" in dc.

9. Luc, Robinet de, "Les poésies de Robinet de Luc brodeur de François Ier", edited by Eugénie Droz, *Bibliothèque d'humanisme et renaissance*, III (1943), 43-50.

Luc composed an epistolary elegy (dc.) in 1536 concerning the death of his new-born son right after the death of the dauphin.

1537

10. Saliat, Pierre, *Elegie nuptiale*, written for the marriage of François Ier's daughter, Madeleine, to King James V of Scotland. This poem, mentioned by La Croix du Maine, II, 320, is thought to be lost, but the B. N. owns a *plaquette* of four leaves without special title-page, containing an anonymous *Elegie Nuptiale Presentee A Tresnoble & tresillustre Princesse Madame Magdaleine premiere fille de France, le lendemain de ses nopces & mariage celebré avec le Roy d'Escoce* (np., nd.), in-8 (Rés. Ye. 3955).

The poem tries to persuade Madeleine of her good fortune in 198 ll. of dc.

11. Bouchet, Jean, *Les angoysses & remedes damours Du Trauerseur en son adolescence* (Poitiers, Marnef [Iehan & Enguilbert], 1536 [1537 ns.]), in-4 (B. N. Rés. Ye. 360).

The work appeared as well in 1538 (ns.), 1545 (with the *Annales d'Acquitaine*), 1550, in an undated edition and again at the end of the century; it is based on a very early work which appeared at the beginning of the century in pirated editions, such as *Lamoureux transy sans espoir* (Paris: Jehan Janot), in-4 (B. N. Rés. Ye. 364). Only two of the four elegies of 1537 appear in these early editions, and then in very different form and without the title elegy. The four elegies have the following forms:

I: A10A10A10B4, B10B10B10C4 etc.; II: the stanzas alternate in lines of 10 and 8 syllables but the rhyme-scheme is always AABAABBBABBA; III: AABAABBBCC, decasyllables; IV: AABAABBCCDCCD, decasyllables.

12. Sagon, Françoys, *Deffense de Sagon Contre Clement Marot, On la vend au mont Sainct Hylaire deuant le College de Reims* (nd.), in-8 (B. N. Fonds Rothschild 2594 [IV, 5, 17]).

Contains "Elegie par Francoys de Sagon, se complaignant a luy mesmes daucuns que ne prennent bien lintention de son Coup d'essay, dont il frappa Marot", 314 lines, dc.

1538

13. Marot, Clément, *Les Œuvres de Clement Marot de Cahors, valet de chambre du Roy. Augmentées de deux Livres d'Epigrammes, Et dung grand nombre d'aultres Œuvres par cy devant non imprimées. Le tout songneusement par luy mesmes reveu, et mieulx ordonné* (Lyon: Dolet, 1538), in-8 (B. N. Rés. Ye. 1457-1460).

Six new elegies, which accompany the twenty-one published in the *Suite de l'Adolescence Clementine*. Of the new poems, half deal with love but the remaining three deal with death. In Guiffrey's edition these poems are numbered XXI-XXVI.

1540

14. Sainte-Marthe, Charles de, *La Poesie Francoise de Charles de Saincte Marthe natif de Fontevrault en Poictout. Diuisée en trois Livres. Le tout addressé à tres noble & tresillustre, Princesse Madame la Duchesse d'Estampes & Contesse en Poinctievre. Plus, Vn Livre de ses Amys* (Lyon: chés le Prince, 1540), in-8 (B. N. Rés p. Ye. 193).

Contains six elegies, sometimes epistolary, dealing with serious themes generally of a moral nature. Four are in dc., one in ac., and one in quatrains (A10A10A10B4; BBBC etc.).

1544

15. Colet, Claude, *L'oraison de Mars aux Dames de la Court. Ensemble la Response des Dames à Mars, par Claude Colet Champanoys* (Paris: Chrestien Wechel, 1544), in -4 (B. N. Rès p. Ye. 390).

One elegy of 48 lines in quatrains (A10A10A10B4; BBBC etc.). A second edition in 1548 gives a title clearly indicating the subject: "Elegie du bien de la guerre, au peuple Francoys".

16. Deheris, Guillaume, *Elegie delectable et fructueuse de la guerre & victoire de Vertu contre Fortune contenant la mort & Epitaphe de la dicte Fortune par Guillaume deheris de Bourges en Berri* (Anvers: Iehan Loe, 1544), in-4 (B. N. Rés. Ye. 347).

Long allegorical *débat* in dc.

1545

17. Fontaine, Charles, *La Fontaine d'Amour* (Lyon: Jean de Tournes, 1545), in-8 (B. M. 1073. d. 34). A second edition appears in 1546 (Paris: Marnef), in-16 (B. N. Rés. Ye. 1609).

The book devotes a whole section to twenty-two elegies. All are in dc., between about 30-80 lines in length, epistolary in character. Love is the theme with only one exception ("La XVIII. Elégie faite pour le Receveur de Glatigny, adressée à Monsieur du Brueil", a poem of praise and compliments but not of love in any sentimental way). Fontaine's elegies are difficult to date, but stylistically they seem to be later than his poems of 1536 and 1537, and, since there is no trace of the platonism which becomes important after his 1541 *Contr'amye de court*, it is likely that at least the bulk of the poems were composed between 1538 and 1541, just before and after his trip to Italy.

1546

18. Du Guillet, Pernette, *Les Rithmes et Poesies de Gentile et Ver-*
    tueuse Dame D. Pernette Du Guillet Lyonnoise. Auecq' le
    Triumphe des Muses sur Amour; Et autres nouuelles composi-
    tions (Paris: Jeanne de Marnef, 1546), in-12 (B. N. Rés. Ye.
    1342).

    In the posthumous edition of the preceding year no poem bears
    the title elegy. In 1546 the title is used twice, for "Combien de
    fois ay-je en moy souhaicté" and very curiously for a series of
    epigrams, "Autre Elegie par dixains et huitains". Love is the
    subject throughout; the *épître* is nowhere in evidence. Since
    Saulnier's study on Pernette it is usual to consider a number
    of other poems as elegies, but there is no sixteenth-century
    source involved.

19. Aurigny, Gilles d', *Le Tuteur d'Amour, auquel est comprise*
    la fortune de l'Innocent en amours, ensemble un livre où sont
    epistres, elegies, complainctes, epitaphes, chants royaulx, bal-
    lades et rondeaux. Avec un aultre livre d'épigrammes (Paris:
    Arnoul l'Angelié, 1546), in-8 (B. N. Rés. Ye. 1615).

    In the second edition (Lyon: Jean de Tournes, 1547), in-8
    (B. N. Rés. Ye. 1616), the three elegies are set off more clearly
    from the preceding thirteen *épîtres* by the title *ELEGIES* in
    large print. D'Aurigny's poems are not, in fact *épîtres*, but
    they deal with the theme of love in dc.

1547

20. Bardin, Medard, *Elegie de Feu Vatable, Lecteur en Hebreu,*
    pour le Roy en l'Vniversité de Paris. Auecq' l'épitaphe d'iceluy.
    Par Medard Bardin, Chanoyne Oyssery en Brie (Paris: Estienne
    Groulleau, 1547), in-8 (B. N. Fonds Rothschild 2598 [IV. 3.
    184]).

    A poem of 78 lines in dc. The poem is quite biblical in its
    decoration, and the importance of Hebrew as a study is em-
    phasized at the expense of the deplorative element.

1548

21. Forcadel, Etienne, *Le Chant des Sereines. Avec plusieurs compositions nouvelles* (Paris: Corrozet, 1548), in-8 (B. N. Rés. Ye. 4021).

Contains two elegies which reappear in 1551 (Catalogue 26) as elegies II and III.

(before 1550)

22. Marion, Jehan, *Rondeaulx et Vers d'Amour par Jehan Marion Poëte Nivernois du XVIe siècle. Publiés pour la première fois par Prosper Blanchemain* (Paris: Leon Willem, 1873).

There is one elegy in dc., an *épître* complaining of his lady's lack of favour. Marion is a completely unknown poet.

1550

23. Jamet, Lyon, "Elegie sur le trespas de feu monsieur Charles de valoys duc d'Orleans", in *Traductions de Latin en Françoys, Imitations, et Inventions nouvelles, tant de Clement Marot, que d'autres des plus excellens Poetes de ce temps* (Paris: Estienne Grouleau, 1550), in-8 (B. N. Rés. p. Yc. 1646).

The elegy probably dates from 1545; 24 lines in dc. No other poem in the section called "Elegies" bears the title elegy; the poems are in fact generally in recognizable fixed forms or resemble epigrams. "D'vn Cordelier et d'aucuns soldatz" by Eustorg de Beaulieu and "Les conditions de l'amye moderne" by Mellin de Saint-Gelais could perhaps be regarded as elegies, but they are not so called in other editions of the works of these authors.

1551

24. Papillon, Almanque, one elegy in *Le Mespris de la court auec la commendation de la Vie Rustique, Nouuellement traduict d'Espagnol en Francoys. L'Amye de Court, la Parfecte Amye, La Contr'amye. L'Androgyne de Platon, L' Expérience de l'Amye*

de Court, contre la Contr'amye. L'Honneste Amant. Le Nouuel Amour. Auec plusieurs Epistres, Elegies & Dizains, au propos que dessus (Paris: Iehan Ruelle, 1550 [1551 ns.]), in-16 (Ars. 3245S).

Papillon's "Le Nouuel Amour" begins with a superscription "Epistre allez…" but it ends with: "Fin de l'Elegie douloureuse". An edition of the poem in 1543 (an anthology, *Les questions problématiques du pourquoy d'Amours…*, see Lachèvre, 60) has no mention of the word elegy anywhere. On the other hand the 1568 anthology *Le Mespris de la Court avec la Vie Rustique* (Lachèvre, 153-4) gives as a running title at the top of the page *L'Elegie Douloureuse* as well as "Fin de l'Elegie douloureuse, enuoyee d'une dame de Rouen à son amy qui est en court". The poem is a typical *épître* in dc.

25. La Tour d'Albenas, Bérenger de, *Le Siècle d'or, Et autres vers diuers* (Lyon: Jean de Tournes, 1551), in-8 (B. N. Rés. Ye. 1653).

    Thirteen elegies, uncomplicated *épîtres amoureuses* in dc.

26. Forcadel, Etienne, *La Poesie d'Estienne Forcadel* (Lyon: Jean de Tournes, 1551), in-8 (B. N. Rés. Ye. 1824).

    Contains in more elaborate form the two elegies of 1548 (Catalogue 21) and eight new elegies. Very weak link with the *épître*; love themes in dc. A posthumous edition, *Les Œuvres poétiques* (Paris: Chaudière, 1579), in-8, gives the same ten poems in considerably more ornamented form.

1553

27. Du Bellay, Joachim, *Recueil de poésie…Reveu et augmenté depuis la première édition* (Paris: G. Cavellat, 1553), in-8 (B. N. Rés. Ye. 1854).

    Contains one love-elegy, epistolary, in dc.

28. Des Autels, Guillaume, *Amoureux Repos de Guillaume des*

Autelz Gentilhomme Charrolois (Lyon: Iean Temporal, 1553), in-8 (B. N. Rés. Ye. 1405).

Contains a single elegy, which attemps to be classical in inspiration and form. The love-theme here is not very characteristic of the Latin elegy, however, and the poet contents himself by indenting every second dc. so that the eye has the impression of a form reminiscent of the classical distich.

1554

29. Tahureau, Jacques, *Sonnetz, Odes, Et Mignardises Amoureuses de l'Admiree* (Poitiers: Chez les de Marnefs et Bouchetz freres, 1554), in-8 (B. M. 1073. d. 32).

Contains two elegies, the first (dc.) based on Propertius II, i (concerning the choice of love as a poetic theme) and the second (ac.) a very narrative poem on the death of Françoise Belot.

30. Le Caron, Louis, *La Claire ou De la prudence de droit, Dialogue Premier. Plus La clarté amoureuse* (Paris: Guillaume Cauellat, 1554), in-8 (B. N. F. 38413).

Contains an "Elegie de l'amoureus desesperé", not epistolary and in quatrains (ABBA, decasyllables).

1555

31. Fontaine, Charles, *Sensuyvent les ruisseaux de Fontaine: Oeuure contenant Epitres, Elegies, Chants diuers, Epigrammes, Odes & Estrenes pour cette presante annee 1555* (Lyon: T. Payan, 1555), in-8 (B. N. Rés. Ye. 1610).

Two elegies, on the death of his sister (about 1540) and on the death of his son (about 1547), dc. but very different in style.

32. Labé, Louise, *Euures de Louize Labe lionnoize* (Lyon: Ian de Tournes, 1555), in-8 (B. N. Rés. Ye. 1651).

Three elegies in dc. about love, only II in the *épître amoureuse* style; the other two are more *épîtres artificielles*, addressing the women of Lyons. The poems were composed between 1549 and 1555.

33. Tahureau, Jacques, *Oraison de Jaques Tahureau au Roy: de la grandeur de son règne, de l'excellence de la langue françoyse. Plus quelques vers du mesme autheur, dédiez à Madame Marguerite* (Paris: Chez la veufue Maurice de la Porte, 1555), in-4 (B. N. 4° Lb.[31] 62).

After the *Oraison*, one elegy lamenting a death in ac.

34. La Péruse, Jean, *La Medee, Tragedie. Et autres diverses Poesies, Par I. de La Peruse* (Poitiers: les de Marnefz et Bouchetz freres, nd.), in-4 (B. N. Yf. 504). In handwriting on this copy is the generally accepted date 1555; Banachévitch (See Bibliography) is inclined to think 1556 more accurate (65-72). The edition is posthumous in any case since La Péruse died in 1554.

The poems date from 1553-54. The section of elegies presents problems: no poem is called elegy but the running title ELEGIES at the top of the page unites seven poems presumably as elegies. There is, however, an exception made for the fifth poem: the running title momentarily becomes ORAISON for the "Oraison Pour Auoir Santé". The fourth poem, a short "Epitaphe d'Anne de Poulignac Contesse de Sancerre & de la Roche-focaud" can also be safely eliminated. The seventh poem is also scarcely like any elegy: it is a ten-line *odelette* on the *carpe diem* theme. Three of the four remaining poems which we regard as elegies are on the theme of death, two in ac. and one (on the death of a child) in a curious quatrain system of 7-syllable lines: the poem begins and ends with a quatrain of the type ABAB, A-rhyme feminine and B masculine; the rest of the poem is then formed by alternating a pair of masculine couplets with a pair of feminine couplets. The fourth elegy is in sextains (A7A7B5C7C7B5) and is a poem of farewell to a friend. According to Banachévitch (207) it is more like an ode, and we agree.

35. Habert, François, *La Louange et Vitupere de Pecune; Elegie morale sur deux vers d'Horace; Priere à Dieu faites (sic) par Manassès, Roi de Juda; Cantique sur l'Avant-naissance du huitieme enfant du Roi Henri II, né à Fontainebleau, en l'an 1555, nommé Hercules, Duc d'Anjou: Epigrammes: le tout imprimé à Paris audit an.*

Lost, mentioned by Du Verdier. See Henri Franchet's edition of Habert's *Le Philosophe parfaict et le Temple de Vertu*, xxix. La Croix du Maine mentions an edition of 1558 but it is no longer an elegy but an *Eglogue morale sur Horace* that is mentioned. This edition appears to be lost as well.

1556

36. Tahureau, Jacques, an "Elegie" prefacing: *Cinq premiers Livres de l'Histoire Françoise traduits en François du Latin de Paul Aemile, Par Jean Regnart Angevin* (Paris: Fezandat, 1556), in-fol. (B. N. Rés. L. ³⁵ 26).

The poem is a verse preface (ac). which praises Regnart but deals generally as well with matters of a literary nature.

37. Flory, Iehan, one elegy in *Elegies ou Deplorations sur le trespas de monsieur Philibert de Rye, prince & euesque de Geneue: Et de tresillustre seigneur René de Chalon, Prince d'Orenge & seigneur de Nozeret &c. Auec celle du trespas de tres uertueuse dame Antoyne de Monmartin, iadis femme de messire Iehan de Popet, cheualier & seigneur de la Chaux* (Lyon: Zachee Quadrier, 1556), in-4 (Besançon Bel. let. 2948).

Flory's poem, "Elegie et Funebre histoire sur le trespas de Philibert de Rye, prince & Euesque de Geneve" is the longest poem (and only elegy) of the anthology: 1224 lines in dc. The poem is a typical deploration. Lachèvre (234) dates this work 1553 but he was unable to find a copy of it.

1557

38. Bugnyon, Philibert, *Erotasmes De Phidie Et Gelasine Plus, Le*

chant Panegyrique de l'Isle Pontine: avec la gaieté de May (Lyon: Iean Temporal, 1557), in-8 (B. N. Rés. Ye. 1683).

An *épître* in dc. asking for a letter during the regretted absence of the poet's beloved.

39. Des Masures, Louis, *Œuures Poëtiques de Louïs Des Masures Tournisien* (Lyon: Iean de Tournes & Guillaume Gazeau, 1557), in-4 (B. N. Rés. Ye. 366).

One elegy in dc. which expresses the joy that his "mutuelle flamme" has brought him.

1558

40. Du Bellay, Joachim, *Divers Ieux Rustiques et autres oeuures poetiques de Ioachim Du Bellay* (Paris: F. Morel, 1558), in-4 (B. N. Rés. Ye. 412).

Contains two love-elegies, epistolary, dc.

41. Julyot, Ferry, *Elegies de la belle fille, lamentant sa Virginité perdue auec plusieurs Epistres, Epigrammes, Instruction & Traductions morales. Composees par Ferry Iulyot de la Cité imperiale de Bezanson. Imprimé aux despens d'Antoine Ludin, escuyer, citoyen dudit Bezanson, au moys de Mars, 1557* (1558 ns.), in-8 (B. N. Rés. p. Ye. 96).

Eight elegies recount the misadventures of the hapless girl, two monologues and six *épîtres*, mainly *artificielles*. A ninth elegy is a prayer to God that He free Besançon from plagues (1544). All the poems are in dc.

1559

42. Doublet, Jean, *Elegies de Ian Doublet Dieppoys* (Paris: Langelier, 1559), in-4 (B. N. Rés. p. Ye. 378).

Twenty-six elegies, all using a quatrain which was intended by the author to be an equivalent of the classical distich: A10B10A8B8. Fourteen poems deal with love, but not par-

ticularly in the classical erotic style. The other twelve poems
are on a great variety of themes.

43. Magny, Olivier de, *Les Odes d'Olivier de Magny de Cahors en
Quercy* (Paris: André Wechel, 1559), in-8 (B. N. Rés. Ye.
1706).

Two elegies in dc., one a simple *épître amoureuse* about his
lady's absence, and the other a long (172 lines) allegorical
narrative involving the poet's meeting with Cupid.

1560

44. Habert, François, *Les Epistres Heroïdes Pour seruir d'exemple
aux Chrestiens, Reueues & amplifiées depuis la première impression* (Paris: Michel Fezandat, 1560), in-8 (B. N. Rés. p.
Ye. 248).

Contains "Elegie de l'auteur à monseigneur le Mareschal de
Termes...", which does not appear with the 1550 or 1551 editions of *Les Epistres Heroïdes*. The poem (58 lines, dc.) is one
of fulsome praise of the maréchal. At a much earlier date
Habert uses the word elegy in a confused but more conventional way: in his *Deploration Poetique de Feu M. Antoine du
Prat...* (Lyon: Iean de Tournes, 1545), in-8, he says at one
point that he put aside writing "ioyeuses elegies, / Dont les
amours des Amans sont regis" (p. 13, ll. 2-3); later on he says
"Ie changeray toute epistre amoureuse / En elegie amere &
douloureuse" (p. 19, ll. 14-5). To add to the general confusion,
cf. Catalogue 35.

45. Grévin, Jacques, *L'Olimpe de Iaques Grevin de Cler-mont en
Beauuaisis. Ensemble les autres oeuures Poëtiques dudict Au-
teur, Gerard L'Escuyer Prothenotaire de Boulin* (Paris: Robert
Estienne, 1560), in-8 (B. N. Rés. Yf. 2958).

Contains five elegies: "Elegie à son Olimpe" comes at the
beginning of the section *Les Ieux Olimpiques*; the fourth section of the volume, *Les Elegies*, contains the remaining four.

According to Pinvert's study of Grévin, 269-270, the poems were probably written 1559-1560. All five poems are in ac. The poems tend to be concerned with ideas (one is an epitaph, however), serious of tone and only twice at all closely connected with the *épître*. "Elegie à son Olimpe" is a prefatory poem.

1561

46. Aubert, Guillaume, *Elégie sur le trespas de feu Ioch. Du Bellay Ang. par G. Aubert de Poictiers, Aduocat en la Court de Parlement de Paris* (Paris: Morel, 1560 [1561 ns.]), in-4 (B. N. Rés. Ye. 900). There is another edition dated 1561 (B. N. Rés, Ye. 397).

A very florid expression of commonplaces in ac. ending in a short epitaph.

1562

47. Grévin, Jacques, *Le Theatre de Iaques Grevin de Cler-mont en Beauuaisis, A Tresillustre et Treshaulte Princesse Madame Claude de France, Duchesse de Lorraine. Ensemble La Seconde Partie de L'Olimpe & de la Gelodacrye* (Paris: Vincent Sertenas and Guillaume Barbé, 1562), in-8 (B. N. Rés. Yf. 2955-2956).

Two elegies in *Le Second Livre de la Gelodacrye*, one in ac. and one in couplets of alternating alexandrine and decasyllabic lines. Only one is an *épître*. Again Grévin deals with ideas in serious style: the "misère des hommes", man's talents and the nature of poetry etc.

[1563]

48. *Elegie sur La Mort Conspiree Au Seigneur Duc De Guise, Lieutenant general de la Maiesté du Roy. Avec les Exhortations faictes par le Clergé aux Citoyens de Paris. M. L. Mon M sans L ne peult voller* (Paris: Guillaume de Niuerd, nd.), in-8 (B. N. Rés. Ye. 3949).

Lament and reflexion on the troubled times in dc.

1567

49. Jodelle, Etienne, one elegy found at the end of *Le Premier des Meteores de Ian Antoine de Baif* (Paris: Robert Estienne, 1567), in-4 (B. N. Yf. 506).

   A poem of flattery and treating the importance of knowledge. It is written in *vers mesurés* imitating the classical elegiac distich.

1568

50. Amboise, François d', *Elegie sur le trépas d'Anne Duc de Montmorency, Pair, & Connestable de France. Avec vn Panegiric Latin, & vne Ode françoise, sur le desastre de la France agitée des troubles, & reuoltes ciuiles, l'an 1568. Le tout par François d'Amboyse, Parisien* (Paris: Pour Ph.-G. de Rouille par Denys du Pré, 1568), in-4 (B. N. Rés. m. Yc. 954 [5 et 7]).

   The poem (ac.) is highly literary but has some lines devoted to the historical moment.

51. Sorel, Pierre, *Plaincte sur la mort de tres vertueux & trespuissant seigneur, Anne de Montmorency, Pair & Connestable de France: Traduicte du Latin de M. Legier du Chesne professeur du Roy. Ensemble plusieurs Elegies & Sonnets. Par P. Sorel Chartrain* (Paris: Ph.-G. de Roville, 1568), in-4 (B. N. Rés. m. Yc. 945 [3]).

   There is one elegy, in ac. Like the preceding poem by d'Amboise, this poem is both very literary and somewhat concerned with the troubled times. A single person is addressed throughout.

1569

52. Pontoux, Claude de, *Harangues Funebres, Sur la mort de diuers animaux, extraictes du Toscan, rendues & augmentées*

en nostre vulgaire: Ou sont representez au vif les naturels des-
dits animaux, & les proprietez d'iceux, auec vne rhetorique
gaillarde (Lyon: Benoist Rigaud, 1569), in-16 (Ars. B. 30. 712).

Contains at the end of the translation of Ortensio Landi's
deplorations an "Elegie sur la Mort d'vn Couchon nommé
Grognet" in oct. c., 402 lines. The poem is also contained in
Catalogue 86.

53.   Pontoux, Claude de, *Le philopoleme, ou exhortation à la guerre.*
A tous les chefs et capitaines de l'armée du roy, afin de se mon-
strer vaillans à la bataille, pour extirper les ennemys et oster
toute sedition hors du royaume de France. Avec une elegie des
troubles et miseres de ce temps (Lyon, 1569), in-8.

One elegy in ac. on the state of the country. We have not been
able to locate this edition. The poem is reprinted in Catalogue
86.

54.   Pontoux, Claude de, *Elegie funebre sur le deces et trepas d'Isa-*
belle de France regne d'Hespagne (Lyon, 1569), in-8.

Couplets of alternating alexandrine and decasyllabic lines.
This lengthy poem is much concerned with France in the throes
of the third religious war. We have not been able to locate this
edition. The poem is reprinted in Catalogue 86.

55.   *Elegie ou deploration des morts tués en la bataille d'Hervaux,*
et de ce temps calamiteux (Tours: René Siffleau, 1569), in-8.

We have not been able to locate this poem, mentioned by J.-C.
Brunet in his *Manuel du libraire*, II, col. 959.

56.   Du Tronchet, Etienne, *Lettres Missives et Familieres d'Es-*
tienne Du Tronchet, Secretaire de la Royne Mere du Roy A
Messire Albert de Gondy, Conte Doyen Baron de Rectz, de
Sainct Seigne de Dompierre, Marquis des Isles d'or, Cheualier
de l'ordre du Roy, premier Gentilhomme de sa chambre et
Capitaine de cinquante hommes d'armes (Paris: Nicolas du
Chemin, 1569), in-4 (B. N. Rés. Z. 801).

Contains two elegies. The first (ac.) ,plagiarized from Mellin de Saint-Gelais, is a *discours* on "le vray bien"; the second, in *terza rima,* describes the beauties of a lady.

57. *Elegie Ov Complainte, que la France fait aux François, montrant trois causes des guerres & miseres de ce Royaume. Item le vray remede de les appaiser: Auec vne instruction de bien cognoistre & remarquer les amateurs de la Paix, & repos d'icelluy, & les aucteurs des guerres & vrays ennemys de la Couronne. Item monstrant que tous en general, tant d'vne, que d'autre Religion, sont vne des causes d'icelles guerres, aduenues despuis l'Edict de Ianuier. Plus quelques Epigrammes au derriere. Le Tout addressé à Tres-haut, Tres-puissant, & vertueux Comte, François de la Roche-foucaut. D. R., Imprimé nouuellement* (np., 1569), in-8 (B. N. Rés Ye. 3953).

834 lines in ac., by a Reformer. Harsh lines criticizing Catherine de Médicis and the Cardinal de Guise.

58. Baïf, Antoine de, one elegy in *Les Premières Œuures de Scevole de Sainte-Marthe, Gentilhomme Lodunois. Qui contienent ses Imitations & Traductions recueillies de diuers Poëtes Grecs & Latins. Le tout diuisé en quatre Liures, & dedié à Monseigneur le Cheualier d'Angoulesme* (Paris: Federic Morel, 1569), in-8 (B. N. Rés. Ye. 2118).

A poem of flattery and concerning peace and justice. It is written in *vers mesurés* imitating the classical elegiac distich.

[c. 1570]

59. Brantôme (Pierre de Bourdeille, seigneur de), *Recueil d'aulcunes Rymes de mes Jeunes Amours* (B. N. ms. N. A. Fr. 11688; not published until the Lalanne edition of Brantôme's works, 1864-1882).

One elegy, an *épître amoureuse* with an important autobiographical element along with the conventional poses.

1570

60. Belleforest, F. de, one elegy in *Le Tumbeau de messire Gilles Bourdin, Chevalier, Seigneur d'Assy, Conseiller au priué Conseil du Roy, & Procureur general de sa Maiesté au Parlement de Paris. En plusieurs Langues, Recueilli de plusieurs scauans personnages de la France* (Paris: Robert Estienne, 1570), in-4 (B. N. Rés. Ye. 447).

The lament somewhat broadens out to include history. Although written in dc. the lines are set off in sextains.

1572

61. *Elegie Satyrique Sur la Mort de Gaspar de Colli-gny Qui Fut Admiral De France, A laquelle chacun carme commence par la fin de l'autre, autrement appellez carmes serpentins* (Paris: Anthoine Houic, 1572), in-8 (B. N. Rés. Ye. 3955 bis).

The tone is violent, the style almost *rhétoriqueur* and the form ac.

62. Turrin, Claude, *Les Œuures poetiques de Claude Turrin Diionnois, Diuisé en six liures. Les deux premiers sont d'Elegies amoureuses & les autres de Sonets, Chansons, Eclogues, & Odes. A sa Maistresse* (Paris: Iean de Bordeaux, 1572), in-8 (B. N. Rés. Ye. 1811).

Despite the title, only the first book of elegies (13) deals with love; the second book (5) presents a variety of themes. Either dc. or ac. except one poem in couplets of alternating alexandrine and decasyllabic lines and one poem in quatrains. This edition is posthumous; the poems no doubt belong to about the middle 1560's although the style is verging on the neo-Petrarchan vein of the 1570's.

1573

63. La Taille, Jean de, *La Famine, ou les Gabeonites, Tragedie prise de la Bible, & suiuant celle de Saül. Ensemble plusieurs*

autres Œuures poëtiques de Iehan De La Taille de Bondaroy
gentilhomme du pays de Beauce, & de feu Iaques de la Taille
son frere, desquels oeuures l'ordre se void en la prochaine page
(Paris: Federic Morel, 1573), in-8 (Rés. Ye. 1818-1822).

A book of six elegies composed probably during the preceding
decade. All are in dc., only one is not an *épître*. Love and death
involving lovers are the themes with an interesting background
of the troubled times. Generally unadorned style.

64. La Jessée, Jean de, *Le Tombeau De Feu Tres-Noble Seigneur*
Henri de Foix, Conte de Candale, d'Esterac, & Benauges en
Guiene, & Cheualier de L'Ordre: n'aguiere occis au Siege de la
Ville de Somiere en Languedoc, a present rendue sous l'obeis-
sance du Roi. Le tout compris sous vne Deploration des miseres
de la France, Par I. de La Gessée Mauuesinois, Paris, *On les*
vend au Clos Bruneau à l'image saincte Catherine (1573), in-8
(B. N. Rés. Ye. 4232).

Ac. addressing Paul de Foix but containing especially important apostrophes. References to the battle and the "Pro-
testans". Slightly more than the first third of the poem (66
lines) is an apostrophe to *Elégie* expressing the commonplace
that she should return to her original song, lament of death.

65. Tyard, Pontus de, *Les Œuures Poetiques de Pontus de Tyard*
Seigneur de Bissy: A Sçauoir, Trois liures des Erreurs Amou-
reuses Vn liure de Vers Liriques. Plus Vn recueil des nouvelles
œuures Poëtiques (Paris: Galiot du Pré, 1573), in-4 (B. N.
Rés. Ye. 572-574).

Contains an "Elégie à Pierre de Ronsard" probably composed
shortly after 1555; a long *épître* in ac. concerning the poet's
misfortunes in love. Contains as well the curious "Elégie Pour
Une Dame Enamourée d'une Autre Dame", probably composed shortly before its publication; an *épître* in ac.

66. Garnier, Robert, *Hippolyte, tragedie de Rob. Garnier* (Paris:
Robert Estienne, 1573), in-8 (B. N. Rés. Yf. 3953).

Contains an elegy in quatrains (ABAB, alexandrines) addressing Nicolas Ronsard about a new love-affair.

67. Boton, Pierre, *La Camille de Pierre Boton Masconnois. Ensemble les resueries & discours d'vn Amant desesperé* (Paris: Iean Ruelle, 1573), in-8 (B. N. Ye. 12416).

Five elegies only vaguely *épîtres* dealing with love and forming a rather unified group. Extremely florid style.

68. Desportes, Philippe, *Les Premieres Œuures de Philippes Des Portes Au Roy de Pologne* (Paris: Robert Estienne, 1573), in-4 (B. N. Rés. Ye. 580).

Twenty-one elegies, sixteen of them forming a book, one with the *Amours de Diane* (in modern edns, elegy I, 3) and four in the *Amours d'Hippolyte* (elegy I, 18 and the three that remain always with the Hippolyte poems). All poems are love complaints in ac. Probably belonging to this period are the three elegies published by Jacques Lavaud in *Les Imitations de l'Arioste...*, pp. 127, 153 & 163: two of these poems are published by him for the first time and the third first appeared in an anthology published in 1653. These three elegies are exactly like the 1573 poems. For Desportes' other elegies, see Catalogue 71, 78, and 105.

1574

69. Saint-Gelais, Mellin de, *Œuvres Poétiques de Mellin de S. Gelais* (Lyon: Antoine de Harsy, 1574), in-8 (B. N. Rés. Ye. 1702).

This posthumous edition contains three elegies, of which the first is a translation of Ovid (*Amores*, III, iv) and the other two seemingly original works in *terza rima*. These three poems are already so grouped in a ms., B. N. Fds. fr. 885, which Blanchemain in his edition of the poet dates as about 1555 (I, 46-7). Rigaud's edition of 1582 makes no changes concerning the elegies. Mellin is also responsible for a translation of the Bion

idyl of Venus weeping for the death of Adonis; this much reprinted poem bears the title elegy in the important 1547 edition of Mellin's works. A final poem of Mellin is called elegy
at the end of the century: see Catalogue 129.

70. Jodelle, Etienne, *Les Œuures & Meslanges Poetiques d'Es-
tienne Iodelle Sieur du Lymodin. Premier Volume* (Paris:
Nicolas Chesnau & Mamert Patisson, 1574), in-4 (B. N. Rés.
Ye. 450).

Contains one elegy, ac., epistolary, addressing a lady. In his
recent edition of Jodelle, Enea Balmas adds another elegy
(p. 366) hitherto unpublished: it appears to belong to the same
experience as the published poem, so similar are the two
elegies.

1575

71. Desportes, Philippe, *Les Premières Œuvres de Philippes Des
Portes Au Roy de France et de Pologne* (Paris: Robert Estienne,
1575), in-4 (B. N. Rés. Ye. 581-582).

One new elegy (I, 17 in modern editions), a love complaint in
ac.

72. Jamyn, Amadis, *Les Œuures Poetiques d'Amadis Iamyn. Au
Roy de France et de Pologne* (Paris: Mamert Patisson [Robert
Estienne], 1575), in-4 (B. N. Ye. 1045 & Rés. Ye. 484).

Thirty-four elegies, mainly love complaints, in ac. or dc.
Mainly close to the *épître* tradition; about 70 lines in length
(shorter than Ronsard and Desportes). Highly decorated style.

1576

73. Bretin, Filber, *Poésies Amoureuses Reduites en forme d'vn Dis-
cours de la nature d'Amour. Par Filber Bretin, Bourgongnon
Aussonois. Plus les meslanges du mesme Auteur* (Lyon: Benoist
Rigaud, 1576), in-8 (B. N. Rés. Ye. 1670).

One elegy justifying the theme of love in poetry. No address; dc.

74. Brach, Pierre de, *Les Poemes de Pierre de Brach Bourdelois. Diuisés en Trois Livres* (Bordeaux: Simon Millanges, 1576), in-4 (B. N. Rés. Ye. 865).

The *privilège* is dated August 5, 1574 and certainly many of the elegies date back to the beginning of the 1570's. There are twelve elegies: an "A son livre", eight about love (but one of them is really a pastoral poem) and three form a rather personal correspondence on various themes. All in ac. or dc. There are six more elegies by Brach not published until the edition of Reinhold Dezeimeris in 1861-2. They date probably from slightly before 1586 until 1595. Not so much in the usual love-plaint style but discoursing on love, referring to his happy marriage, his sorrow over the death of his wife etc.

75. Le Loyer, Pierre, *Erotopegnie, ou Passetemps d'amour – Ensemble une Comédie du Muet insensé* (Paris: A. L'Angelier, 1576), in-8 (B. N. Rés. Ye. 2146).

One long elegy (312 lines) praising the beauty of Anjou women in a pastoral style (the poem becomes an *idylie* in 1579). It is nevertheless an *épître* in ac.

1577

76. d'Aubigné, Théodore-Agrippa, one elegy, published for the first time in vol. III of the *Œuvres complètes* prepared by Réaume & Caussade, 6 vols. (Paris: Lemerre, 1873-92).

According to the editors of the 1969 Gallimard edition, the poem was written during the months that followed the *paix de Bergerac* (17 Sept. 1577). An intimate confession of the author's disappointments and bad fortune. Ac., mainly in the *épître* style but some use of apostrophe.

77. Anon.: "Elegie de la France se complaignant de la dissolution

des Damoyselles Françoises" in *la Remonstrâce charitable aux Dames & Damoyselles de France, sur leurs ornemens dissolus, pour les induire à laisser l'habit du Paganisme, & prendre celuy de la femme pudique & Chrestienne* (Paris: Sebastien Niuelle, 1577), in-8 (Maz. 62.763).

The *privilège* is dated 5 Nov. 1570. Only the elegy, 2 sonnets and an epigram remain of the book in the Mazarine collection – everything preceding folio 33 recto is missing. The elegy is a rather colourful sermon teaching Christian sobriety in dress and adornment. 128 lines in ac. The volume ends with the initials F. P. N. and the motto "I'espere ou i'aspire".

78. Desportes, Philippe, *Les Premieres Œuvres de Philippes Des Portes* (Paris: pour Robert le Mangnier, 1577), in-12 (B. M. C. 39. a. 43).

One new elegy, with the *Meslanges* (the future II, 3). A love-complaint in ac.

79. Jamyn, Amadis, *Les Œuures Poetiques d'Amadis Iamyn Reueuës, corrigees & augmentees pour la seconde impression. Au Roy de France et de Pologne* (Paris: Mamert Patisson [Robert Estienne], 1577), in-12 (B. N. Rés. Ye. 1875).

One new elegy about love in ac.

1578

80. Boyssières, Jean de, *Les Premieres Œuures Amoureuses De Iean de Boyssieres, Montferrandin. A Monsieur, Duc d'Aniou, Fils de France, et Frere Vnique de* (sic) *Roy* (Paris: Claude de Montreuil, 1578), in-12 (B. N. Rés. Ye. 3618).

Seven elegies about the poet's love for Sylvie but not necessarily addressing Sylvie; the elegies form part of the narrative only. Another elegy tries to reconcile a young lady to a fate of marriage with an elderly man; and a final elegy is praise of the duc d'Anjou, to whom the volume is dedicated. All are in ac. except for one in sextains (A10A10B6C10C10B6).

81. Boyssières, Jean de, *Les Secondes Œuures Poetiques de I. de Boyssieres de Mont-Ferrand en Auuergne. Dediees Aux Princes de l'Illustre Sang de France. Meslanges* (Paris: Iean Poupy, 1578), in-4 (B. N. Rés. Ye. 512).

    Three elegies in ac., all addressing royalty. Praise and request for help.

82. La Jessée, Jean de, *La Grasinde de Iean de La Gessee* (Paris: Galliot Corrozet, 1578), in-4 (B. N. Rés. Ye. 464).

    Contains a section of six elegies, all love-plaints in couplets addressing Grasinde. The poems are republished with many more elegies in 1583 (see Catalogue 103).

83. Belliard, Guillaume, *Le Premier Livre des poèmes de Guillaume Belliard, secretaire de la Royne de Nauarre. Contenant les delitieuses Amours de Marc Antoine, & de Cleopatre, les triomphes d'Amour, & de la Mort, & autres imitations d'Ouide, Petrarque, & de l'Arioste. A la Royne de Nauarre* (Paris: Claude Gautier, 1578), in-4 (B. N. Rés. Ye. 351).

    One elegy dedicating his book in flattering terms to Marguerite de Navarre. Simple and narrative; ac.

1579

84. Sainte-Marthe, Scévole de, *Les Œuures de Scevole de Sainte-Marthe* (Paris: Mamert Patisson [R. Estienne], 1579), in-4 (B. N. Ye. 1098).

    Eight poems are called *élégie*, of which: two had appeared as translations of his Latin in 1569; one will be said to be a translation in 1600; only two of the remaining five are still called elegies in 1600; in 1629 the four original elegies that appear at all have lost their generic title. The poems are mostly in various ways about love (one of the translations is about women's clothing). The forms are varied: only three are in dc.; another is in couplets of an alexandrine followed by a line of six syllables; the remaining poems are in sextains and quatrains.

85. Le Loyer, Pierre, *Les Œuvres et meslanges poétiques de Pierre
     Le Loyer, Angeuin. Ensemble La Comédie Nephelococugie, ou
     la Nuee des Cocus, non moins docte que facetieuse* (Paris: J.
     Poupy, 1579), in-12 (B. N. Rés. p. Ye. 146).

     One elegy (ac.) addressing his lady and justifying his writing
     love-poetry.

86. Pontoux, Claude de, *Les Œuures De Claude de Pontoux Gen-
     tilhomme Chalonnois Docteur en Medecine. Le contenu desquel-
     les se void en la page suyuante. Et dont l'Idee contenant enuiron
     300 Sonnetz n'a esté par cy deuant imprimee* (Lyon: Benoist
     Rigaud, 1579), in-16 (B. N. Rés. Ye. 1845).

     Contains the three elegies published in 1569 (Cat. 52, 53, and
     54).

87. Boyssières, Jean de, *Les Troisiesmes Œuures de Iean de Boys-
     sieres De la Ville de Montferrand en Auuergne. A Monsieur le
     Duc de Mercoeur son Mecoene* (Lyon: Loys Cloquemin, 1579),
     in-4 (B. N. Rés. Ye. 513-517).

     Four new epistolary love-elegies in ac. Also an elegy of in-
     terested flattery.

88. Jamyn, Amadis, *Les Œuures Poetiques D'Amadis Iamyn. Re-
     ueuës, corrigees & augmentees en ceste derniere impression.
     Au Roy de France et de Pologne* (Paris: Robert le Mangnier,
     1579), in-12 (B. N. Rés. Ye. 1876).

     One new elegy, praise and development of ideas, in ac.

1581

89. Romieu, Marie de, *Les Premières Œuures Poetiques de Ma
     Damoiselle Marie de Romieu Viuaroise, Contenant vn brief
     Discours, que l'excellence de la femme surpasse celle de l'hom-
     me non moins recreatifque (*sic) plein de beaux exemples. Le
     Tout A tres-haute & tres-illustre princesse ma dame Marguerite*

de Lorraine Duchesse de Ioyeuse (Paris: Lucas Breyer, 1581), in-12 (B. N. Rés. Ye. 1877).

Contains a narrative elegy, without address, about love, in ac.; and a very long deplorative elegy in elegiac distichs (an alexandrine followed by a decasyllabic line).

1582

90. Habert, Isaac, *Les Œuures Poetiques d'Isaac Habert Secretaire du Roy. Dediées à Monseigneur de Laussac* (Paris: Abel l'Angelier, 1582), in-4 (B. N. Rés. Ye. 1021).

Contains four elegies all in ac; three are epistolary in nature. Two are love-plaints, one is a *discours* mixed with flattery; one an elaborate pseudo-classical deploration.

91. Le Fèvre de la Boderie, Guy, *Diverses Meslanges Poetiques. Par Guy Le Fevre de la Boderie, Secretaire de monseigneur frere du Roy* (Paris: Robert le Mangnier, 1582), in-16 (B. N. Rés. Ye. 1918).

Contains three elegies of different types: a death-lament in dialogue form (*Passant & Esprit*), couplets of alternating alexandrine & decasyllabic lines; a poem of praise in ac.; an autobiographical poem in dc. set off in quatrains, very long and without a personal address.

92. Du Buys, Guillaume, *L'Oreille du Prince Ensemble Plusieurs Autres Œuures Poetiques de G. du Buys Quercinois* (Paris: Iean Febrier, 1582), in-8 (B. N. Rés. Ye. 1879).

This edition is extremely faulty: one must consult the text of his two elegies in: *Les Œures (sic) De Guillaume Du Buys Quercinoys. Contenant plusieurs & diuers traictez: le discours desquel n'apporte moindre vertueux fruict qu'il est agreable, & plain de tout contenant pour la diversité des matieres dont il traicte* (Paris: Guillaume Bichon, 1585), in-12 (B. N. Rés. Ye. 1927).

Both elegies concern the civil wars, have a rather vague address and are written in sextains (AABCCB, the first in octo-syllables & the second in lines of six syllables).

93. Anon., one elegy in *L'Amoureux Passetemps, Declaré en ioy-yeuse Poésie, par plusieurs Epistres du Coq à l'Asne, & de l'Asne au Coq, auec Balades, Dizains, Huitains, & autres ioyeusetez* (Lyon: Benoist Rigaud, 1582), in-16 (B. N. Rés. Ye. 2721).

This edition is thought to be a copy of the one that appears in 1570 (See Lachèvre, 52). The elegy is an epistolary love-plaint in dc.

1583

94. Rapin, Nicolas, *Les Plaisirs du Gentilhomme Champestre. Augmenté de quelques nouueaux Poemes & Epigrammes* (Paris: la vefue Lucas Breyer, 1583), in-12 (B. N. Rés. Ye. 1836).

Two elegies: one in quatrains in pastoral style, a poem of adieu to two "shepherdesses"; one in quatrains but an epistolary discourse.

95. Rapin, Nicolas, one elegy in *V. Ampliss. Christophori Thuani Tumulus In Iac. Aug. Thuani Amerii pietatem* (Lutetiae: Apud Mamertum Patissonium Typographum Regium, in officina Rob. Stephani, 1583), in-4 (B. N. Rés. m. Yc. 925 [14]).

Rapin's poem is called "Vers Elegiaques Rymez A La Cesure"; it is written in *vers mesurés*.

96. Anon., one elegy in *V. C. Ian. Morelli Ebredun. Consiliarij Oeconomíq; Regij, Moderatoris illustrissimi principis Henrici Engolismaei, magni Franciae Prioris, Tumulus* (Parisiis: Apud Federicum Morellum, Typographum Regium, 1583), in-4 (B. N. Rés. m. Yc. 925 [20]).

The one French elegy (signed L. M.) is as much praise of Morel's daughter as it is a lament of his death. Ac.

97. Avost, Hierosme d', *Poésies de Hierosme d'Avost de Laval.*
    En faveur de plusieurs illustres & nobles personnes (np., 1583),
    in-8 (B. N. Rés. Ye. 1880).

    Contains two elegies, one of praise in ac., another in couplets
    of alternating alexandrine and decasyllabic lines lamenting
    the death of Belleforest.

98. Durant, Gilles and Amadis Jamyn, each has an elegy in *La*
    Main Ou Œuures Poetiques Faits Sur La Main de Estienne Pas-
    quier Aduocat au Parlement de Paris (Paris: Michel Gadouleau,
    1583), in-4 (B. N. Rés. 525).

    Each of the poets provides an elegy explaining the absence of
    Pasquier's hands in a portrait done by a Flemish master.
    Both are in ac.

99. Béroalde de Verville, *Les Soupirs Amoureux De F. B. de*
    Veruille. Auec vn discours Satyrique de ceux qui escriuent d'A-
    mour, par N. le Digne (Paris: Pour Timothee Iouan, 1583), in-12
    (B. N. Rés. R. 2718).

    Five love-plaints in ac. but not all addressing the beloved.

100. Du Pont, Gratien, one elegy in Etienne Tabourot's *Les Bigar-*
     rures du Seigneur Des Accordz (Paris: Jean Richer, 1583),
     in-16 (B. N. Rés. Z. 2760).

     The poem dates back to Du Pont's *Controverses des Sexes*
     Masculin et Feminin of 1534, but it is not until Tabourot gives
     his somewhat abbreviated version that the poem is called an
     elegy. It is a satirical lover's complaint made humorous by
     the constant improper rhyme. Ac.

101. Blanchon, Ioachim: *Les Premières Œuures Poetiques de Ioa-*
     chim Blanchon, Au Treschrestien Henry III. Roy de France et
     de Pologne (Paris: Thomas Perier, 1583), in-8 (B. N. Rés. p.
     Ye. 177).

     Six elegies, love-plaints in ac. except for the last one which is in sextains (AABCCB, alexandrines). The epistolary nature of the poems is somewhat confused by the presence of apostrophes.

102. Cornu, Pierre de, *Les Œuures Poétiques de Pierre de Cornu, dauphinois, contenant sonnets, chansons, odes, discours, eclogues, stances, épitaphes, et autres diverses poésies* (Lyon: Jean Huguetan, 1583), in-8 (B. N. Rés. p. Ye. 212).

One elegy of complaint to his lady in ac.

103. La Jessée, Jean de, *Les Premières Œuures Françoyses de Iean de La Iessée, Secrétaire de la Chambre de Monseigneur*, 2 vols. (Anvers: Christofle Plantin, 1583), in-4 (B. N. Rés. Ye. 486-487).

Contains the six elegies of *La Grasinde* (see Catalogue 82) in addition to forty-three new elegies (probably composed by 1578). The poems concern three different ladies and each time form a separate book in the *Amours* devoted to the poet's loves. Ac. or dc. There is a certain vagueness about the epistolary nature of the poems.

104. Du Monin, Jean Edouard, *L'Vranologie, ou Le Ciel de Ian Edouard Du Monin PP. Contenant, outre l'ordinaire doctrine de la Sphaere, plusieurs beaus discours dignes de tout gentil esprit, A Monseigneur M. Philippes Des-Portes* (Paris: Guilhaume Iulien, 1583), in-12 (B. N. 8° Ye. 5537).

Contains two elegies in ac., without personal address, in praise of a city (Amiens) and of the family tree of the Bourbons.

105. Desportes, Philippe, *Les Premières Œuures de Philippes Des Portes* (Paris: Mamert Patisson [Robert Estienne], 1583), in-12 (B. M. C. 39. a. 39).

Four new elegies, which form a new second book of elegies (plus the poem first published in 1577). A total now of 27 elegies, all that were published during Desportes' life. Again the poems are love-complaints in ac.

106. Bertaut, Jean, an "Elegie sur les Dernieres Amours de Monsieur Desportes" in Desportes, Catalogue 105.

A poem of praise in ac.

1584

107. Romieu, Jacques de, *Les Melanges de Iaques de Romieu Vivarois, Secretaire ordinaire de la chambre du Roy. Ou sont comprises les louanges heroïques dudit païs de Viuarois. A tres-illustres* (sic), *& tres-genereux Seigneur, Iust, Lois, Baron de Tournon, Comte de Rossillon, Cheualier de l'ordre du Roy, & Capitaine de cinquante hommes d'armes de sa Majesté* (Lyon: Benoist Rigaud, 1584), in-12 (B. N. Rés. Ye. 1878).

Three elegies of love-plaint, ac. or dc. In one case the address is very confused.

108. Morenne, Claude de, *Poésies profanes de Claude de Morenne*, edited by L. Duhamel (Caen: Le Cost-Clérisse, 1864).

This is the first edition of a manuscript dated 1584. Three elegies of love-plaint, ac. or dc. In one case a series of apostrophes rather than epistolary.

109. Jamyn, Amadis, *Le Second Volume des Œuures d'Amadis Iamin, Secretaire & Lecteur ordinaire de la Chambre du Roy. Au Roy de France & de Pologne* (Paris: Robert le Mangnier, 1584), in-12 (Ars. 8° B. 8875).

Ten elegies: eight are couplet love-poems in Jamyn's early style but two are satirical poems, one in the form of a dialogue.

1585

110. Birague, Flaminio de, *Les Premières Oeuures Poétiques de Flaminio de Birague, Gentil-homme ordinaire de la Chambre du*

Roy. Au Tres-Chrestien Roy de France & de Pologne (Paris: Thomas Perier, 1585), in-12 (B. N. Rés. Ye. 1883).

Ten elegies in ac. or dc. Nine deal with love, only some of them epistolary. The tenth elegy is a letter to Cardinal Birague asking for guidance.

1586

111. Debaste, Nicolas, *Les Passions D'Amour, De Nicolas Debaste, Chartrain. A Monsieur d'Esclimont fils aisné de Monseigneur de Chiuerny, Chancelier de France. Plus les Meslanges de Carmes Latins & François, A Monsieur Ligier sieur de Lauconieres Conseiller, Secretaire du Roy* (Rouen: Thomas Mallard, 1586), in-12 (B. N. Rés. Ye. 3795).

There are nine elegies and only one deals with love. Several are not epistolary but all are in couplets. The themes of Debaste are reminiscent of Ronsard's elegies: "A son livre", poems of dedication and flattery, poems about his poetry, about religious matters and the troubles of the times.

112. Garnier, Robert and R. Cailler, each has an elegy in *Discours de la Vie de Pierre de Ronsard, Gentilhomme Vandomois, Prince des Poëtes François, Avec Vne Eclogue Representee en ses obseques, par Claude Binet. Plus Les Vers Composez Par ledict Ronsard peu auant sa mort: Ensemble Son Tombeau Recueilli de plusieurs excellens personnages* (Paris: Gabriel Buon, 1586), in-4 (B. N. Rés. m. Yc. 925 [21]).

Garnier's poem is very long, in quatrains (A12B6A12B6); Cailler's poem is still longer, in ac.

113. *Elegie A La France Sur Le Larmoiable trespas de Pierre de Ronsard, Gentilhomme Vandomois, vnique Poëte François. Par D. I. E. M.* (Paris: Berenguié Chalabre, 1586), in-8 (B. N. Rés. Ye. 3952).

Classical allusions in profusion and an important biographical element. Much criticism of Ronsard's supposed neglect by the French. Ac.

114. Granchier, François, *Les Larmes, Regrets et Déplorations sur la Mort de Jean Edouart du Monin, excellent poëte Grec, Latin & François. Composé par François Granchier, Marchois, son nepueu & escolier* (Paris: P. Ramier, 1586), in-8 (B. N. X. 18911 [5]).

One elegy in ac., a poem of adieu to the murdered uncle.

115. *Elegie Sur La Mort Du Sieur Iean Edouart Du Monin Tres-exellent poëte Philosophe* (Paris: Estienne Preuosteau, 1586), in-4 (B. N. Rés. Ye. 1928).

Anonymous poem in formal style, ac., full of apostrophes and supposedly spoken at the graveside.

1587

116. Iacquet, Gabriel, P. Philipon, and Iacques de Lutreyne, each has one elegy in *Recueil D'Epita(p)hes En Diverses Langues Composez par plusieurs doctes hommes de France & autres, sur le trespas de Iean Edoard du Monin, & de Iean des Cauvres Principal du college d'Amiens, tous deux intimes amis & scauants personnages* (Paris: Estienne Preuosteau, 1587), in-18 (B. N. Ln. ²⁷ 6670)

Each poem is commonplace; ac. or dc.

117. Anon., one elegy in *De Iezabelis Anglæ Parricidio Varii Generis Poemata Latina et Gallica* (np., nd.), in-4 (B. N. Rés. m. Yc. 858).

The elegy is a dialogue between the *Passant* and the *Muse* in ac.

118. Le Poulchre de La Motte-Messemé, François, *Les Sept Livres des Honnestes Loisirs de Monsieur de La Motte Messemé, Cheuallier de l'ordre du Roy, & Capitaine de cinquante hommes d'armes des Ordonnances de sa Majesté. Intitulez*

chacun du nom d'vn des Planettes. Qui est vn Discours en forme de Chronouiologie où sera veritablement discouru des plus notables occurances de noz guerres ciuiles, & des diuers accidens de l'Autheur. Dedié au Roy. Plus, vn meslange de diuers Poëmes, d'Elegies, Stances & Sonnets (Paris: Marc Orry, 1587), in-12 (B. N. Rés. Ye. 1934).

Five elegies in ac., four of which deal with the poet's love but not necessarily in epistolary style. One elegy is a familiar letter on a great variety of subjects.

119. Trellon, Claude de, *La Muse Guerriere. Dediée à Monsieur le Conte d'Aubijoux. Par le Sr. de Trellon* (Paris: Abel L'Angelier, 1587), in-8 (B. N. Rés. Ye. 2111).

Contains sixteen elegies, all in ac. Eleven concern his love-affair with Sylvie; one elegy of flattery and one inciting the courageous to fight for God and King. There is also a section called *l'Hermitage* which contains three elegies of religious confession, criticism of worldly life, preparation for death.

1588

120. Cholières, Nicolas de, *La Guerre des masles contre les femelles représentant en trois dialogues Les prérogatives et dignitez tant de l'un que de l'autre sexe Avec les meslanges poétiques du Sieur de Cholières* (Paris: Pierre Chevillot, 1588), in-12 (B. N. Rés. R. 2169).

Two elegies in ac. but both are borrowed from Ronsard: "Le bain de Calirée" and the "Elegie du Poète à Eurymedon" (no. 72 in our list). The third poem that Cholières gives to celebrate the love of Eurymedon and Calirée, a *chanson*, is borrowed from Jamyn (see Catalogue 72). In all three cases the variants are insignificant; the two elegies are slightly longer.

121. Vitel, Ian de, *Les Premiers Exercices Poëtiques de Ian de Vitel Avranchois. Contenans l'Hymne de Pallas, La prinse du Mont sainct Michel, L'Imitation de deux Idyll. du Grec de Theocrite,*

Discours, Eclogues, Odes, Elegies, & Tombeaux. A Tres-Illustre Prince et Reverendissime Prelat Monseigneur Charles de Bourbon Cardinal de Vandome, Archeuesque designé de Rouen. &c. (Paris: Estienne Preuosteau, 1588), in-12 (B. N. Rés. Ye. 2101).

Contains three elegies of different types, none of them closely epistolary: a poem of flattery and request for help; a death-lament highly ornamented with classical allusions; a personal poem concerning a plague and its effects on his activity as poet. The last poem is in dc., the other two are in ac.

1590

122. Sallière, Pierre Lucas, *Le Tombeau de Feu Missire Francois Du Parc, en son viuant Cheualier de l'ordre du Roy, Gentil-homme ordinaire de sa Chambre, Gouuerneur d'Auranches, Baron des Biards, Sieur des Cresnais, de Morferuille, de Cain-dolle, etc. Par P. L. S.* (np., 1590), in-4 (B. N. Rés. Ye. 1131).

Contains one elegy in ac., an apostrophe to the dead man.

123. La Roque, Siméon-Guillaume de, *Les Premières Œuures de S. G. De La Roque, de Clermont en Beauuoisis* (Paris: Mamert Patisson, 1590), in-8 (B. N. Rés. Ye. 1951).

One elegy in ac. apostrophizing sinners on religious themes.

1591

124. Le Chevalier, Antoine, one elegy in *Le tombeau de Robert et Antoine le Chevalier, frères, sieurs d'Aigneaux doctes et ex-cellens Poetes François, de Vire en Normandie. Ledit Tombeau recueilli de plusieurs doctes Poëtes Par P. L. S.* (P. Lucas Sallière). *Avec quelques beaux poemes trouvez en leur estude, Le tout mis par ordre comme on peut veoir en la page suyvante* (Caen: Pierre le Chandelier, 1591), in-8 (Ars. B. L. 9103).

The poem is in ac., apostrophizes the dead brother, the Muses etc. No doubt the grief is sincere but the expression of it is highly literary and predictable.

1594

125. Le Cauchois, Estienne, *Le Tombeau De Noble, Et Vertueux Seigneur, Feu Monsieur de la Noüe. Qui deceda au grand regret des hommes d'honneur, le quatriesme iour d'Aoust, 1591. Par Estienne le Cauchois, Chirurgien ordinaire du Roy* (Melun: np., 1594), in-8 (B. N. Rés. Ye. 4291).

La Noüe died in 1591. The one elegy is a real curiosity because it is a double sonnet. No address.

1595

126. Papon, Loys, *Œuures du Chanoine Loys Papon Seigneur de Marcilly Poète Foresien du XVIe Siècle. Imprimées pour la première fois sur les manuscrits originaux. Par les soins et aux frais de Mr. N. Yemeniz, Membre de la Société des Bibliophiles françois. Précédé d'une Notice sur la Vie et les Œuvres de Loys Papon, par Guy de La Grye* (Lyon: Louis Perrin, 1857).

One elegy addressing Anne d'Urfé in ac. Various themes: decadence of times, praise of d'Urfé and his new country house.

127. Trellon, Claude de, *Les Œuures Du Sieur De Trellon. Diuisees en quatre Liures. Reueuës & corrigees de nouueau par l'Autheur, & augmentees du Pelerin, des Amours de Felice, et autres Poësies* (Lyon: Thibaud Ancelin, 1595), in-12 (B. N. Rés. Ye. 2011).

Eliminates one of the elegies of 1587 (see Catalogue 119) but adds five new ones for Félice. All in ac. One is a dialogue; in the others, there is varied use of address.

128. La Roque, Siméon-Guillaume de, *Les Amours de Caristée. Par le Sieur de la Rocque, de Clermont en Beauuoisin* (Rouen: Raphaël du Petit Val, 1595), in-12 (B. N. Rés. Ye. 1953).

Twelve elegies about the poet's love for Caristée. Not all of the love-plaint type: some are narratives and *discours*. Vague use of direct address; ac.

1596

129. Marot (Mellin de Saint-Gelais), one new elegy (Elégie XXVII) in *Les Œuures De Clement Marot de Cahors en Quercy, Valet de chambre du Roy* (Rouen: Thomas Mallard, 1596), in-12 (B. N. Rés. Ye. 1525).

The poem, here attributed to Marot, is Mellin de Saint-Gelais' "A une malcontente, d'avoir esté sobrement louee et se plaignant non sobrement". This poem appeared first in 1546 with the *Rymes* of Pernette du Guillet and was associated with Marot after its inclusion in the *Epigrammes de Clement Marot...* (Poitiers: Marnef, 1547). It also appeared in Saint-Gelais' works in 1547 (see Catalogue 69) on p. 30 and was listed in the table of contents as an *opuscule*. Let it be emphasized that it is never called an elegy before this 1596 edition of Marot.

130. Expilly, Claude, *Les Poëmes du Sieur d'Expilly, A Madame la Marquise de Monceaux* (Paris: Abel Langelier, 1596), in-4 (B. N. Rés. p. Ye. 174).

Six elegies in ac. all dealing with love in a variety of ways. Vague use of address.

1597

131. Passerat, Jean, *Le Premier Livre des Poemes de Iean Passerat* (Paris: Mamert Patisson [Robert Estienne], 1597), in-4 (Ars. 4° B. 2927).

Contains twelve poems constituting a book of elegies. A distinct classical influence and very little connection with the *épître amoureuse*. All are in ac. or dc. Two poems lament the death of pet birds.

132. Trellon, Claude de, *Le Cavalier Parfait, Dedié A Monseigneur Le Duc de Guyse. Diuisé en quatre liures. Où sont comprinses les Amours de Syluie, les Amours de Felice, les Meslanges, &*

l'Hermitage (Lyon: Thibaud Ancelin, 1597), in-12 (B. N. Ye. 7465).

Three elegies of 1587 and 1595 disappear but eight new love-elegies in ac. are added. Some epistolary connections.

133. Sponde, Jean de, one elegy in *Recueil de diverses poésies, tant du feu sieur de Sponde, que des sieurs du Perron, de Bertaud, de Porcheres, et autres non encore imprimées. Recueillies par Raphaël du Petit Val* (Rouen: Petit Val, 1597), in-12 (this first edition appears to be lost; the edition of 1599 is the earliest available: see the edition of Sponde by Boase and Ruchon, pp. 163-7, for details concerning the *Recueil*).

The elegy no doubt belongs to Sponde's early years. It is a curious work. The first part (in couplets) apostrophizes the poet's verse; the second part (in stanzas of six couplets containing two lines of refrain) discusses the effects of his lady's absence.

134. La Roque, Siméon-Guillaume de, *Diverses Poesies Du Sieur De La Roque, De Clermont En Beauuoisis, composees durant son sejour à Fontainebleau. A Madame* (Rouen: Raphaël du Petit Val, 1597), in-4 (B. N. Rés. Ye. 535).

Four elegies in the "Diverses Poésies". All concern love; not always epistolary; ac.

135. Papillon de Lasphrise, Marc, *Les Premières Œuures Poetiques Du Capitaine Lasphrise. A Cesar Monsieur* (Paris: Iean Gesselin, 1597), in-12 (B. N. Rés. Ye. 2017).

Contains thirteen elegies, two for Théophile, five for Noémie, and six miscellaneous poems, dispensing praise or *discours* in character. All are in ac.; address is vague.

1598

136. Guy de Tours, Michel, *Les Premières œuures poétiques et soupirs amoureux de Guy de Tours* (Paris: I. Du Carroy, 1598),

in-12 (B. N. Ye. 7467). The same year (Paris: N. Louvain), in-12, another edition (B. N. Rés. Ye. 2015).

Contains eight love-elegies in ac. Vague use of address.

137. *Elegie Sur L'Heureux Succez De La Paix. Dedié aux Dames de Lyon* (Lyon: Ionas Gautherin, 1598), in-8 (B. N. Rés. Ye. 3954).

In ac. a series of apostrophes in praise of peace, women, and various important people.

1599

138. Papillon de Lasphrise, Marc, *Les Premières Œuures Poetiques Du Capitaine Lasphrise. Reueuës et augmentées par l'Auteur. A Tres-Illustre & tres-excellent Prince Cæsar de Bourbon Duc de Vendosme Gouuerneur des Païs de Bretaigne & Lyonnois* (Paris: Iean Gesselin, 1599), in-12 (B. N. Rés. Ye. 2018).

Three new elegies in ac., one autobiographical apostrophizing his book, two of flattery and request.

139. Virbluneau, Scalion de, *Les Loyalles et Pudicques Amours de Scalion de Virbluneau A Madame de Boufflers* (Paris: Iannet Mettayer, 1599), in-12 (B. N. Rés. Ye. 2020).

Contains a curious elegy in octosyllabic *huitains* (ABAB-BCBC). The poem asks his lady for mercy.

140. Perault, Philippes, one elegy contained in Virbluneau, Catalogue 139.

This poem is a preface praising Virbluneau and his Angélique. The poem addresses the reader; ac.

1600

141. Vauquelin des Yveteaux, Nicolas, one elegy as a liminary poem in *Les Premières Œuures de Philippe Des Portes,*

Dernière Edition reveüe et augmentee (Paris: Mamert Patisson, 1600), in-8 (B. M. C. 39. a. 13).

The poem (ac.) is in the Ronsardian style of the *discours-*flattery combination but the address is largely absent or confused.

1601

142. Bertaut, Jean, *Recueil des Œuvres Poétiques de I. Bertaut, Abbé d'Aunay, et Premier Aumosnier de la Royne* (Paris: la veuve Mamert Patisson, 1601), in-8 (B. N. Ye. 7706).

Contains one elegy in ac., on the death of Mr. de Noailles.

1602

143. Passerat, Jean, *Le Premier Livre des Poemes de Iean Passerat. Reueus & augmentez par l'Autheur en ceste derniere edition* (Paris: la veufue Mamert Patisson, 1602), in-8 (B. N. Yc. 8437).

Contains the book of elegies which appeared in 1597 (Catalogue 131) and two new elegies (see Blanchemain's edition, I, 72 and 75).

144. Bertaut, Jean, *Recueil de Quelques Vers Amoureux* (Paris: la veuve Mamert Patisson, 1602), in-8 (B. N. Ye. 11435).

Contains five elegies numbered 1 to 4 plus a "Response". Ac., theme of love, not invariably in the epistolary style. The poems are thought to have been written at a considerably earlier date.

1606

145. Passerat, Jean, *Recueil des œuvres poetiques de Iean Passerat* (Paris: Langelier, 1606), in-8 (B. N. Rés. Ye. 4545).

Contains all the elegies of Passerat, thirty in number (plus one translation of Solon) of which fourteen had already appeared (Catalogue 131 and 143). All in ac. or dc. except for one, in quatrains (ABAB, alexandrines). More than half deal in some way with love; the rest are on a considerable variety of themes.

1607

146. Pasquier, Etienne, one elegy appears in *Les Recherches de la France d'Estienne Pasquier, reveues et augmentées d'un livre et de plusieurs chapitres par le mesme autheur* (Paris: L. Sonnius, 1607), in-4 (B. N. 4° L. ⁴⁶ 1. I).

The elegy is to be found in the eleventh chapter of the new book, VII. The elegy is in *vers mesurés* imitating the classical elegiac distich and is dated 1556, probably somewhat imprecisely. The theme of the elegy is love.

1609

147. La Roque, Siméon-Guillaume de, *Les Œuvres de sieur de La Roque. Reveues et augmentées de plusieurs poésies outre les précédentes impressions* (Paris: Vve C. de Monstr'œil, 1609), in-16 (B. N. Ye. 25588).

Seven new elegies, all on themes of love but not always complaints and often without direct address; ac.

1610

148. Pasquier, Etienne, *La Ieunesse d'Estienne Pasquier et Sa Suite* (Paris: Iean Petit-Pas, 1610), in 8° (B. N. Z. 19831).

Nine elegies are contained in the section called *Les Ieus Poetiques d'Estienne Pasquier*. They run from 34 to 358 lines; all are in ac. or dc., except for one in lines of seven syllables. The elegies are found in various sections of the depiction that Pasquier gives of the ages of man and their effect on his sentimental life. The first five are rather typical love-poems but there is also a long *discours* on the rôle of women in marriage.

149. Rapin, Nicolas, *Les Œuures Latines et Françoises de Nicolas*

Rapin. Tombeau de l'autheur, avec plusieurs éloges (Paris: P. Chevalier, 1610), in-4 (B. N. Ye. 1059).

Contains one elegy in elegiacs of *vers mesurés*, a non-epistolary love-plaint. The poem probably was written at a much earlier date. In 1583 Rapin had published another elegy in elegiacs (Catalogue 95).

CATALOGUE OF RONSARD'S *ÉLÉGIES*

The following list of elegies is arranged and annotated according to these principles:

(a) The order of the poems is determined by their first appearance as *élégies* in the works of Ronsard.

(b) The first *incipit* given is its first form. If it has changed in the 1584 edition, the new version is given as well.

(c) The title given is that of the poem's first appearance as an *élégie*. Any other significant title-changes are also given, but, if the change does not affect the genre of the poem, it has not been mentioned.

(d) After its first appearance, the poem is to be presumed to have appeared in all collective editions after it unless there is a note to the contrary.

(e) After the *incipit* there are two page references. The first is to the Laumonier edition prepared for the Société des Textes Français Modernes and the second to his 1584 edition published by Lemerre.

(f) The notes set forth all details of title, date and appearance which interest our subject.

1. Non Muret, ce n'est pas daujourdui   V 224; I 112
    "Elegie A M. A. De Muret" in *Le Cinquiesme Des Odes* (1553, 2nd ed.).

2. Si quelquefois le dueil, & les grieves tristesses   V 243; V 273
   "Elegie Sur Le Trepas d'Antoine Chateignier, Poete Elegiaque..." in *Le Cinquiesme des Odes* (1553, 2nd ed.).

   "Epitaphe" in *Œuvres* 1567-1578.

   "Elegie en forme d'Epitaphe..." in *Œuvres* 1584-1587.

3. Encore Dieu, dit Arate, n'a pas   V 259; V 34
   1584: Encore Dieu par sa grace n'a pas
   "Elegie A J. De La Peruse" in *Le Cinquiesme des Odes* (1553,
   2nd ed.).

   In 1567 and in all subsequent editions, the word "Elegie" is
   dropped; in 1560 the poem is found in the section called
   Poëmes, where it remains in all following editions.

4. Mon œil, mon cœur, ma Cassandre, ma vie   VI 57; I 110
   "Elegie A Cassandre" in *Le Bocage* (1554 and 1555).

5. Aus faits d'amour Diotime certaine   VI 149; IV 87
   1584: Des faits d'amour Diotime certaine
   "Elegie A Ian Brinon" in *Meslanges* (1555).

   Rejected in 1587.

6. Pein moi, Janet, pein moi je te supplie   VI 152; I 119
   "Elegie A Janet Peintre du Roi" in *Meslanges* (1555).

7. Ceus que la Muse aimera plus que moi   VI 165; III 315
   1584: Ceus que les Soeurs aimeront plus que moi
   "Elegie Du Verre A Jan Brinon" in *Meslanges* (1555).

   "Discours du Verre" in *Œuvres* 1584; simply "Le Verre" in
   1587 edition.

8. Quand le fameux Jason & la fleur de la Grece VI 225; VIII 351
   1584: Quand Jason et la fleur de la meilleure Grece
   "A Jean de Morel, Ambrunois, Mareschal Ordinaire des Logis

de la Reine. Elegie" in *Nouvelle Continuation des Amours* (1556).

In the collective editions from 1560 to 1573 and in 1587, the word "Elegie" is dropped and the title is purely dedicatory. In 1578, the poem is again called "Elegie"; in 1584, it is called "Discours". In all editions from 1560 to 1587 it is placed among the *Poëmes*.

9. Au beuf qui tout le jour a trainé la charue   VII 231; VI 297
"Elegie" in *Nouvelle Continuation des Amours* (1556).

This poem appears in print only once after this: in the *Continuation des Amours* of 1557.

10. Quand j'estois libre, ains que l'amour cruelle   VII 234; I 190
1584: Quand j'estois libre, ains qu'une amour nouvelle
"Elegie" in *Nouvelle Continuation des Amours* (1556).

From the *Continuation des Amours* of 1557 to 1587 the poem is called simply "Chanson".

11. Non, je ne me deulx pas qu'une telle abondance VIII 351; V 184
"Elegie de Pierre de Ronsard, A Chretophle de Choiseul, Abbé de Mureaux" in *Odes D'Anacréon Teien, traduites de grec en françois par Remi Belleau* (Paris, Wechel, 1556).

The poem appears in all the collective editions, but only in 1560 is it called "Elegie". In the other editions its title is dedicatory. It appears among the *Poëmes* throughout.

12. L'homme ne peut sçavoir de qui parfaictement   X 5; V 179
1584: L'homme ne peut sçavoir s'il est parfaitement
"Elegie A Monseigneur Le Reverendissime Cardinal de Chatillon" in *Second Livre des Meslanges* (1559).

From 1567 to 1584 the poem is called "Discours"; in 1587 the word "Discours" is dropped.

13. Nous ne sommes pas nez de la dure semence   X 101; V 228
"Elegie" in *Second livre des Meslanges* (1559).

After 1567 the word "Elegie" is dropped.

14. Quiconques peut oster une jeune pucelle   X 109; IV 71
    1584: Quiconque oste par force une jeune pucelle
    "Elegie Traduitte du Grec d'Ergasto" in *Second livre des Meslanges* (1559).

15. Depuis que je suis amoureus   VI 147; I 118
    "Elegie A Cassandre" in *Œuvres* (1560).

    This poem has a most complicated story. It continues to appear as an "Elegie" in the editions between 1567 and 1573, but it first appeared in *Les Meslanges* of 1555 as "Ode à Cassandre" and with the *incipit* "Du jour que je fus amoureus". It will remain in this form in the editions of 1560 and 1567, and thus we have in these two editions the same poem appearing twice with different titles and slight variants in the text. The matter is simplified in the editions between 1578 and 1587 where the poem appears only once with the *incipit* "Du jour que je fus amoureus" but this time with the title "Chanson". Laumonier's note in his edition for STFM (vol. X, pp. 199-200) is incorrect since it is the "Ode" which does not appear in the 1571-73 editions.

16. Cherche, Cassandre, un poëte nouveau   X 202; I 367
    1584: Cherche, maistresse, un poëte nouveau
    "Elegie" in *Œuvres* (1560)

    The poem is rejected in 1587.

17. Mon fils, si tu sçavois que lon dira de toy   VII 315; I 125
    1584: Mon fils, si tu sçavois ce qu'on dira de toy
    "Elegie à son livre" in *Œuvres* (1560)

    The poem had already appeared in *Nouvelle Continuation des Amours* (1556) and in *Continuation des Amours* (1557) simply as "A Son Livre".

18. Marie, à celle fin que le siecle advenir   X 238; VIII 341

1584: Ma seconde ame, à fin que le siecle advenir
"Elegie à Marie" in *Œuvres* (1560).

19. Mon l'Huillier, tous les ars qu'on apprend en jeunesse
                                        X 292; III 312
1584: Trousily, tous les arts appris en la jeunesse
"Elegie Au Seigneur L'Huillier" in *Œuvres* (1560).

In 1584 and 1587 the word "Elegie" is dropped and the title
becomes purely dedicatory.

20. Puis que Dieu ne m'a faict pour supporter les armes
                                        X 300; V 174
"A Pierre L'Escot, Conseiller, & Aumonier Ordinaire du Roy.
Elegie" in *Œuvres* (1560).

In 1578 and 1584 the poem is called "Discours"; in 1587 the
dedication forms the title.

21. Si j'estois à renaistre au ventre de ma mere   X 315; IV 91
"A Robert de la Haye, Conseiller du Roy en son Parlement à
Paris. Elegie" in *Œuvres* (1560).

22. Tout ce qui est enclos soubz la voulte des cieux   X 333; V 226
"Elegie A Tresillustre et Reverendissime Cardinal de Chastillon" in *Œuvres* (1560).

In 1573 the poem has no title; in 1578 and 1584 it is called
"Discours à Odet de Coligny, cardinal de Chastillon" and in
1587 the word "Discours" is dropped.

23. Des Autelz, que la loy, & que la rethoricque   X 348; V 355
"Elegie A Guillaume Des Autels Gentilhomme Charrolois" in
Œuvres (1560).

From 1578 to 1587 the poem is called "Discours".

24. Comme celuy qui voit du haut d'une fenestre   X 362; V 362
"Elegie A Loïs Des Masures Tournisien" in *Œuvres* (1560).

From 1578 to 1587 the poem is called "Discours".

25. Comme un beau pré depoüillé de ses fleurs   XII 193; V 17
    "Elegie sur le despart de la Royne Marie retournant à son
    royaume D'Escosse" Lyon, 1561 (published alone anony-
    mously).

    This *élégie* appears in *Recueil des Nouvelles Poesies* in 1564 and
    in all the collective editions after 1567. In 1587 the word
    "Elegie" is dropped, and "Regret" is used in its place.

26. Grevin,en tous mestiers on peult estre parfaict XIV 193;VI 404
    "Elegie de Pierre de Ronsard à J. Grevin", published at the be-
    ginning of the *Théâtre de J. Grevin*, Paris, 1561 (Vincent
    Sertenas and Guillaume Barbé).

    This poem is not included in any of Ronsard's editions.

27. Celuy debvoit mourir de l'esclat d'un tonnerre XII 87; IV 45
    "Elegie Au Seigneur Baillon, Tresorier de l'Espergne du Roy"
    in *Les Quatre saisons de l'an...* (1563), then in the *Recueil des
    Nouvelles Poesies* (1564) and all collective editions.

28. L'Huillier, si nous perdons cette belle Princesse XII 189; V 15
    "Elegie A H. L'Huillier, Seigneur de Maisonfleur" in *Recueil
    des Nouvelles Poesies* (1564).

    In 1587 "Regret" is substituted for "Elegie".

29. Si le ciel, qui la foy des amans favorise   XII 200; IV 43
    1584: Si la foy des amans qui l'Amour favorise
    "Elegie" in *Recueil des Nouvelles Poesies* (1564).

30. Douce Maitresse, à qui j'ay dedié   XII 208; IV 49
    1584: Madame, oyez le mal que je reçoy
    "Elegie. Vers Communs" in *Recueil des Nouvelles Poesies*
    (1564).

    Rejected in 1587.

31. De vous, & de fortune, & de moy je me deuls XII 215; IV 51
    1584: De moy seul ennemy, vostre traistre, je suis
    "Elegie" in *Recueil des Nouvelles Poesies* (1564).

32. J'avoy toujours & creint & voulu tout ensemble
    XII 223; VIII 330
    1584: J'ay cherché mille fois & fuy tout ensemble
    "Elegie" in *Recueil des Nouvelles Poesies* (1564).

33. Bien que l'obeissance & l'amour que je doy   XII 229; IV 60
    "Elegie" in *Recueil des Nouvelles Poesies* (1564).

34. Ou soit que les marets de l'Egypte feconde   XII 238; III 304
    "Elegie des Armaires A René de Sanzay, Chevallier, Fils Aisné
    de René Seigneur de Sanzay, Chevallier, Chambellan et
    Conseiller du Roy, Gouverneur et son Lieutenant A Nantes"
    in *Recueil des Nouvelles Poesies* (1564).

    In 1584 the poem is called "Discours" and nothing more, and
    in 1587 it bears the title "Les Blasons ou Armoiries".

35. L'autre jour que j'estois assis aupres de vous XII 245; VIII 327
    1584: Hier quand bouche à bouche assis aupres de vous
    "Elegie" in *Recueil des Nouvelles Poesies* (1564).

36. Oyant un jour redoubler mes souspirs   XII 251; IV 98
    "Elegie" in *Recueil des Nouvelles Poesies* (1564).

    Rejected in 1587.

37. Le jour que vostre voyle aux vagues se courba   XII 277; V 4
    1584: Le jour que vostre voyle aux Zephyrs se courba
    "Elegie A la Royne d'Escosse" in *Recueil des Nouvelles Poesies*
    (1564).
    In 1584 the poem is called "Discours" and in 1587 "Regret".

38. Ce me sera plaisir, Genevre, de t'escrire   XII 284; IV 37
    "Elegie" in *Recueil des Nouvelles Poesies* (1564).

In 1584 the title is "Second discours de Genevre en forme d'Elegie", but in 1587 it becomes simply "Elegie à Genevre".

39. Mon cœur esmeu de merveille se serre   XIII 39; III 242
     "Elegie A La Majesté De La Royne D'Angleterre" in *Elegies, Mascarades et Bergerie* (1565).

     In 1578 it becomes "Discours"; in 1587 the title has only the dedication.

40. Quand Juppiter, le grand pere des Rois   XIII 63; III 253
     "Elegie à Mylord Robert Du-Dlé Conte de l'Encestre" in *Elegies, Mascarades et Bergerie* (1565).

     In 1584 the title is "Discours"; in 1587 the poem is rejected.

41. Si les souhaitz des hommes avoient lieu   XIII 131; III 237
     "Elegie A La Magesté Du Roy Mon Maistre" in *Elegies, Mascarades et Bergerie* (1565).

     In 1584 "Elegie" is dropped.

42. Comme une mere ardente en son courage   XIII 141; VIII 317
     1584: Comme une belle & jeune fiancée
     "Elegie A La Magesté De La Royne Ma Maistresse" in *Elegies, Mascarades et Bergerie* (1565).

     In 1584 "Elegie" is dropped.

43. Ton bon conseil, ta prudence & ta vie   XIII 150; III 280
     "Elegie A Monsieur De Foyx Ambassadeur Du Roy En Angleterre Et Maistre De Ses Requestes" in *Elegies, Mascarades et Bergerie* (1565).

     In 1584 the title is "Discours"; in 1587 there is only the dedication.

44. Pour vous montrer que j'ay parfaitte envie   XIII 170; VI 349
     "Elegie" in *Elegies, Mascarades et Bergerie* (1565).

Rejected in 1584.

45. Je suis certain que vostre bon esprit   XIII 177; III 302
"Elegie A Mademoiselle de Chasteaubrun" in *Elegies, Mascarades et Bergerie*, (1565).

46. Ce Diamant, maitresse, je vous donne   XIII 203; VI 354
"Elegie pour une Mascarade" in *Elegies, Mascarades et Bergerie* (1565).

Rejected in 1578.

47. Fameux Ulysse, honneur de tous les Grecs   XIV 81; I 200
"Elegie A Amadis Jamin" in *Œuvres* (1567).

In 1584 the title becomes "Le chant des Serenes".

48. Je veus, mon cher Belleau, que tu n'ignores point VI 61; IV 95
"Elegie à Remy Belleau" in *Œuvres* (1567).

The poem had first appeared in the *Bocage* of 1554 with the name Pascal in the *incipit* instead of Belleau. The title "Elegie" will remain in all the editions after 1567.

49. Au grand Hercule animé de courage   XIV 133; III 230
"Elegie au Roy" in *Œuvres* (1567).

In 1584 the word "Elegie" is dropped.

50. Genevre, je te prie, escoute par pitié   XII 256; IV 12
1584: Genevre, je te prie, escoute ce discours
"Elegie" in *Œuvres* (1567).

The poem had appeared in the *Recueil des Nouvelles Poesies* in 1564 bearing the title "Discours Amoureux de Genevre". In 1584 it becomes "Discours I. En Forme d'Elegie", and in 1587, "Elegie, à Genevre".

51. Docte Cecille, à qui la Pieride   XIII 159; III 306
"Elegie au S. Secille Anglois" in *Œuvres* (1567).

The poem first appeared in *Elegies, Mascarades et Bergerie* (1565) with a dedicatory title only. In 1584 it becomes "Discours"; in 1587 there is only the dedication.

52. Sus, dépan, Charbonnier, de son croc ta musette VI 73; IV 65
   1584: Sus, dépan, mon Daurat, de son croc ta musette
   "Elegie" in *Œuvres* (1567).

   The poem first appeared in *Bocage* (1554) with the title "Le Narssis, Pris d'Ovide, A François Charbonnier, Angevin". From 1567 to 1573 it is called simply "Elegie"; in 1578 its title is "Le Narcis". In 1584 the word "Elegie" comes back: "La mort de Narcisse en forme d'Elegie", and in 1587 it is simply called "Elegie XIIII".

53. J'ay ce matin amassé de ma main   XIV 148; IV 74
   "Elegie" in *Œuvres* (1567).

54. Bien que le trait de vostre belle face   XIV 152; V 8
   "Elegie" in *Œuvres* (1567).

   In 1584 the word "Elegie" disappears. In 1587 the title becomes "Fantaisie. A elle mesme".

55. Vous qui passez en tristesse le jour   XIV 160; III 322
   "Elegie" in *Œuvres* (1567).

   In 1578 it is called "Discours"; in 1587 it is rejected.

56. Je n'ay voulu, Madame que ce livre   XIV 177; V 13
   "Elegie à la Royne" in *Œuvres* (1567).

   The poem is "Discours" in 1584 and "Envoy" in 1587.

57. Soit que l'homme autrefois d'argille retastée   XV 371; VI 418
   "Elegie de P. de Ronsard A N. de Nicolay" published at the beginning of: *Quatre premiers livres des Navigations et Peregrinations Orientales, de M. de Nicolay Dauphinoys, seigneur d'Arfeuille, varlet de chambre, & Geographe ordinaire du Roy* (Lyon, Guillaume Roville, 1568).

The poem does not appear in any collective edition.

58. Comme un guerrier refroidy de prouësse   XV 104; IV 125
"Elegie" in *Sixieme livre des Poëmes* (1569).

59. Pource, mignon, que tu es jeune & beau   XV 122; IV 146
"Elegie" in *Sixiesme livre des Poëmes* (1569).

In 1578 and 1587 the poem is simply called "Invective" but is
included in the book of *Elegies*; in 1584 it is called "Elegie, en
forme d'invective".

60. Du Lac, qui joins la gentille carolle   XV 167; V 95
"Elegie Au Seigneur Pierre Du Lac Seigneur du Petit-Bourg"
in *Septiesme livre des Poëmes* (1569).

In 1578 the poem is called "Discours à Pierre du Lac" and in
1584-87, simply "A Pierre du Lac".

61. Le Gast, je suis brulé d'amour & de chaleur
                                            XV 206; VIII 332
1584: Je suis brulé, le Gast, d'une double chaleur
"Elegie ou Amour Oyseau Au Capitaine Le Gast de Daufiné"
in *Septiesme livre des Poëmes* (1569).

62. Pour vous aymer, Maitresse, je me tuë   XV 213; IV 129
"Elegie" in *Septiesme livre des Poëmes* (1569).

63. Couvre mon chef de pavot, je te prie   XV 253; VI 376
"Elegie A Am. Jamin" in *Septiesme livre des Poëmes* (1569).

The poem is rejected in 1578.

64. Seule apres Dieu la forte destinée   XV 254; IV 105
"Elegie" in *Septiesme livre des Poëmes* (1569).

The poem is rejected in 1587.

65. Belot, afin que mort tu puisses vivre   XV 261; V 395

"Elegie A monsieur Nicolas Segretaire du Roy" in *Septiesme livre des Poëmes* (1569).

The poem is rejected in 1578.

66. Le temps se passe & se passant, Madame   XV 326; IV 107
"Elegie" in *Œuvres* (1571).

In 1578 the poem becomes "Discours" but in 1584 and 1587 it is again entitled "Elegie".

67. C'estoit au poinct du jour, que les songes certains.
                                                    XIII 3; IV 117
"Elegie à la Royne" in *Œuvres* (1571).

The poem had first appeared by itself in 1564 with the title "La Promesse Par Pierre de Ronsard Vandosmois A la Royne". After appearing in 1571 as an "Elegie" it was to undergo several changes: in 1578 it is called "Discours", in 1584 it is an "Elegie" again and in 1587 it is called "Elegie XXVII. Promesse".

68. Charles, en qui le ciel toutes graces inspire XVII 46; III 179
"Response à vne Elegie du feu Roy Charles Neufiesme, envoyée à Ronsard..." in *Les Estoilles A Monsieur de Pibrac* (Paris: Gabriel Buon, 1575).

In all later editions the poem of Charles is simply called "Vers du Roy Charles IX. à Ronsard" and the latter's poem "Reponse Aux Vers Precedens du feu Roy Charles neufieme".

69. Charles, tel que ie suis, vous serez quelque iour
                                                    XVII 50; III 182
"Response à vne autre Elegie de sadicte Majesté, qui se commence..." in *Les Estoilles A Monsieur de Pibrac* (1575).

Same note as in 68.

70. A vous race de Rois, Prince de tant de Princes
                                                    XVII 85; III 204

"Au Roy Henry III Elegie I". This poem first appeared in the *Estrennes au Roy Henri III* of 1575, but since this book is not to be found today the first copy of the poem is in the edition of 1578.

In 1584 and 1587 editions the poem is placed in the *Bocage Royal* and is simply called "A luy-mesme".

71. Le jour que la beauté du monde la plus belle   XVII 134; I 220
    "Elegie" in *Œuvres* (1578).

72. Prince, de qui le nom m'est venerable et sainct XVII 158; I 238
    "Elegie du Poete A Eurymedon" in *Œuvres* (1578).

73. Ce Dieu qui se repaist de nostre sang humain XVII 174; II 67
    "Elegie" in *Œuvres* (1578).

    In 1584 the poem is called "L'Amour Amoureux. A Elle-Mesme".

74. Printemps, fils du Soleil, que la terre arrousée XVII 191; I 255
    "Elegie Du Printemps A La Sœur d'Astrée" in *Œuvres* (1578).

75. Un long voyage ou un courroux, ma Dame XVII 320; I 360
    "Elegie" in *Œuvres* (1578).

76. Belot, parcelle, ains le tout de ma vie   XV 15; V 44
    "Elegie" in *Œuvres* (1578).

    With its first appearance in 1569 in the *Sixiesme livre des Poëmes* and in all collective editions except that of 1578, the poem has only a dedicatory title.

77. Voicy le temps, Candé, qui joyeux nous convie
                                          XVII 380; IV 58
    1584: Voicy le temps, Hurault, qui joyeux nous convie
    "Elegie" in *Œuvres* (1578).

78. Le fort cheval & l'aigle genereux   XIV 180; III 276

1584: Le petit aigle, après avoir esté
"Elegie" in *Œuvres* (1578).

When it first appeared in 1567 and in the editions that appeared before 1578, the poem was placed with the *Elegies* but had a dedicatory title only. In 1584 and 1587 it is placed in the *Bocage Royal* and in 1584 it is called "Discours". In its final appearance it bears only the dedicatory title again.

79. Six ans estoient coulez, & la septiesme annee   XVIII 33; I 337
     "Elegie" in *Œuvres* (1584)

80. Soit que ce liure icy ne viue qu'un Prin-temps   XVIII 58; III 177
     "Elegie sur Le Livre De La Chasse Du Feu Roy Charles IX. Recueilly & ramassé par la diligence de Monseigneur de Villeroy" in *Œuvres* (1584).

81. Ie resemble, mon Prince, au Prestre d'Apollon
                                            XVIII 120; IV 6
     "Au Roy. Elegie I" in *Œuvres* (1584).

82. Je chante icy, de Bray, les antiques fais d'armes XII 126; IV 77
     "L'Orphée, en forme d'Elegie" in *Œuvres* (1584).

It is only in this edition that the word *élégie* is attached to the poem. It first appeared in the *Quatre Saisons...* of 1563 with the title "L'Orphée" and a dedication. Although it is placed among the *Elegies* in all collected editions between 1567 and 1584 it is never numbered as one. In 1587 it is placed at the end of the *Bocage Royal* and bears the title "Orphée" and a dedication.

83. Nous fismes vn contract ensemble l'autre iour XVIII 124; IV 89
     "Elegie XIII" in *Œuvres* (1584).

84. Sans ame, sans esprit, sans pouls & sans haleine
                                            XVIII 126; IV 90

"Elegie XIIII" in *Œuvres* (1584).

85. Quiconque aura premier la main embesognée

XVIII 143; IV 143

"Elegie XXIIII" in *Œuvres* (1584).

86. Nous deuons à la Mort & nous & nos ouurages

XVIII 247; VI 23

"Elegie II. A Philippes des-Portes Chartrain" in *Œuvres* (1587).

87. Fictes, qui n'est point fein aux enfans de la Muse

XII 108; IV 26

"Elegie V. Adonis" in *Œuvres* (1587).

This poem appeared as early as 1563 and, from the collective edition of 1567 on, was always included in the book of *Elegies*. It is not until 1587, however, that the word "Elegie" actually occurs in the title.

88. Cinq jours sont ja passés, Denizot mon amy   VII 198; II 369
"Elegie IX" in *Œuvres* (1587).

This poem was called "Ode" in the *Continuation des Amours* of 1555 and in all the collective editions from 1560 to 1584.

89. D'où vient cela (mon Prelat) que les hommes   II 1; II 286
1560-87: D'où vient cela (Pisseleu) que les hommes
"Elegie XXII" in *Œuvres* (1587).

Like the preceding poem, this one was called "Ode" when it first appeared in 1550 and in all succeeding editions. Even in 1587 it still appears as an *ode* as well as an *élégie*.

90. Quand l'homme ingrat feroit tous les jours sacrifice

VII 22; II 229

"Elegie XXIII" in *Œuvres* (1587).

Appeared as "Ode" in 1555 (*Les quatre premiers livres des Odes*) and in all editions before 1587.

91. Nous vivons, mon Panjas, une vie sans vie   VI 116; II 228
1584-7: Nous vivons, mon Belleau, une vie sans vie
"Elegie XXV" in *Œuvres* (1587).

The poem was called "Odelette" in *Le Bocage* of 1554 and
"Ode" in the collective editions from 1560 to 1584.

92. Doncques voici le iour qu'en triomphe est menée
XVIII 128; IV 134
"Elegie XXXI" in *Œuvres* (1587).

This poem first appeared in 1584 as "Discours", but it was
placed in the book of *Elegies*.

93. Si mes vers semblent doux, s'ils ont eu ce bon heur
VI 113; II 226
"Elegie XXXIII' in *Œuvres* (1587).

From its first appearance in *Le Bocage* of 1554 and in all the
collective editions from 1560 to 1584, the poem bore the title
"Ode".

94. Del-Bene (second Cygne apres le Florentin) XVIII 253; VI 26
"Elegie XXXV. Au sieur Barthelemi Del-Bene, Gentilhomme
Florentin, Poëte Italien excellent, pour response & reuanche à
deux de ses Odes Italiennes" in *Œuvres* (1587).

95. Ainsi qu'on voict le vefue tourterelle   XVIII 424; VI 492
"Elegie" attributed to Ronsard in a manuscript at the Bibliothèque Nationale de Paris (fonds français 1663).

BIBLIOGRAPHY

The bibliography is divided in the usual way, the Primary Sources separated from the Secondary and the latter arranged according to their publication as books or articles. An unusual feature of the Primary Sources, however, is our decision not to repeat all the bibliographical information which has already appeared in the Catalogue of Elegies. Instead, beside the author's name a number (or numbers) will be found which refers the reader to the Catalogue. In the Primary Sources, therefore, one finds in detail mainly the modern editions which were used, usually for their critical apparatus.

The Secondary Sources might easily have become intolerably unwieldy since we have consulted for each writer virtually all the critical material that has been produced in the last hundred years. We mention here only those works which were of particular benefit to our study; we have also omitted most well-known general studies of the sixteenth century.

Abbreviations used are the following:

BBB — *Bulletin du Bibliophile et du Bibliothécaire*
BHR — *Bibliothèque d'humanisme et renaissance*
MLN — *Modern Language Notes*
RHLF — *Revue d'Histoire Littéraire de France*
RR — *Revue de la Renaissance*
RSS — *Revue du Seizième Siècle*
UP — University Press

I. PRIMARY SOURCES

anonymous: 48, 55, 57, 61, 77, 93, 96, 113, 115, 117, 137.
Alamanni, Luigi: *Opere Toscane*, Roma, Cætani, 1806 (2 vols.).
Amboise, François d': 50.
Aneau, Barthélemy: in *Art Poetique Francoys, Pour L'Instruction des ieunes studieux, & encore peu auancez en la Poësie Françoyse: Auec le Quintil Horatian sur la defense & illustration de la langue Françoyse. Auquel est inseré à la fin vn recueil de Poësie Françoyse, pour plus facilement entendre ledict art*, Paris, la veufue Françoys Regnault, 1555, in-8.
Ardenne, Remacle d': *Remacli Arduenne florenatis amorum libri, venundantur in ædibus Ioannis parui: & Iodici Badii Ascensii*, Parisiis, 1513, in-4.

Aubert, Guillaume: 46.

Aubigné, Agrippa d': 76.

———: *Œuvres*, edited by H. Weber, J. Bailbé and M. Soulié, Paris, Gallimard, 1969.

Aurigny, Gilles d': 19.

Auton, Jean d': 1, 2.

———: *Chroniques*, edited by Paul Lacroix, Paris, Silvestre, 1834 (4 vols.).

Avost, Hierosme d': 97.

Baïf, Jan Antoine de: 58.

Bardin, Medard: 20.

Belleforest, François de: 60.

Belliard, Guillaume: 83.

Béroalde de Verville: 99.

Bertaut, Jean: 106, 142, 144.

———: *Recueil de Quelques Vers Amoureux*, edited by Louis Terreaux, Paris, Didier, 1970.

Birague, Flaminio de: 110.

Blanchon, Ioachim: 101.

Boissière, Claude de: *Art poétique réduict en abrégé en singulier ordre et souverain méthode, pour le soulas de l'apréhension et récréation des espritz. Faict et composé par Maistre Claude de Boissière Davlphinois*, Paris, Annet-Briere, 1554, in-8.

Boton, Pierre: 67.

Bouchet, Jean: 11.

———: *Epistres Morales & Familieres du Traverseur*, Poitiers, Jacques, Jehan and Enguilbert de Marnef, 1545, in-fol.

Boyssières, Jean de: 80, 81, 87.

Brach, Pierre de: 74.

———: *Œuvres poétiques de Pierre de Brach, Sieur de la Motte Montussan*, edited by Reinhold Dezeimeris, Paris, Aug. Aubry, 1861-2 (2 vols.).

Brantôme (Pierre de Bourdeille, seigneur de): 59.

Bretin, Filber: 73.

Bugnyon, Philibert: 38.

Cailler, Robert: 112.

Callimachus: *Callimachus and Lycophron*, translated and edited by A. W. Mair, London, Heinemann, 1921.

Catullus: *Catullus, Tibullus and Pervigilium Veneris*, translated and edited by F. W. Cornish, London, Heinemann, 1912.

Cholières, Nicolas de: 120.

Colet, Claude: 15.

Cornu, Pierre de: 102.

Corrozet, Gilles: 7.

Debaste, Nicolas: 111.

Deheris, Guillaume: 16.

Des Autels, Guillaume: 28.

Des Masures, Louis: 39.

Desportes, Philippe: 68, 71, 78, 105.

———, *Elégies*, edited by Victor E. Graham, Genève, Droz, 1961.

———: *Les Imitations de l'Arioste par Philippe Desportes, Suivies de Poésies*

Inédites ou Non Recueillies du Même Auteur, by Jacques Lavaud, Paris, Droz, 1936.

Dolce, Lodovico: *I Quattro Libri Delle Osservationi Di M. Lodovico Dolce, Di Nuouo Da Lui Medesimo ricorrette, & ampliate, & con le postille*, Venegia, Giolito De'Ferrari, 1562, in-8.

Doublet, Jean: 42.

——: *Elegies de Ian Doublet Dieppoys*, edited by P. Blanchemain, Rouen, Société des Bibliophiles normands, 1869.

Du Bellay, Guillaume: *Guillemi Du Bellay, Peregrinatio Humana. Item de beatissimæ Virginis mariæ natiuitate elegia De dominica annunciatione Sapphicum Carmen De sancto betrando Sapphicum Carmen De capessenda virtute Sapphicum Carmen De venere & auaricia Asclepiadæum Carmen Ad sanctam genouesam Ode dicolos distrophos*, Paris, Gilles de Gourmont, 1509, in-4.

Du Bellay, Joachim: 27, 40.

——: *La Deffence et Illustration de la Langue Francoyse*, edited by Henri Chamard, Paris, Fontemoing, 1904.

——: *Œuvres Poétiques*, edited by Henri Chamard, Paris, Cornély, 1908-31 (6 vols.).

——: *Poésies Françaises et Latines de Joachim Du Bellay*, edited by E. Courbet, Paris, Garnier, 1918 (2 vols.).

——: *Divers Jeux Rustiques*, edited by V.-L. Saulnier, Genève, Droz, 1947.

Du Buys, Guillaume: 92.

Du Guillet, Pernette: 18.

——: *Rymes*, edited by Victor E. Graham, Genève, Droz, 1968.

Du Monin, Jean Edouard: 104.

Du Pont, Gratien: 100.

Durant, Gilles: 98.

Du Tronchet, Etienne: 56.

Du Verdier, Antoine: See La Croix du Maine.

Expilly, Claude: 130.

Fabri, Pierre: *Le Grand et vrai art de pleine rhétorique de Pierre Fabri*, edited by A. Héron, Rouen, Cagniard, 1889-1890 (3 vols.).

Flory, Iehan: 37.

Fontaine, Charles: 17, 31.

Forcadel, Etienne: 21, 26.

Gaguin, Robert: *De variis vite humane incommodis Roberti gaguini elegia*, Parisiis, apud D. Gerlier, nd., in-4.

Garnier, Robert: 66, 112.

——: *Œuvres Complètes (Théâtre et Poésies) de Robert Garnier*, edited by Lucien Pinvert, Paris, Garnier, 1923 (2 vols.).

——: *Les Juifues, Bradamante, Poésies Diverses*, edited by Raymond Lebègue, Paris, Société Les Belles Lettres, 1949.

Granchier, François: 114.

Grévin, Jacques: 45, 47.

Guy de Tours, Michel: 136.

Habert, François: 35, 44.

——: *Le philosophe parfait et le Temple de vertu*, edited by Henri Franchet Paris, Champion, 1923.

Habert, Isaac: 90.

Iacquet, Gabriel: 116.

Jamet, Lyon: 23.

Jamyn, Amadis: 72, 79, 88, 98, 109.

Jodelle, Etienne: 49, 70.

——: *Œuvres complètes*, edited by Enea Balmas, Paris, Gallimard, 1965 (vol. I).

Julyot, Ferry: 41.

Labé, Louise: 32.

La Croix du Maine, François Grudé de: *Les Bibliothèques françoises de La Croix du Maine et de Du Verdier sieur de Vauprivas*, edited by Rigoley de Juvigny, Paris, Michel Lambert, 1772 (6 vols.).

La Jessée, Jean de: 64, 82, 103.

La Péruse, Jean de: 34.

La Roque, Siméon-Guillaume de: 123, 128, 134, 147.

La Taille, Jean de: 63.

——: *Œuvres de Jean de la Taille Seigneur de Bondaroy*, edited by René de Maulde, Paris, Léon Willem, 1878-82 (4 vols.).

La Tour d'Albenas, François Bérenger de: 25.

Laudun d'Aigaliers, Pierre de: *L'art poétique français*, edited by Joseph Dedieu, Toulouse, au siège des Facultés libres, 1909.

Le Blond, Jean: 8.

Le Caron, Louis: 30.

Le Cauchois, Estienne: 125.

Le Chevalier, Antoine: 124.

Le Fèvre de la Boderie, Guy: 91.

Le Loyer, Pierre: 75, 85.

Le Poulchre de La Motte-Messemé, François: 118.

Luc, Robinet de: 9.

Lutreyne, Iacques de: 116.

Magny, Olivier de: 43.

——: *Les Odes Amoureuses de 1559*, edited by Mark S. Whitney, Genève, Droz, 1964.

Marion, Jehan: 22.

Marot, Clément: 6, 13.

——: *Les Œuvres de Clément Marot de Cahors en Quercy*, edited by Georges Guiffrey and Jean Plattard, Paris, Jean Schemit, 1875-1931 (5 vols.).

——: *Œuvres Lyriques*, edited by C.-A. Mayer, London, The Athlone Press, 1964.

Michel de Tours, Guillaume: 3, 4, 5.

Morenne, Claude de: 108.

Ovid: *Heroides and Amores*, translated and edited by Grant Showerman, London, Heinemann, 1947.

Papillon, Almanque: 24.

Papillon de Lasphrise, Marc: 135, 138.

Papon, Loys: 126.

Pasquier, Etienne: 146, 148.

——: *Les Œuvres d'Estienne Pasquier contenant ses Recherches de la France, son Plaidoyé pour M. le duc de Lorraine: celuy de Me Versoris pour les jésuites contre l'Université de Paris; Clarorum vivorum ad Steph. Pasquierium carmina; Epigrammatum libri sex; Epitaphiorum liber; Iconum liber cum nonnullis Theod. Pasquierii in Francorum Regum icones notis; ses lettres; ses œuvres meslées; et les lettres de Nicolas Pasquier fils d'Estienne*, Amsterdam, la compagnie des libraires associés, 1723, in-fol. (2 vols.).

Passerat, Jean: 131, 143, 145.

——: *Les Poésies Françaises de Jean Passerat*, edited by Prosper Blanchemain, Paris, Lemerre, 1880 (2 vols.).

Peletier du Mans, Jacques: *Art poétique*, edited by André Boulanger, Paris, Les Belles Lettres, 1930.

Perault, Philippes: 140.

Philipon, P.: 116.

Pontoux, Claude de: 52, 53, 54, 86.

Propertius: *Elegies*, translated and edited by H. E. Butler, London, Heinemann, 1912.

——: *Elegies*, edited by H. E. Butler and E. A. Barber, Oxford, Clarendon Press, 1933.

Rapin, Nicolas; 94, 95, 149.

Romieu, Jacques de: 107.

Romieu, Marie de: 89.

Ronsard Pierre de: *Œuvres Complètes*, edited by P. Laumonier, completed by I. Silver & R. Lebègue, Paris, S. T. F. M. (Hachette-Droz-Didier), 1914-1967 (18 vols.).

——: *Les Œuvres de Pierre de Ronsard, Texte de 1587*, edited by Isidore Silver, Published for the Washington University Press by the Univ. of Chicago Press, 1966 (vol. I).

Sagon, Françoys: 12.

Sainte-Marthe, Charles de: 14.

Sainte-Marthe, Scévole de: 84.

Saint-Gelais, Mellin de: 69, 129.

——: *Œuvres Complètes de Melin de Sainct-Gelays*, edited by Prosper Blanchemain, Paris, Daffis, 1873 (3 vols.).

Saliat, Pierre: 10.

Sallière, Piere Lucas: 122.

Sebillet, Thomas: *Art poétique françoys*, edited by Félix Gaiffe, Paris, Cornély, 1910.

Sorel, Pierre: 51.

Sponde, Jean de: 133.

——: *Poésies*, edited by Ruchon & Boase, Genève, Cailler, 1949.

Tabourot, Estienne: 100.

Tahureau, Jacques: 29, 33, 36.

——: *Poésies de Jacques Tahureau*, Paris, Librairie des Bibliophiles, 1870 (2 vols.).

Tasso, Bernardo: *Libro primo de gli Amori di Bernardo Tasso – Hinni et ode di Bernardo Tasso*, Vinegia, Joan. Ant. de Sabio, 1534, in-8.

Tibullus: *Catullus Tibullus and Pervigilium Veneris*, translated and edited by J. P. Postgate, London, Heinemann, 1912.

Trellon, Claude de: 119, 127, 132.

Turrin, Claude: 62.

Tyard, Pontus de: 65.

———: *Œuvres Poétiques Complètes*, edited by John C. Lapp, Paris, Didier, 1966.
Vauquelin de La Fresnaye, Jean: *L'art poétique*, edited by Georges Pellissier, Paris, Garnier, 1885.
Vauquelin des Yveteaux, Nicolas: 141.
Virbluneau, Scalion de: 139.
Vitel, Ian de: 121.

II. SECONDARY SOURCES

1. *Books*

Balmas, Enea: *Un poeta francese del Rinascimento: Etienne Jodelle*, Florence, Olschki, 1962.
Banachévitch, Nicolas: *Jean Bastier de La Péruse (1529-1554) Etude biographique et littéraire*, Paris, Presses Universitaires de France, 1923.
Bauer, Constantin: *Die Elegien Pierre de Ronsarts*, Leipzig, Seele, 1907.
Baur, Albert: *Maurice Scève et la Renaissance lyonnaise*, Paris, Champion, 1906.
Becker, Ph.-Aug.: *Mellin de Saint-Gelais*, Wien, Hölder-Pichler-Tempsky, 1924.
———: *Clément Marot, sein Leben und seine Dichtung*, München, Kellerer, 1926.
———: *Aus Frankreichs Frührenaissance*, München, Kellerer, 1927.
Bowra, C. M.: *Early Greek Elegists*, London, Oxford UP, 1938.
Brunet, Jacques-Charles: *Manuel du Libraire*, Paris, Firmin Didot, 1860-65 (6 vols.).
Cameron, Alice: *The Influence of Ariosto's Epic and Lyric Poetry on the Work of Amadis Jamyn*, Baltimore, John Hopkins Press, 1933.
Carré de Busseroles, J.-K.: *Dictionnaire géographique, historique et biographique d'Indre-et-Loire*, Tours, Société archéologique de Touraine, 1878-88 (7 vols.).
Chamard, Henri: *Histoire de la Pléiade*, Paris, Didier, 1939-40 (4 vols.).
Cioranescu, Al.: *L'Arioste en France Des origines à la fin du XVIII siècle*, Paris, Editions des Presses Modernes, 1939 (2 vols.).
Clements, Robert J.: *Critical Theory and Practice of the Pléiade*, Cambridge, Harvard UP, 1942.
Couat, Auguste: *La Poésie Alexandrine sous les trois premiers Ptolémées*, Paris, Hachette, 1882.
Daley, Tatham Ambersley: *Jean de La Taille (1533-1608) Etude Historique et Littéraire*, Paris, Gambier, 1934.
Day, Archibald A.: *The Origin of Latin Love-Elegy*, Oxford, Blackwell, 1938.
Delboulle, A.: *Matériaux pour servir à l'histoire du français*, Paris, Champion, 1880.
Desonay, Fernand: *Ronsard Poète de l'Amour*, Bruxelles, Duculot, 1952-59 (3 vols.).
Frey, Dora Elisabeth: *Le genre élégiaque dans l'œuvre de Ronsard*, Liège, Thone, 1939.
Goujet, C.-P.: *La Bibliothèque françoise*, Paris, P.-J. Mariette, 1740-56 (18 vols.).
Graur, Theodosia: *Un Disciple de Ronsard Amadis Jamyn 1540(?)-1593 Sa Vie, Son Œuvre, Son Temps*, Paris, Champion, 1929.
Guy, Henricus: *De fontibus Clementis Maroti pœtæ*, Fuxi, Gadrat, 1898.

Guy, Henry: *Histoire de la poésie française au XVIe siècle*, Paris, Champion, 1910-26 (2 vols.).

Hallowell, Robert E.: *Ronsard and the Conventional Roman Elegy*, Urbana, Illinois UP, 1954.

Hamon, Auguste: *Un grand rhétoriqueur poitevin: Jean Bouchet, 1476-1557?*, Paris, Oudin, 1901.

Hartmann, Hans: *Guillaume des Autels (1529-1581?) ein französischer Dichter und Humanist*, Zürich, Leeman, 1907.

Hardison, O. B.: *The Enduring Monument, A Study of the Idea of Praise in Renaissance Literary Theory and Practice*, Chapel Hill, North Carolina UP, 1962.

Hauvette, H.: *Un exilé florentin à la cour de France au XVIe siècle: Luigi Alamanni*, Paris, Hachette, 1903.

Hawkins, Richmond Laurin: *Maistre Charles Fontaine Parisien*, Cambridge, Harvard UP, 1916.

Héritier, Jean: *Catherine de Médicis*, Paris, Fayard, 1959.

Hudson-Williams, T.: *Early Greek Elegy*, Cardiff, Wales UP, 1926.

Hulubei, Alice: *L'églogue en France au XVIe siècle, époque des Valois (1515-1589)*, Paris, Droz, 1938.

Hutton, James: *The Greek Anthology in France and in Latin Writers of the Netherlands to the year 1880*, Ithaca, Cornell UP, 1946.

Jebb, R. C.: *The Growth and Influence of Classical Greek Poetry*, London, Macmillan, 1893.

Jourda, Pierre: *Marot, L'homme et l'œuvre*, Paris, Boivin, 1950.

Keeler, Sœur Mary Jerome: *Etude Sur la Poésie et Sur le Vocabulaire de Loys Papon Poète Forézien du XVIe siècle*, Washington, Université Catholique d'Amérique, 1930.

Kühnholtz, H.: *Des Spinola de Gênes, et de la Complainte, depuis les temps les plus reculés jusqu'à nos jours: suivis de La Complainte de Gennes sur la Mort de Dame Thomassine Espinolle, Geneuoise, Dame intendyo du Roy, auecq's l'Epitaphe et le Regrect*, Paris, Delion, 1852.

Lachèvre, Frédéric: *Bibliographie des Recueils Collectifs de Poésies du XVIe Siècle*, Paris, Champion, 1922.

Laumonier, Paul: *Table chronologique des œuvres de Ronsard*, La Flèche, 1911.

——: *Ronsard poète lyrique*, Paris, Hachette, 1932.

Lavaud, Jacques: *Un poète de cour au temps des derniers Valois Philippe Desportes (1546-1606)*, Paris, Droz, 1936.

Lebègue, Raymond: *La Poésie française de 1560 à 1630*, Paris, Société d'édition d'enseignement supérieur, 1952 (2 vols.).

Luck, Georg: *The Latin Love Elegy*, London, Methuen, 1959.

Mayer, C.-A.: *Bibliographie des Œuvres de Clément Marot*, Genève, Droz, 1954 (2 vols.).

Mojsisovics, Edgar von: *Jean Passerat, sein Leben und seine Persönlichkeit*, Halle, Niemeyer, 1907.

Müller, Richard: *Motivkatalog der Römischen Elegien*, Zürich, Juris-Verl., 1952.

Murarasu, D.: *La Poésie Néo-Latine et la Renaissance des Lettres antiques en France (1500-1549)*, Paris, Gamber, 1928.

Nolhac, Pierre de: *Ronsard et l'humanisme*, Paris, Champion, 1921.

Oulmont, Charles: *Estienne Forcadel*, Toulouse, Edouard Privat, 1907.

Patterson, Warner Forrest: *Three Centuries of French Poetic Theory*, Ann Arbor, Michigan UP, 1935 (2 vols.).

Picot, Emile: *Les Français italianisants au XVIe siècle*, Paris, Champion, 1906-7 (2 vols.).

Pinvert, Lucien: *Jacques Grévin (1538-1570) Etude Biographique et Littéraire*, Paris, Fontemoing, 1899.

Plattard, Jean: *Marot – Sa carrière poétique, son œuvre*, Paris, Boivin, 1938.

Raymond, Marcel: *L'Influence de Ronsard Sur La Poésie Française (1550-1585)*, Paris, Champion, 1927 (2 vols.).

———: *Baroque et renaissance poétique*, Paris, Corti, 1955.

Roedel, Alfred: *Studien zu den Elegien Clément Marots*, Meiningen, Keyssner'-schen, 1898.

Rucktäschel, Theodor: *Einige Arts Poetiques aus der Zeit Ronsard's und Malherbe's*, Leipzig, Fock, 1889.

Ruutz-Rees, C.: *Charles de Sainte-Marthe*, Paris, Champion, 1914.

Sandys, J. E.: *A History of Classical Scholarship*, Cambridge, UP, 1903-08 (3 vols.).

Saulnier, V.-L.: *Maurice Scève*, Paris, Klincksieck, 1948-49 (2 vols.).

———: *Les Elégies de Clément Marot*, (Nouvelle édition augmentée), Paris, Société d'enseignement supérieur, 1968.

Scollen, Christine M.: *The Birth of the Elegy in France 1500-1550*, Genève, Droz, 1967.

Spingarn, J. E.: *A History of Literary Criticism in the Renaissance*, New York, Columbia UP, 1924.

Sutherland, George M.: *Etude littéraire comparée de la poésie latine et française de J. du Bellay*, Thèse de doctorat d'université, Paris, 1952 (not published).

Thickett, D.: *Bibliographie des Œuvres d'Estienne Pasquier*, Genève, Droz, 1956.

Van Tieghem, Paul: *La littérature latine de la renaissance*, Paris, Droz, 1944.

Vianey, Joseph: *Le Pétrarquisme en France au XVIe siècle*, Montpellier, Coulet, 1909.

———: *Les épîtres de Marot*, Paris, Malfère, 1935.

Villey, P.: *Tableau chronologique des publications de Marot*, Paris, Champion, 1921.

———: *Rabelais et Marot*, Paris, Champion, 1923.

Wagner, Albert: *Clément Marot's Verhältnis zur Antike*, Leipzig, Seele, 1906.

Weber, Henri: *La création poétique au XVI siècle en France: De Maurice Scève à Agrippa d'Aubigné*, Paris, Nizet, 1956 (2 vols.).

Weinberg, Bernard: *Critical Prefaces of the French Renaissance*, Evanston, Northwestern UP, 1950.

Wilson, D. B.: *Descriptive Poetry in France from Blason to Baroque*, Manchester, Manchester UP, 1967.

2. *Articles*

Armstrong, Elizabeth: "Notes on the works of Guillaume Michel, dit de Tours", *BHR*, XXXI (1969), pp. 257-281.

Bailbé, Jacques: "Le thème de la vieille femme", *BHR*, XXVI (1964), pp. 98-119.

Balmas, E.: "Poesie inedite di Jodelle. A proposito del ms. f. 25455", *Revista di letterature moderne e comparate*, 14 (1961), pp. 45-104.

Baron, Hans: "The 'Querelle' of the ancients and the moderns as a problem for Renaissance scholarship", *Journal of the History of Ideas*, 20 (1959), pp. 3-22.

Becker, Ph.-A.: "Clément Marots Liebeslyrick", *Kaiserlichen Akademie der Wissenschaften in Wien: Philosophisch-historische Klasse, 5te Abhandlung*, 1917.

——: "Cl. Marots Buch der Elegien. Sein Sinn und seine Bedeutung", in: *Romanica, Festschrift, Prof. Dr. Fritz Neubert, Berlin zum 60. Geburtstag am 2. Juli 1946*, Berlin, Stundenglas-Verlag, 1948, pp. 11-54.

Bouchereaux, S. M.: "Recherches bibliographiques sur Gilles Corrozet", *BBB*, 1948: pp. 134-151; 204-220; 291-301; 324-336; 393-411; 470-478. 1949: pp. 35-51; 93-107; 147-154; 196-202. 1954: pp. 260-295. 1955: pp. 20-48.

Cameron, Alice: "Desportes and Ariosto: Additional Sources in the *Orlando* and the *Liriche*", *MLN*, L (1935), pp. 174-178.

Charlier, Gustave: "Jean Le Blond et son apologie de la langue française (1546)", *Revue de L'Instruction Publique en Belgique – Extrait – (1912?)*.

Desonay, Fernand: "Les manifestes littéraires du XVIe siècle en France", *BHR*, XIV (1952), pp. 250-265.

——: "Les Variations métriques de Ronsard, poète de l'amour", in *Lumières de la Pléiade* (9e Stage International d'Etudes Humanistes, Tours 1965), Paris, Vrin, 1966, pp. 363-390.

Faisant, Claude: "Les relations de Ronsard et de Desportes", *BHR*, XXVIII (1966), pp. 323-353.

Fromage, Robert: "Clément Marot, son premier emprisonnement. Identification d'Isabeau et d'Anne", *Bulletin de la société de l'histoire du protestantisme français*, 1910, pp. 52-71; 122-129.

Gaillon, Vicomte de: "Notice Biographique et littéraire sur Jean Doublet Dieppois", *BBB*, 1856, pp. 739-756.

Galletier, Ed.: "L' 'Idylle Du Loir' du Poète Angevin Pierre Le Loyer et ses sources antiques", *RSS*, V (1917-1918), pp. 147-161.

Guérin, Charles: "Les éditions de Ronsard', *Portiques*, IV (1946), pp. 129-143.

Hutton, James: "Michel Guy de Tours: Some Sources and Literary Methods", *MLN*, LVII (1943), pp. 431-441.

Joukovsky-Micha, F.: "Clément et Jean Marot", *BHR*, XXIX (1967), pp. 557-565.

Lacretelle, Pierre de: "Notes sur Claude de Trellon", *BBB*, 1905, pp. 541-551; 1906, pp. 29-38; 133-138.

Lebègue, R.: "De la Brigade à la Pléiade", in *Lumières de la Pléiade*. (Neuvième Stage International d'Etudes Humanistes, Tours 1965), Paris, Vrin, 1966, pp. 13-20.

Mahieu, Robert-G.: "L'Elégie au XVIe siècle. Essai sur l'histoire du genre", *RHLF*, XLVI (1939), pp. 145-179.

Mayer, C.-A.: "Le Texte de Marot", *BHR*, XIV (1952), pp. 314-328; XV (1953), pp. 71-91.

Mayer, C.-A. & D. Bentley-Cranch: "Le Premier pétrarquiste français, Jean Marot", *BHR*, XXVII (1965) pp. 183-5.

——: "Clément Marot, poète pétrarquiste", *BHR*, XXVIII (1966), pp. 32-51.

Moncaut, Cénac: "Jean de La Jessée", *Revue d'Aquitaine*, VII (1862), pp. 365-375; 442-449; 490-496; 549-553; 584-589.

Morrison, Mary: "Ronsard and Desportes", *BHR*, XXVIII (1966), pp. 294-322.

Oulmont, Charles: "Un chantre de l'Amour au XVI siècle (Claude Turrin)", *La Nouvelle Revue*, VIII (1913), pp. 433-452.

Picot, Emile: "Les artistes italiens en France", *Bulletin Italien*, IV (1904), pp. 61-75; 160-184.

Saulnier, V.-L.: "Etude sur Pernette Du Guillet", *BHR*, IV (1944), pp. 1-119.

——: "La Mort du Dauphin François et son tombeau poétique (1536)", *BHR*, VI (1945), pp. 50-97.

——: "L'Oraison funèbre au XVIe siècle", *BHR*, X (1948), pp. 124-157.

——: "Remarques sur la tradition des textes de Mellin de Saint-Gelais", *Bulletin de l'Association Guillaume Budé*, 1953, juin, pp. 13-19.

Sayce, R. A.: "Ronsard and Mannerism: the *Elégie à Janet*", *Esprit Créateur*, VI, 4 (Winter 1966), pp. 234-247.

Schmidt, Albert-Marie: "Poètes lyonnais du seizième siècle", *L'Information littéraire*, IV (1952), pp. 90-94; 127-130.

——: "Pontus de Tyard on l'amour famélique", *Table Ronde*, 1956, pp. 84-88.

Silver, Isidore: "Ronsard Studies (1936-1950)", *BHR*, XII (1950), pp. 332-364.

Smith, M. C.: "Ronsard and Queen Elizabeth I", *BHR*, XXIX (1967), pp. 93-119.

Thickett, D.: "L'Elegie au Jésuite est-elle un inédit de Ronsard?", *BHR*, XIX (1957), pp. 44-50.

Thomasson, Lieutenant-colonel de: "La poésie métrique aux XVIe-XVIIIe siècles", *Le Français Moderne*, V (1937), pp. 41-54.

Van Bever, A.: "Un capitaine poète du XVI siècle Marc Papillon de Lasphrise (1555-1600?)", *L'Ermitage*, IV (1905), tome I, pp. 231-241; 269-309.

Vaschalde, H.: "Le poète Bérenger de La Tour et ses œuvres", *Revue du Lyonnais*, XII (1891), pp. 46-60; 99-116; 173-190; 228-247.

Villey, P.: "Recherches sur la chronologie des œuvres de Marot", *BBB*,
    1920: pp. 185-209; 238-249
    1921: pp. 49-61; 101-117; 171-188; 226-252; 272-287
    1922: pp. 263-271; 311-317; 372-388; 423-432
    1923: pp. 48-54.

INDEX